The
Splendor Seekers

The Splendor Seekers

AN INFORMAL GLIMPSE OF AMERICA'S MULTIMILLIONAIRE SPENDERS — MEMBERS OF THE $50,000,000 CLUB

Allen Churchill

GROSSET & DUNLAP

Publishers • New York

"The country, at this moment, is just beginning to be astonishing."

—MR. VANDERBILT'S HOUSE AND COLLECTION, 1882

"A fortune of only a million is respectable poverty."

—WARD MCALLISTER

"They came to the place where they could best display their money to the gaping multitude, and advertised their arrival in the most obvious manner by erecting palaces, buying art, and all the exhibitionism they could invent."

—CHARLES A. BEARD

"God gave me my money."

—JOHN D. ROCKEFELLER

Contents

List of Illustrations

1

The Terrifying Commodore

IN May of the year 1876 the shadow of death at long last began hovering over the oaklike figure of Commodore Cornelius Vanderbilt. This famous man, known over half a century for such diverse distinctions as having accumulated $100 million in personal wealth and speaking with mangled grammar and a wonderfully profuse profanity, was at the time a ripe eighty-one years of age. Since the demise of John Jacob Astor in 1848, Vanderbilt had stood forth as the richest man in New York City, merely another way of saying the richest individual in the United States and one of the wealthiest persons—if not *the* wealthiest —in the entire world.

Until his health began to fail, the rugged, still handsome man had continued to do a full day's work as head of the New York Central and so many other railroads that he was called the Railroad King of the East. He also found time and energy to direct the manifold shipping interests, among them trans-Atlantic steamers, that had formed the basis of his fortune, as well as functioning as a formidable practitioner of the kind of Wall Street stock-cornering rampant at the time.

His only apparent idiosyncrasy of age had been that he wore a heavy overcoat, indoors and out, winter and summer. No one, not even his family, dared ask the terrifying oldster why he found this necessary; men as titanic as Vanderbilt just did such things. But presumably he felt a chill in his bones, no matter what the temperature.

If so, the chill did not seem a portent of actual illness until the day in May when the Commodore admitted to his wife that he had suddenly begun feeling his years. This Mrs. Vanderbilt was the old fellow's second helpmeet. His first wife had lived long enough for the couple to spend a golden wedding anniversary together, surrounded by their twelve children and an uncountable number of grandchildren. Shortly afterward, the first wife had died.

A year later the Commodore, vigorous at seventy-four, took as his bride a well-born Southern lady named Frankie Crawford, who was forty years his junior. A few of his privileged contemporaries boldly suggested that it might have been more seemly for him to marry her mother, of whom he also seemed fond. The Commodore's reply to this was surpassing in its logic. "Oh, no!" he exclaimed. "If I had married her mother, Frankie would have gone off and married someone else. Now I have them both!"

A doctor was called in 1876 when the Commodore admitted to feeling poorly. Throughout his life Vanderbilt had distrusted medical men, preferring to depend on unqualified quacks and patent-medicine nostrums promising long life and added vitality. But now the Croesus submitted meekly to the doctor's ministrations and, with only token mutterings of profane protest, agreed to stay in bed. The old Commodore, a legend in his own time, was indeed on the decline.

Yet there was life in the old boy. Word soon traveled around New York—then a metropolis of just over a million—that the Commodore and his overcoat had been missing from usual haunts, and the various newspapers of the day sent reporters to unearth the reason. For a time the newsmen stood uncertainly before the imposing red-brick Vanderbilt residence at 10

Washington Place, off Washington Square; then as a group they bravely moved to the door and banged the knocker. Mrs. Vanderbilt answered and politely invited them in. Indoors, the gentlemen of the press noted that the carpets on the floor were badly worn in spots, while the pictures adorning the walls were tasteless chromos. Only in the gold and silver models of his favorite ships and railroad locomotives—one of each bearing his name—did the owner's massive wealth manifest itself.

The entry of the newspapermen was audible upstairs in the sickroom and suddenly the Commodore, attired in a heavy bathrobe, stood at the head of the stairs demanding to know what was going on. His wife called upward that the press had come to find out about his health. This produced a reaction, for the patient summoned his strength to shout, "I ain't a-gonna die, I ain't a-gonna die!"

For eight long months, he didn't. Day after day he lay in bed, mind clear, only body and spirit weakening. Batteries of doctors huddled in consultation around him. Even as death approached, the Commodore was a penny pincher. When a desperate medico recommended champagne as an energizer, Vanderbilt croaked from between the sheets, "Won't sody water do?" Each night his devoted wife called the entire Vanderbilt clan to stand around the Commodore's bed and sing hymns while she played a portable organ.

However, diversions were few. For the most part the dying man lay half awake, thinking his thoughts. He had been close to death once before, in a far more dramatic fashion. As a young man he had ridden the pioneering Camden & Amboy Railroad on the occasion of the first recorded rail wreck in American history. The axle of a car had broken, plunging the entire train off a thirty-foot embankment. Vanderbilt had been seriously injured, but everyone else in his car had been killed. Plainly the Almighty had better things in store for him.

After that he had vituperatively hated railroads. Not until age sixty-eight, the possessor of a $40-million ships-and-shipping fortune, did his hatred subside, allowing him to begin buying small railroads like the Camden & Amboy and merge them into

the mighty New York Central, which linked the Eastern Sea-
board with the Midwest. Profits from railroading had more than
doubled his great steamboat fortune.

There was so much else to ponder in his four-score years!
Most satisfying, of course, was reliving the numerous triumphs
over his fellow man that had enabled him to become the Railroad King of the East, with his full-size statue embellishing the
Grand Central Terminal.

But with good came the bad. For all his majestic ruthlessness,
he had sometimes behaved foolishly. Not only had he persis-
tently consulted medical quacks, but fear of death had propelled
him to spiritualist mediums. His last involvement had been with
young, beautiful Tennessee Claflin, who with her sister Victoria
Woodhull had involved him in all kinds of lunatic schemes.
These girls actually believed women were as good as men. Yes,
they were suffragettes and Victoria had even run for the presidency of the United States. One day Tennessee had sat on his
lap, pulled his whiskers, and made him promise to set the girls
up as Wall Street stockbrokers. To the delight of press and
public, he had done so. These unlikely events had taken place
just prior to his second marriage. Thoughts of Tennie and Vic-
kie, who had tenderly called him "Old Boy," must have made the
sick man shudder.

Other recollections were more rewarding. If the nearness of
death brought uncanny insight, the Commodore could see himself as the prototype of the financial plunderers who had lately
become so vital a part of the American scene. In the new climate
of the nation, people were beginning to worship wealth, with
self-made millionaires turning into national heroes. In the era of
the Commodore these men were fondly known as the Barefoot
Millionaires, for in the best rags-to-riches tradition most of them
had risen from shoeless poverty to colossal wealth. A more polite
name for the breed was the Suddenly Rich. Later on, a President
of the United States would brand them malefactors of great
wealth; High Society came to refer to them as the Bouncers
because they bounced back after social rebuffs; and a social his-
torian would pay tribute to their splendid audacity, rhinoceros

hides, and sharp financial bite. Finally, the author Matthew Josephson dubbed them Robber Barons, a name that stuck.

Whatever the designation, Commodore Vanderbilt established the pattern. His old adversary John Jacob Astor may have piled up more money in a lifetime by investing millions made from the fur business in New York real estate. In fact, Astor's last words before death reputedly were, "Could I begin life all over again, knowing what I do now, and had money to invest, I would buy every foot of Manhattan Island."

But Astor, though superbly greedy and grasping, had been a Teutonic type to whom few legends clung. The opposite was true of the Commodore. His early money-making precocity had become as famous as his conquest of the financial citadels of Wall Street. Fellow countrymen well knew that he had been born on Staten Island and earned his first childhood pennies by tilling land. While still a burly boy in his late teens he had bought a periauger, or two-masted sailing barge, with money he had saved and he began operating a ferry between Staten Island and the lower tip of Manhattan Island. His ferry carried more produce than human beings and the young man, already bent on making a fortune, got off to a quick start by guaranteeing to deliver goods to the destination, rather than dumping it on the docks like his competitors. Soon he was operating three ferries and his furious energy, coupled to a mind teeming with money-making ideas, won him the ironic title of Commodore.

As years passed irony gave way to deep respect. Vanderbilt was a handsome man, standing an erect six-foot-two of well-muscled height. Until he opened his mouth to speak a crassly untutored English, he had the look of a fine-visaged aristocrat on the order of George Washington. On the one hand he seemed oblivious to the rest of humanity; on the other he nursed a compulsion to outdo his fellow man in every possible manner. His first biographer credited a innate pugnacity for his success, and to this other writers added such adjectives as *fearless, self-centered, relentless, overpowering,* and *overbearing.*

So endowed, he moved from barge-ferries to schooners, battering his way to supremacy as a shipper in and around New

York harbor. The Commodore was never a pioneer—nor were many of the Robber Barons who followed in his footsteps. Instead, he preferred to let others do the groundwork in new fields, as Robert Fulton and his partner Chancellor Livingston had done with steamboats.

At first the Commodore, like most sailing men, considered the steamboat a rich man's toy. But one morning he arose with different ideas. Dramatically disposing of his schooner fleet, he offered his services as captain of the oddly named steamboat *Mouse-of-the-Mountain,* plying its way between New York City and New Brunswick, New Jersey. For the next twelve years Vanderbilt served as captain of this and other craft, learning so much about steamboats that he could design them himself, and sometimes did. "Boats is my line," he liked to boast, thumping a brawny chest.

In three decades he forged his iron control over shipping along the East Coast, and on trans-Atlantic lines. Those who dealt with him told tales of his callousness, ruthlessness, and inspired profanity. He was uncouth, shrewd, tireless, sly, and heartless, but most of all arrogant. Once an associate dared warn him that a scheme hatching in his mind was against the law. Vanderbilt erupted. "The law!" he bellowed. "Who in the goddamn Hades needs the law? Hain't I got the power already?"

Vanderbilt had stepped into railroads at an age when another multimillionaire might entertain thoughts of retirement. But he worked harder than ever to attain his Eastern rail monopoly. Others used identical methods, but none on the same vast scale. "His foible was opposition," wrote an early biographer, "and whenever his keen eye detected a line that was making a profit . . . he swooped down and drove it to the wall, by offering better service and lower rates."

With the coming of the Civil War, along with its opportunities for profit and profiteering, the number of Robber Barons noticeably increased. Philip Armour of Chicago made a profit of $2 million out of a single deal furnishing meat to the Union armies. Even J. P. Morgan, a man of respectable antecedents, was involved in a transaction whereby defective carbines were bought from the army and sold back at a profit of more than

$100,000. Vanderbilt, too, did his share of profiting and profiteering, undeterred by the rumblings of a congressional committee:

> Worse than traitors in arms are the men who, pretending loyalty to the flag, feast and batten on the misfortunes of the nation while patriot blood is crimsoning the plains of the South and bodies of their countrymen are moldering in the dust.

Chastisement like this never hindered the Barefoot Millionaires, most of whom capitalized in one way or another on the Civil War. Nor did their number decrease as the conflict ended. Rather, these men found greater opportunities for aggrandizement in monopolies like the one Commodore Vanderbilt was busy creating with his New York Central.

In these areas, the Commodore stood forth a notable victor, but in personal affairs the smile of fortune was not so bright.

At age nineteen, he married a strapping girl named Sophia Johnson who was the daughter of his father's sister—his own first cousin. At the time of the marriage Sophia was said to be doing housework for Staten Island families. The girl had many homely virtues which the Commodore came to appreciate; for one, she added to the family income by running a tavern in New Brunswick during the lean years when her husband was a steamboat captain.

But he soon found out that his first-cousin spouse did not join his dreams of fortune and fame. From then on he consoled himself sexually with female strays, while utilizing his wife as unpaid housekeeper and broodmare. The couple produced thirteen children; nine of them, to the Commodore's profane fury, being girls. To make matters worse, one of the four sons died young.

Neither wife nor children brought the Commodore abiding satisfaction. He had little use for his daughters, since their progeny would not perpetuate the Vanderbilt name. Yet he perversely insisted on keeping them under the family roof. He did so by giving their husbands jobs and paying them such tiny salaries that they could not maintain their own homes.

His oldest son was named William Henry, after President
Harrison, a man the Commodore admired. The Commodore's
namesake, Cornelius Jr., grew up to be an epileptic
ne'er-do-well. The third son who survived made the Commodore proud by attending West Point. But after that he did little
in life.

Wealthy American families practiced primogeniture as rigidly
as the English aristocracy. So if and when the Commodore died
the oldest son, William Henry, would inherit the major portion
of the estate and be expected to run the far-flung Vanderbilt
enterprises. Yet William Henry was a pallid, frightened chap
who early in life earned his father's open contempt. The Commodore insultingly refused to employ William Henry, and let
him labor as an ill-paid bookkeeper for his business rival Daniel
Drew. The old man's heart even failed to melt when William
Henry married Maria Louisa Kissam, a clergyman's daughter
well connected in New York and Brooklyn society.

When William Henry suffered a nervous breakdown the stern
parent grudgingly allowed him to run the family farm on Staten
Island. The Commodore believed in cheating his offspring in
money transactions—it was good for them to learn not to trust
anyone! One day he discovered that William Henry had cheated
him in a deal involving a boatload of manure. It brought slight
respect for his son, and slowly be began giving William Henry
authority in Vanderbilt affairs. On the Commodore's death, William Henry was to inherit $60 million and become president of
the New York Central.

Another of the Commodore's frustrations had been his inabil-
ity to break into New York Society. For in the breast of this
rough man smoldered a desire to be part of the select group
christened the Knickerbocracy by the snobbish writer Nathaniel
Parker Willis, since the roots of so many of its best families extended back to pre-Revolutionary Knickerbocker days. In the
eighties and nineties, the Knickerbocracy would be rechristened
(by Ward McAllister) the Four Hundred, because this was the
number that could be squeezed into Mrs. William Astor's sac-
rosanct ballroom.

Money was Vanderbilt's god, and he failed to comprehend why possession of a fortune did not automatically allow him to mix on equal terms with the blue-bloods of Gotham. Life had, of course, been good to him, but this highly competitive character felt it would be better with entrée to Society's costume balls and exclusive clubs. Besides, he knew members of the Knickerbocracy considered themselves the most fortunate people in the United States. Their city was in closest contact with the culture of Europe and boasted more concert halls, theaters, museums, and luxury shops than any other community in the land. With all this, people in the Knickerbocracy had each other. Vanderbilt, like many millionaires after him, wanted to enjoy New York as part of the city's proud aristocracy.

The Commodore did have a means of penetrating this golden circle. Because of his ever-growing wealth and power, he could exert pressure on well-born Wall Street males, forcing them to make their wives invite him to their rarefied homes.

He tried this for the first time in 1836, and duly received cards inviting him for tea in the residences of several of the better families. The Commodore chose to arrive alone, leaving Sophia at home. Feeling euphoric and relaxed, he made no effort to improve on his customary behavior. Happily spitting streams of tobacco juice on expensive rugs, he used his awful profanity before the ladies of the house, and cheerfully tweaked the bottoms of pretty servant girls passing the cakes. In this crude behavior he resembled John Jacob Astor who, when invited to dine with the Albert Gallatins, ate peas with his knife and wiped sticky fingers on the clean white dress of a daughter of the house.

The men of the Knickerbocracy might have been able to tolerate Vanderbilt's uncouth manners, but their womenfolk were outraged and flatly refused to invite him again. Sensing this, the Commodore in turn experienced his own outrage. The world knew he had no education, but he could buy and sell nearly every husband in the Knickerbocracy. What matter, then, if he lacked grammar and depended heavily on profanity to express himself? As for spitting on the rugs, there had been no spittoons in the homes of his hosts! And pinching the serving wenches

—why, young girls were a known weakness of his; it was part of son William Henry's job to hire young, willing maids for the backstairs regions of Vanderbilt residences.

No matter how the Commodore excused himself, the raw fact remained that he got no further invitations from Knickerbocracy families. His fury over this triggered a curious reaction, for the resentful man decided to remove himself and family to Staten Island. If nothing else, this pleased his downtrodden wife, who looked forward to returning to the scenes of her childhood. More important, though, was the Commodore's decision to erect a home on Staten Island that would be a stunning showplace.

What gave this boorish man the sensitivity to conceive such a project? No doubt an architect persuaded him, for certainly he utilized the services of one of the few knowledgeable ones in and around Manhattan. If an architect did influence him, the man deserves a niche in history, for few ever swayed the mind of the iron-willed Vanderbilt. This architect must have studied abroad—a rare thing in those days—for the home he built for the Vanderbilts not only went back to the Renaissance and Middle Ages for inspiration, but to ancient Greece as well.

Obviously the Commodore gave his architect *carte blanche* in creating so stately a mansion, and this too was out of character. Thus the question remains: What hidden sensitivity gave this ignoble man the depth to approve plans for what came to be called a "noble marine villa." The reasons are hard to fathom. Vanderbilt's mother has been called a remarkable woman, but this was for strength of character rather than culture. Or perhaps Vanderbilt suddenly became house-proud because of his recollection of the fine mansions of lower Manhattan, which he had seen as an impressionable young man.

Oddly enough, these graceful homes, with balconies, palladian windows, and wide lawns, had been one of the hidden causes of the American Revolution. When erratic King George ascended the throne of Britain, he listened avidly while his generals and admirals described the mansions of Little Old New York, in which meals were served by black servants dressed in colorful livery. The quixotic monarch promptly decided that every citizen of the thirteen colonies was rich, and began imposing heavier tax levies on commodities like tea and sugar.

Five years after the Revolution, New York had become the capital city of the country—the Federal Town, it was called. President George Washington occupied a handsome residence on lower Broadway and revealed an unsuspected side of his nature by personally buying additional furniture needed for the executive mansion and himself supervising its delivery and arrangement.

New York's early mansions had been of graceful Georgian design, stemming from the lovely homes of London. But they began to disappear as, with the opening of the Erie Canal in 1825, the city turned into a bustling metropolis. Suddenly the downtown streets were too noisy for the discriminating socialites who dwelled in urban mansions, and they started to build homes in the area north of City Hall—Canal, Prince, and Spring Streets, and others as far up as Eighth.

In doing this, the upper crust of the city displayed a reverse kind of snobbery. Whereas the mansions of lower Manhattan had been striking to behold, the owners of the new houses saw fit to frown on exterior ostentation, deeming it bad taste. The finest new houses of the city offered bare and uninteresting facades of brownstone, with only a few carvings or colonnades as token decoration.

Still, luxury abounded inside. High-ceilinged rooms were both decorated and heated by white marble fireplaces, built low (as were sofas and chairs) to give the illusion of extra height to ceilings. Heavy furniture was of mahogany, rosewood, or walnut. Horsehair sofas were much in vogue. Draperies of crimson, purple, plum, and sea-green arched back to reveal lace or muslin curtains and spanking-clean windows. Walls were covered with expensive paper and spotted with oil paintings, oval ormolu mirrors, and sentimental chromos.

Carpets were thick, chandeliers heavy and complex, floors shiny parquet. Every room had a profusion of furbelows: draperies held back by elegantly contrived gold lilies; plaster cherubs in corner nooks; footstools before each chair; scatter rugs; artificial blooms under glass; and sea shells on marble-top tables.

These were the type of homes Commodore Vanderbilt entered during his brief foray into High Society and they too must have played a part in moving him toward expensive living. Or he may have been nudged in that direction by the few luxury hotels of the time, indoors and out the most ornate edifices in the land. One boasted twenty-two-foot ceilings alive with curlicues and scrolls, sofas and chairs upholstered with French tapestry material, gilt-edged mirrors on every wall, and Turkish rugs and window hangings of damask and silk; its embroidered draperies cost $1,000 apiece and window curtains came to $700. The best-known hotel of the moment was the Astor House in New York, with travelers spreading tales of its satin, brocade, and crystal-chandelier opulence. Its lobby fairly glistened with gilt.

Almost as ostentatious were the salons of Commodore Vanderbilt's new steam-and-sailboats, capable of covering greater distances with each launching. His boats also brought paintings and *objets d'art* from abroad to wealthy Americans, art patrons, and art galleries. So the Commodore knew that valuable items could be crated in cork and transported safely to this country.

All these factors—or at least some—merged to create the marine villa into which Vanderbilt moved his family in 1839. The striking residence stood on a family-owned hillside between Tomkinsville and Stapleton and it must have been a dramatic sight from the harbor below, emerging with cameo-clarity from the surrounding underbrush and woods. But few facts remain about this noble dwelling, which eventually burned to the ground. It must have been large, with at least fourteen bedrooms, for the Commodore still liked to keep as many of his flock as possible under the patriarchal roof. The design was of Gothic derivation, modified by a Grecian portico with six fluted columns in front. This and other architectural embellishments brought the flavor of great wealth and of Europe's golden past.

Indoors, the decor was ornate. Solid, heavy mantelpieces over the fireplaces (each room required one for heat) were of Egyptian marble; the plate glass throughout was fresh from France; colored glass on the massive front door delineated the contours of the Commodore's favorite steamer, *Cleopatra*; the elegant staircase had been built—or perhaps created is a better word —by artisans expressly brought over from England for the purpose.

The beauties of his hillside villa were enough to satisfy the Commodore for ten years. True, he spent long periods in New York and did much traveling, but the villa on Staten Island still represented home. Then, in 1849, he abruptly informed the family that he planned to move them back to Manhattan, where another Vanderbilt residence was already under construction. The Staten Island jewel of a villa would from now on serve as a summer residence.

One family member who failed to appreciate this move was the Commodore's wife; she had enjoyed the relaxing decade in the locality of her birth. Instructed by her husband to commence preparations for the move, the good woman gave way to fits of hysterics. The Commodore responded by packing her into a buggy and depositing her at a mental institution. Sophia remained there until she agreed to move her household without tears.

Though Vanderbilt had shelled out $55,000 for his new home off Washington Square, it was a four-story red-brick residence rather than an old-world mansion. A builder instead of an architect supervised construction, and no one but the family bothered to decorate the interior. It was an imposing residence, but after Staten Island a letdown.

The Washington Place area was aristocratically uptown and in this abode Vanderbilt lived surrounded by Knickerbocker names like Jay, Schuyler, Van Rensselaer, and Rhinelander. Such proximity again turned his mind to breaking down the barriers betwixt him and Society. He may have thought his chances improved because of his oldest son's marriage to Maria Louisa Kissam, but he got no help from her; then and forever Maria Louisa Vanderbilt was a society woman totally uninterested in Society.

Vanderbilt may also have thought the millions of dollars added since his first social venture rendered him a more palatable person. But if a few things had changed, his arrogance remained. Once again he twisted Wall Street arms and won himself invitations within the Knickerbocracy. As before, he spat on rugs and pinched the posteriors of serving wenches. As Oscar Wilde would one day say of Frank Harris, "He was invited to all the best houses—*once!*"

Following this round of social rebuffs, the Commodore again sought solace in a lavish display of wealth. This time the object was a yacht. Vanderbilt had become the real-life Commodore of an ever prospering fleet of sail-and-steam sidewheelers capable of crossing the Atlantic. For himself and family, he personally designed a $500,000 yacht of 2,500 tons, 270 feet long and 38 feet of beam, with four coal-fed boilers, bigger and better looking than any ship on any ocean. It may be hard to believe, but at that point in history no American had yet taken a pleasure cruise. Vanderbilt determined to use his yacht, christened *North Star,* for a restful cruise to Russia with his family and their endless progeny. He also took a doctor and clergyman, the latter a cheery soul who afterward wrote a book on the experience. Said he, "The Commodore did the cursing and I did the praying, so we got along fine."

Again the formidable man stepped aside to let more delicate hands embellish the interior of his yacht. The owner's salon (or saloon) was in the magnificent style of Louis XV with frescoed ceilings and rosewood furniture, including two sofas, four smaller couches, and six armchairs. A large steamheater kept this and the ten adjoining staterooms comfortably warm. The stove was a masterpiece of deception, its ugly inner workings hidden from sight behind a handsome gilded-bronze trellis. Each of the staterooms (large enough for an entire family) was done in a different color. One had red lace curtains over the portholes, red *lambrequins,* red spreads on berths, and red dominant in the upholstered furniture. Other staterooms were similarly decorated in blue, yellow, green, gold, and so on.

Most impressive was the dining salon, where walls were of brightly polished igneous marble, with panels of Naples granite laid against a surface of yellow Greek marble. The ceiling was white with scrollwork of purple, light green, and gold twining around medallion portraits of notable figures in American history, among them Columbus, Washington, Henry Clay, Daniel Webster, and William Henry Harrison. Here too the furniture was Louis XV and the serving china ruby and gold—not until later did maroon become the vaunted Vanderbilt color, used for carpets, equipages, and the livery of butlers, footmen, and chauffeurs. Over the stairway leading from this salon to the passenger quarters hung a painting of the Greek revival mansion on Staten Island.

Vanderbilt's enemies believed this 1853 pleasure cruise to be another attempt to enter Gotham Society. His game plan, they declared, was to arrive in foreign ports aboard a vessel so spectacular that American expatriates and consular officials would swarm aboard, then in gratitude for his hospitality give the Commodore letters of introduction to relatives back home.

Only part of this came true. Vanderbilt certainly attracted attention with his deluxe yacht. Wrote a contemporary, "Both ship and the cruise are so fantastically extravagant as to call wide attention to this great multimillionaire."

But it was Europeans who displayed interest in the yacht and its owner; expatriates and diplomats remained as aloof as the Knickerbocracy. In London, the dean of the American colony did visit *North Star,* and stayed for dinner. But this was the Commodore's only triumph. At Kronstadt, Russia's Grand Duke Constantine was piped aboard, to be awed and amazed by a craft finer than the czar's. In Rome, the party dallied while Vanderbilt and his wife had portraits painted by expatriate artists, but this failed to gain them a foothold in Rome's American colony. Finally, *North Star* returned to New York after covering 15,000 miles in four months and three days.

Vanderbilt had nearly a quarter-century to live following the cruise of his luxury yacht. Even if he had renounced all hopes of social climbing, there was plenty for him to do. Among other things, he found that two men left in charge of his multifarious steamship holdings had betrayed him. "Gentlemen," he scratched out in his illiterate scrawl, "you have tried to cheat me. I won't sue you, for the law is too slow, I'll ruin you. *C. Vanderbilt.*" Of course, he did.

Next he transferred his super-energies to the railroad field, thus multiplying his activities, responsibilities and millions. He jousted with men like Jim Fisk and Jay Gould in million-dollar stock deals. Sophia died after more than fifty years of matrimony, and a year later the lusty widower wed Frankie Crawford, a quiet, wise, sensitive woman despite her flashy name. Attired in his heavy overcoat, the Commodore labored through trojan days to increase his wealth and power.

Then he began to weaken, and meekly obeyed the doctor's orders to stay in bed. Lying there, he may have found satisfaction in being the first of the Barefoot Millionaires, or the Suddenly Rich, since names like Rockefeller, Gould, Huntington, and Carnegie were becoming famous in the land. In part to emulate him, most of these men had established headquarters in New York.

He may also have thought of his social ambitions, and his total lack of success in scaling the walls of the Knickerbocracy. If he pondered this in connection with the Suddenly Rich, he may have allowed himself a wry smile. Vanderbilt knew enough about the emotions of Barefoot Millionaires to be aware that similar hopes of social acceptance beat in the breasts of the competitive souls who had made millions from oil fields, silver mines, or the monopoly of commodities like barbed wire and sugar. These men might never admit it, but their own lust for the recognition of High Society, or the determination of their wives, was high among the impulses that brought parvenus like themselves to Gotham.

No doubt his thoughts ended there, for he had no way of knowing that in years to come the pattern of luxury established by him in both the marine villa on Staten Island and the lavish decoration of *North Star* had provided a fresh and ostentatious way of spending money. Nor could he suspect that his docile son William Henry would continue the great dynasty of the Vanderbilts and their mansions—or that the name Vanderbilt would become a cognomen for extravagance, splendor, and even aristocracy.

Over the next forty years—until the advent of a world war —the vast majority of the population might struggle to keep up with the Joneses. But for a fistful of Robber Barons with their centimillions the challenge was keeping up with the Vanderbilts.

So the old man died in January 1877. He must have pondered many things before his final breath. But he probably never thought of himself as the first of the nation's Splendor Seekers.

2

Greek Columns and Rosa Bonheur's Horse Fair

COMMODORE Vanderbilt lived out the final decade of his life in the uncomfortable knowledge that a rival he professed to like but probably despised had outclassed him in lavish living.

The man who did so was Alexander Turney Stewart, widely known as the Merchant Prince because of two dry goods emporiums, or department stores, operated under the name A. T. Stewart & Company. Stewart was the second richest man in New York City, generally running about $20 million behind the Commodore. But after the riches, similarity between the two men ended. Vanderbilt stood tall and striking; Stewart was bantam-size and homely. Whereas the Commodore was arrogant, Stewart acted servilely and obsequiously in the presence of his so-called betters. Vanderbilt, a penny pincher in personal life, was capable of making huge deals involving millions. Stewart's fortune, large though it might be, involved small, over-the-counter penny profits.

The Merchant Prince was born near Belfast and to him one contemporary writer—but only one—attributed a neat Irish wit and jollity. If this was so, no instance of it appears in the diaries, memoirs, biographies, or newspapers of his time. Stewart's image before the world was that of humorless money grubber. One who observed him in mid-career left this devastating pen-portrait: "His whole manner is hard and repulsive. . . . He is short, with a decided Hibernian face; sandy hair, nearly red; sharp, cold avaricious eyes; a face furrowed with thought, care, and success; a voice harsh and unfriendly even in its most mellow tones."

Even so, Stewart had partisans among the citizens of New York, who greatly admired their local millionaires. Vanderbilt was sometimes to be seen on the winding streets of the downtown financial district. Stewart, on the other hand, could be spotted at nearly any hour of the day prowling the aisles of his department store, greeting his best customers with fawning politeness, and cruelly chastising salespersons whose performance failed to meet his strict standards. The Merchant Prince seemed closer to the people, and those who preferred him to Vanderbilt actually made the claim that Stewart was richer than the Commodore because the fast turnover of his business allowed him to lay his hands on more ready cash than his rival. To some, A. T. Stewart stood enshrined as the wealthiest man in New York.

Of the Merchant Prince it was said, "His foot was sure and his stride rapid in the race for wealth." In 1818, at nearly twenty years of age, he had landed in New York, the precocious bearer of a diploma from Trinity College in Dublin authorizing him to teach the history of ancient Greece and Rome. At this point he aspired only to be a teacher, and found work in a Manhattan seminary. But at the age of twenty-one he returned to Ireland to claim a small inheritance. A well-wisher on this side of the ocean advised him to buy Irish lace, bring it back to New York, and turn it over to an experienced shopkeeper for sale. Stewart did, and the considerable profit from the transaction banished thoughts of teaching forever. Instead, there ignited within him a hard, gemlike flame of avarice that never expired until the moment of his death.

Beginning with an outlay of $3,000, A. T. Stewart opened his own dry goods store on lower Broadway, near Chambers Street. There he sold Irish linen and lace, French cambric, damask, and practical items like diapers. The newly ambitious young man lived upstairs over the store with his bride, born Cornelia Mitchell Clinch, then and later one of the least obtrusive helpmeets in history. Not until her husband's death, when she became the richest woman in the United States, did any kind of identity adhere to Mrs. Alexander T. Stewart.

Stewart and his wife had no children; two sons born to them died in infancy. Thus the merchant's thoughts were free to beam almost exclusively on business. "He thinks money, lives money, makes money; it is the end and aim of his existence," a biographer wrote later on. In those departed days, goods on sale in stores were not marked by price. Rather, each purchase was a fresh undertaking, with buyer and seller engaged in a supposedly friendly game of barter before agreeing on the amount. No one was ever sharper or shrewder than A. T. Stewart in the thrust and parry of a simple sale. In the words of an admiring Elbert Hubbard, "He was an expert in the boggle, banter, and blarney that was part of the game."

Already several hundred dry goods stores existed on the streets of lower Manhattan, and Stewart realized that to become conspicuous among them he had to give his store a personality. Where most of his rivals sought to outdo the customer in the boggle and banter of a sale, Stewart shrewdly found it better to make the customer feel she (or he) had got a bargain. He did this in subtle ways. After a particularly satisfying sale he might wrap a free piece of ribbon, or a spool of yarn or thread, into the package as a bonus. Such gestures were unprecedented in Little Old New York, and word of Stewart's generosity got around.

For a time he employed a male assistant who was told to make extravagant claims about the virtues of goods on sale. Stewart, the boss, would overhear and rise up in false anger, berating his employee and telling the customer the straightforward truth about the material. This well-rehearsed act won him a reputation for abnormal probity. Stewart created further goodwill by offering a ten percent discount to the wives and children of clergymen and schoolteachers.

In addition, an uncanny instinct enabled him to sense when a rival store was in financial trouble. Stewart then appeared with cash in pocket to drive a hard bargain for the entire stock. It was the same when a competing establishment caught fire. Stewart arrived just behind the fire laddies to bid for salvageable goods. For a time he made a practice of buying up the samples of lace used in other stores. These became soiled after handling and usually were thrown away. The crafty Stewart had the pieces laundered and put up for sale at reduced prices. Yet his high road to success was not always smooth. Once he faced bankruptcy and was forced to violate a strict personal code by borrowing money. The experience scarred him so deeply that he began a lifetime policy of paying for everything with cash. This, in turn, won rare discounts.

Stewart himself never perused a best-selling guide to salesmanship, but he could have written the first of them. For the young man's instinctive knowledge of sales techniques was successful enough to set the precepts followed by Captain R. H. Macy, Benjamin Altman, John Wanamaker, the Messrs. Lord and Taylor, and others whose merchandising success brought luster to their names. Stewart's end-accomplishments were based on the fact that he made New Yorkers talk about his stores: Purchasers knew he offered the best buys at the least prices. He seemed alert to everything, and became the first American merchant to use glass show windows for display. "Meet me at Stewart's" became a cliché of the female shopping world.

Stewart's rise in the retail field can be charted by a series of mottos he thought up himself. When he opened his first store, the selling credo of the day was "Never let a customer go." He amended this to "Make sure the customer comes back." So he became the first American in trade to realize that to increase business one must make a friend of the buyer. Later, with a faithful following assured, he worked by the motto "No misrepresentation," and at the peak of his success the Stewart slogan was "Not how cheap, but how good."

Asked his overall secret of success, Stewart liked to reply, "Work, work, work!" The metropolis marveled at his dedication to it. "Work is his idol, his pleasure, his profit," wrote one Julius Henri Browne. It was an era when a credulous world believed money brought happiness and even so level-headed a man as the aristocratic diarist George Templeton Strong wrote of Stewart, "How I envy that man!"

Over the years Stewart's business flourished, with every day dumping a cornucopia of cash into the cupped hands of an intensely greedy man. In slightly over a decade he was worth $1.5 million and from then on his fortune grew enormously. He still tried to greet each customer at the door of his store, but his manner had lost its obsequiousness. Toward lady buyers he was described as friendly but never too friendly. Leading a favored customer toward a counter, he would whisper temptingly into her ear, "I've put something aside for you."

Prosperity exposed another facet in the evolving character of the Merchant Prince. The frosty fellow, it turned out, had an extraordinary flair for outsize publicity. His personal charities were nonexistent and he entertained nothing but contempt for those working for him. Yet he was capable of the kind of grand gesture that made the world talk about him and the store. He sent a boatload of supplies to sufferers from the Irish potato famine, and another to the French after the Franco-Prussian War. At home, he gave $50,000 worth of clothing and blankets to victims of the Chicago Fire.

He was equally inspired where his store itself was concerned. By the early 1840s, the feminine population of New York knew about A. T. Stewart's, but the clever entrepreneur wished to set the whole town talking. He bought Washington Hall, a down-at-the-heels hotel at the corner of Broadway and Chambers Street, the south end of which faced the back of City Hall. Stewart tore down the hotel and began constructing the largest building in the city, a huge, marble, block-size edifice immediately dubbed "Stewart's Folly" by the populace. Laughter turned to awe as the magnificent emporium opened in March 1846. "Nothing in New York can compare with it," enthused ex-Mayor Philip Hone. Wide aisles, high ceilings, noble pillars, glass chandeliers, full-length mirrors, and other features made A. T. Stewart's the wonder of the town.

Stewart's big store (the building still stands at 280 Broadway) brought the forty-three-year-old merchant satisfactions. It had supplanted the Astor House as the most famous building in New York, and Stewart added to its notoriety by festooning the facade with flags and flowers on holidays. On days of national or municipal mourning it was swathed in purple and black. Stewart no longer greeted people at the main door; this was the province of his head ushers, or floor-walkers. Instead, the proprietor tirelessly roamed the aisles of his store. One contemporary wrote that he walked with quiet tread, as if his feet were encased in velvet.

Stewart's sales clerks—all male at that time—worked in terror of his eagle eye, for he seemed to know instinctively when something was wrong. "Never waste a bit of string," he lectured a clerk who was using too much to wrap a package. As often as not, he fired the offender on the spot. A series of fines for lateness, long lunches, wrong change, or misaddressed packages bit deep into weekly pay envelopes. Stewart felt no rapport whatever with the sales force who worked for him from 7:00 A.M. to 7:00 P.M., six days a week. "They are simply machines," he told the prominent New Yorker Peter Cooper during a tour of the store.

In addition to what one writer called elegances, the Stewart emporium boasted other innovations. Here was the first large store in the land (some say the world) to be departmentalized —hence the name department store. Most of the goods on display were imported by the Merchant Prince himself, for he had organized a network of purchasing offices and factories across Ireland, Scotland, England, France, Germany, and even India. Yet it is odd to note that the brilliant innovator never conceived of the one-price policy; that is, each item plainly marked with a price. Instead, he clung to the boggle, banter, and blarney system until 1865. Then John Wanamaker of Philadelphia instituted the one-price system which, among much else, allowed the hard-bitten merchants to employ women sales clerks at wages lower than men. Stewart quickly, and rather shamefacedly, borrowed the idea from Wanamaker.

Stewart's only unhappiness with his fine Broadway store came with the gradual realization that he had located too far downtown. He had begun following in the footsteps of John Jacob

Astor by purchasing large parcels of Manhattan real estate and had become owner of the Randall Farm, which spread around Broadway, Astor Place, Ninth and Tenth Streets. After waiting ten years, he began to erect on this property a large, cast-iron store, the total cost of which, including land, was $2.75 million.

Again mutterings of "Stewart's Folly" were heard and once more they turned to praise as the so-called Business Palace opened in 1861. Each of the eight floors of the building—some will recall it as the north store of a later Wanamaker's—covered two and one-half acres. Hundreds of salespeople were needed to take care of the public, and the annual operating cost was more than $1 million. The daily intake, though, was $100,000. When architect John Kellum suggested painting an A. T. Stewart sign on the store, the proud owner vetoed the idea. "People know whose store it is," he said smugly.

So A. T. Stewart posed before an admiring world as the reigning Merchant Prince. Once shinily clean shaven, he had grown a long grayish beard (while continuing to shave his upper lip) that removed his Hibernian look and made him resemble a Calvinist preacher. At age fifty-eight, his personal fortune was estimated at $30 million. He was retailer, wholesaler, and jobber, for with the opening of the uptown store at Astor Place his downtown Broadway premises were turned into a gigantic wholesale operation. He owned nine factories in Europe where, it was noted, he paid the lowest possible wages.

The Merchant Prince missed nothing. He stood ready to outfit completely hotels, churches, steamboats, clubs, and hospitals, providing everything from his own stock, including beds, rugs, chandeliers, silverware, mattresses, and napkins. During the Civil War he sold uniforms and blankets to the Union armies, and gained more favorable publicity as the only merchant in the North to do it at cost. While others profiteered, the patriotic Stewart refused to play the game. "The stand he took during the Rebellion brought him into further prominence and made him seem more than a tradesman," wrote the journalist Adam Badeau.

Such was the man who at the end of the Civil War decided to

cap his career—and incidentally begin New York's era of neo-Babylonian architecture—by building a splendid mansion in the heart of the metropolis. Multimillionaires of that day were not badgered by newspapermen, as they are today. Instead reporters, like the rest of the world, stood in awe of these great men. They feared them as well, for an irate multimillionaire might complain to a publisher or editor and cost an inquisitive reporter his job. And of these men of colossal wealth, Alexander T. Stewart was by far the most secretive about his private life. "Mr. Stewart had fewer biographies than other men as successful as he," one of his obituaries would state.

Here, as with Commodore Vanderbilt, we can only speculate about what drove a bantam moneybags to visualize a marble palace on the corner of Fifth Avenue and Thirty-fourth Street. A few clues do exist, but none is precisely a clincher. One theory said that he did it for his wife, a woman his associates considered silly and good natured. "I want to call some attention to Mrs. Stewart," he reputedly said, explaining the mansion to a friend. Again, he supposedly confided his plans to build a $1 million white marble residence to a member of the Astor family. Then he nodded his head meaningfully toward Mrs. Stewart and said, "*She* wants it."

Still, it is hard to believe that Stewart himself was not the one who desired a showplace. His youthful studies of Greece and Rome had made him aware of the glories of the past, and a mansion reminiscent of lavish days gone by may have satisfied an inner urge. There is also the matter of immortality. Stewart and others who followed him as Splendor Seekers built mansions in the belief that they would stand forever as solid monuments to the original owners. Finally, there is the fact that Stewart possessed far more money than he knew what to do with.

Of course, a few suggested that, no less than Commodore Vanderbilt, the Merchant Prince wished to break into Gotham Society. But in the cold eyes of the Knickerbocracy he was and always would be a tradesman, even though one of the wealthiest individuals in the city. It would be great irony that his fine mansion stood across Thirty-fourth Street from the large, undistinguished brownstone inhabited by Mrs. William Astor, doyenne of the Four Hundred. By peering out her north windows, Mrs. Astor could feast her eyes on the grand exterior of the Stewart mansion. But despite her curiosity about the interior—and she must have had a little—Caroline Schermerhorn Astor's social eminence precluded anything like a neighborly visit.

One of Stewart's detractors opined that the merchant had a yardstick soul. Yet in the matter of his Fifth Avenue mansion this Midas dreamed on the scale of Aladdin. Nor did he hurry his project. In 1858, he bought the $100,000 showplace of Dr. J. C. "Sarsparilla" Townsend, on the northwest corner of Fifth Avenue and Thirty-fourth Street. For a time residents of the city believed Stewart intended to do no more than remodel this handsome house and live there with his wife. Yet nothing like that happened. "To the astonishment of beholders," says a contemporary account, "he tore down the whole structure, even to the taking of every foundation stone."

Stewart was often seen on the premises with architect John Kellum, the best-known practitioner of his craft in the city. Kellum had done the downtown New York *Herald* building on Park Row and was projecting the Manhattan County Courthouse that figured so prominently in the depradations of Boss Tweed, offering a pattern of municipal graft for Robber Barons to come. Some contemporaries considered Kellum extravagant and wasteful but these qualities, oddly enough, were exactly what the parsimonious Stewart desired.

For now, through numerous fits and starts over the next decade, New Yorkers watched with amazement as a most unlikely dwelling rose on the spot. It appeared to be a glistening marble palace with roots in the Renaissance. But was it Renaissance? The boxlike edifice designed by John Kellum showed evidence of an architect blissfully bemused when faced with a profusion of available styles. The Stewart palace offered a multiplicity of architectural features ranging from the early Greek to the period of François Mansart, originator of the mansard roof, with a few added touches of the up-to-date Victorian. In size and solid dignity, it gave the overall impression of a chateau or palazzo unexpectedly and delightfully discovered amidst the countryside of southern Europe. To some, the mixed styles gave a look of the

French Second Empire. Others considered it bastard Renaissance.

The gleaming building was slightly rectangular, a little longer
on Thirty-fourth Street than on Fifth Avenue. In urban surroundings, its bulk and impressiveness gave it the look of a
museum or library. It was a five-story building with a three-story
facade, topped by a mansard roof giving the illusion of extra
height. Boxlike, without attempted grace, it had no showy ornamentation anywhere. Its beauty—if that word can be used
—was chaste and severe, grand without heaviness, elaborate
without being fanciful. Thirty broad steps led up to the imposing
main entrance on Thirty-fourth Street. The exterior was a profusion of balconies, prominent entablatures and cornices, heavy
stone quoins at corners, and deep ridges (called rustication) between the big building blocks.

Most prominent were the huge, vertical recessed windows,
eighteen facing Thirty-fourth Street alone. Each of these was a
single giant pane of purest French glass. Free-standing Corinthian columns decorated the handsome facades, extending
upward to the third floor. They were purely decorative, a fact
disturbing to purists who felt columns should not exist without
supporting something. "An architectural conundrum," one critic
thought them. Others admired them profusely. "The monumental Corinthian columns are the finest in the country," wrote
one observer.

More than 500 workmen labored to erect an exterior of
weatherproof stone that managed to shine like polished marble.
Indoors, two grand bisecting halls extended straight through the
center of the building to the opposite end, so that visitors could
look down the marble length of the mansion and see out the
mighty window at the other end. At the intersection of these two
main halls rose a marble staircase that had taken seven years to
build.

As the building neared completion, a second army of artisans
took over to decorate the interior. Many of the skilled workers
were recent immigrants to the United States, but the most expert
of them were brought over especially from Italy. Marble-masters
set to work creating floors and walls of blue-veined Carrara mar-

ble. Meanwhile artists from Italy mounted scaffolds to paint frescoes on ceilings and walls, in many cases with designs matching the Aubusson carpets below which had been manufactured especially for the Stewart mansion. With its marble columns, vaulted hallways, and splendid glass chandeliers, the interior was worthy of the palace of a king, a cardinal, or a prince. Of the building as a whole, a new publication called *American Architect* said, "It has caused more surmise and gossip than any other house ever erected in America."

Stewart's mansion eventually cost $1.5 million, in a day when the dollar was worth 100 cents. In all, it contained fifty-five rooms, the huge marble ones on the first floor being called "state" rooms after those in European palazzi used for display only. Rooms on the second floor were only slightly less formal, but could be used for entertaining or family living. The third floor provided sumptuous living quarters for the Merchant Prince and his docile wife. So many rooms were architecturally alike that it became necessary to furnish them in varying styles with names like Oak Room, Lace Room, Gold Room, and Gilt Room.

Stewart had a passion for clocks, and his prize possession was one in his entrance hall that stood twelve feet high and told not only the time but also the day of the week, the month, the temperature, changes in the moon, and atmospheric pressure. Each important room of the edifice had at least three handsome clocks, and it became the full-time job of a servant to make sure all were synchronized and struck simultaneously.

As the interior neared completion no less than 1,011 paintings, statues, and *objets d'art* were tenderly lifted up the steps and across the threshold.

Of interest to the observing populace were the life-size statues destined to line Stewart's entrance halls like a ghostly welcoming committee. Prominent among them was Thomas Crawford's rendering of Demosthenes, standing eight feet high on an imposing pedestal. Nearby stood life-size statues of *Little Nell*; *Eve Tempted*; *Lydia, the Blind Girl of Pompeii;* and a host of others. By far the most celebrated Stewart statue was *The Greek Slave*, by Hiram Powers. This nude maiden with hands bound by a delicate chain had drawn thousands who stood in line to see her when first exhibited in 1847. Somehow *The Greek Slave* was a shocker, though a later critic called her expression so demure and her pose so circumspect that she seemed fully clothed in her own skin.

The public also showed curiosity about Stewart's picture gallery, for the bloodless little man was on the way to becoming the foremost collector of paintings in the United States. His gallery turned out to be a windowless, gaslit vault, fifty feet high, thirty wide, and seventy-five long. It contained 217 paintings, many of them outsize, so that every inch of wall space was covered with works of art hung in intricate, jigsaw-puzzle fashion, with no background showing through. The gallery was further decorated by two lines of marble water nymphs and fishing girls, weaving garlands, staring pensively, or posed on tiptoe clutching modest draperies to rounded bodies—some of them stood on revolving pedestals. Around the room were a profusion of ceramics, vases, and urns. In the center were upholstered circular sofas for those who wished to sit while drinking in the beauty of the surroundings.

Stewart owned a Rembrandt, a Titian *Madonna and Child*, and a Gilbert Stuart portrait of George Washington. But these paled into insignificance in the public mind (and his own) beside his collection of living European painters, among them Meissonier, Detaille, Gérôme, Munkacsy, Bouguereau, August Bonheur, and others.

At first Stewart had bought inexpensive paintings found in the art shops and auction rooms of lower Broadway. Then he learned that William P. Wright of Weehawken, New Jersey, was of a mind to sell Rosa Bonheur's *Horse Fair*, the most celebrated "modern" painting in the western world. Miss Bonheur was an industrious French artist who specialized in grandiose paintings of animals, and of her a critic said, "She hugged the taxidermist too closely and loafed too little along the way." Yet the simple folk of Stewart's era believed that she and her overseas contemporaries had achieved a new pinnacle of art with their lifelike, colorful, almost photographic works of art.

Stewart bought the seventeen-foot-wide *Horse Fair* and with that acquisition instantly became a collector of major importance. Like the majority of the Splendor Seekers who followed him, the Merchant Prince admired large paintings in rich color that "told a story." He and his immediate successors favored battle scenes, pastoral views, hearthside glimpses, and animals of all sorts. Stewart's taste was revealed in a sampling of the paintings carried into his Fifth Avenue residence—*Visit to the Baby*, by Munkácsy; *Natural Park, California,* by Bierstadt; *Chariot Race*, by Gérôme; *Elks Pursued by Wolves*, by Lackenwitz; *New Born Lamb*, by Bouguereau, *Goodbye Grandpa*, by Outin; *Off to the Hunt* and *Return from the Hunt*, both by Chelmiński; *Environs of Fontainbleau*, by August Bonheur; and *Little Red Riding Hood*, by Blondel. Most of them were splendidly encased in extra large baroque frames of carved wood and gilt.

As Stewart's home achieved completion, *Harper's Weekly* made the owner glad by declaring it certain to stand forever; only an earthquake, the magazine opined, could prevent it from remaining as long as Manhattan. But it is to the credit of the citizenry that not all were overpowered by the magnitude of the edifice. A few irreverent souls dubbed it the "Marble Mausoleum," or the "Marble Icebox." One dared write, "It is very elaborate and pretentious, but exceedingly dismal, reminding one of a vast tomb."

The most frequent criticism leveled at this and subsequent Fifth Avenue mansions was that they demanded the proper surroundings of rolling lawns, shrubs, rose gardens, hedges, and driveways accentuating the beauty and ornateness of the buildings. By creating mansions of stone on stone—as it were—the owners belittled their mansions. It was also grotesque to copy houses with centuries of good living behind them. Stewart, of course, was the first offender here. His street-corner palazzo cried out for green grass and landscaping, but all it got was a low marble wall encircling the merest suggestion of greenery.

A. T. Stewart took possession of his Marble Palace in August 1869, only six months after Fate had dealt him a most shattering blow.

During the Civil War he had contributed more than $100,000 to the Union cause, in addition to selling goods to the army

at cost. This largesse won him superior status in the
politico-financial community and when at war's end General
Grant officially visited New York, Stewart headed a group of
distinguished citizens greeting him. The General and Merchant
Prince immediately took to one another. Grant's own prewar
efforts at business had ended in dreary failure, and he was much
impressed by a man who had succeeded so conspicuously in the
field. The wives of the two men also got along famously. Stewart
held firmly to the belief that, given a chance, businessmen could
run the country better than politicians; the simplistic Grant was
inclined to agree. Grant was not impervious to Stewart's practiced flattery, nor was Mrs. Grant left unimpressed by the expensive gifts from the Stewart store lavished on her by the Merchant
Prince.

Stewart became a charter member of the Grant for President
Club, making substantial financial contributions to the cause.
When Grant was triumphantly elected in 1868, Stewart felt
gratified. During the months between election and inauguration,
the President-elect played his cards close to his chest, never indicating who his Cabinet choices would be. But a week before the
Inauguration on March 4, Stewart got whispered word that his
friend had selected him as Secretary of the Treasury.

The man who supposedly had ice water in his veins reacted
like a jubilant child. Among many other things, this honor would
ensure his acceptance by New York Society; the Knickerbocracy
might ignore a Merchant Prince, but it could never disregard a
Secretary of the Treasury, or even an ex-Secretary in its midst.
With his wife and an entourage of admirers, Stewart made haste
to Washington for the Inauguration. Ostensibly he was attending just for the ceremony, since Grant had not yet revealed his
Cabinet officers. For the occasion Stewart took the largest suite
in the ultra-fashionable Ebbitt House.

"The Agony Is Over!" headlined the New York *Herald*, as the
names of Cabinet members were released a day before the
swearing in. But Grant's agony had just begun. He had chosen
his Cabinet on a personal basis, picking only men liked and
admired by him. No politicians or congressmen had been consulted, an unpardonable breach of political etiquette. Grant's

arrogance especially infuriated a group known as the Radical Senators. Determined to strike back, they unearthed the fact that Alexander Hamilton, first Secretary of the Treasury, had put on the books a law barring from that office any person involved in trade or commerce. Stewart, the angry senators told Grant, was ineligible.

The emotions of the man in the Ebbitt House can only be imagined. Hopeful that Grant would put up a strong fight for him, Stewart evolved a plan whereby the profits of his mercantile enterprises would be handed over to trustees and funneled into charity as long as he served in the Cabinet. Grant admitted to liking the idea, but the President, sorely beset by unexpected problems, deemed his merchant friend expendable. He requested Stewart's resignation and, after this tiny moment of glory, a mournful Merchant Prince went back to New York.

Stewart licked his wounds as best he could. He spent his customary long hours at the store, supervised the moving of family possessions into the Fifth Avenue mansion, and invested further in Manhattan real estate. He continued to buy paintings, and soon had so many that it was necessary to lean them against the pedestals of the statues in his gallery.

With the Stewarts ensconced in their mangificent abode, New Yorkers began wondering how two people, along with a battalion of butlers, footmen, and servants, enjoyed life in the Marble Palace. There was no way of finding out, since the Stewarts had few visitors or guests. For a time the only ones who entered the mansion were art lovers who wrote Stewart for permission to view his paintings. He sometimes allowed them to come, one or two at a time, and hustled them in and out of the gallery.

Still, from an occasional visitor, workman, or discharged servant, word got around that, not unexpectedly, the interior of the mansion looked and felt like an American Louvre. One who penetrated the tomblike edifice reported, "It is plain, cold, and severe inside, by reason of the large quantity of Italian marble used, though rich in frescoes by Grimaldi." The only personal touches were in the bathrooms, and not many there. Stewart's bathtub was gold-encrusted and altogether the room was so large that he hung his favorite painting on the wall and savored it during his ablutions.

Slowly the Stewarts seemed to find their favorite rooms in the mansion, and settled down in these. The Grand Drawing Room on the second floor was one so favored, although Stewart felt most at home in the Lace Room, perhaps because his enormous prosperity was based on lace. The Merchant Prince also liked to smoke his cigars in the Picture Gallery, gloating over his masterworks.

In the rooms they came to prefer, man and wife pushed aside *objets d'art* to surround themselves with a clutter of Victorian furniture, knick-knacks, and gew-gaws. A lawyer who had personal business with Stewart recalled the Grand Drawing Room as a welter of intricately carved small chairs and sofas upholstered in yellow satin, marble-topped tables with marquetry, life-size statues, handsome gaslit chandeliers, seven-foot Sèvres vases worth $20,000 a pair, a *vitrine* ornamented with ormolu and stuffed with bibelots, Chinese ivory figurines, German porcelain vases, silver snuff boxes and souvenir spoons, Royal Doulton plates, miniatures of the mistresses of French kings in gilt frames studded with rhinestone, and bits of *cloisonné*. He concluded, "From pedestals of polished granite, marble busts fixed you with a blind stare."

Life amidst marble halls provoked Stewart into thinking on a cosmic scale, for he began hatching plans which appeared to benefit humanity but actually existed to enrich him.

One was a superior hotel for young working women—"to keep them above temptation"—on Park Avenue. Once in operation it would render him a neat profit. Then he dreamed up a complex of factories up the Hudson to manufacture goods hitherto imported; it would give work to many Americans, but the goods would go to Stewart.

By far the most ambitious of his projects was the creation of a City Beautiful on Long Island. For $394,350, the Merchant Prince bought 7170 acres on Hempstead Plains to begin construction of what today is Garden City. Its outstanding feature was (and is) a glorious cathedral with a soaring spire and polygonal crypt to hold Stewart's mortal remains after his death. A credulous public believed the old moneybags when he described Garden City an earthly paradise for working people. In truth, it was one more money-making real estate development.

In 1873, at age seventy, Stewart suffered a kidney attack and recuperated by going abroad to buy more paintings. On this trip he crowned his picture-collecting career by paying Jean Louis Ernest Meissonier $60,000 for the painting *Friedland: 1807.* The artist had spent more than two years on this eight-foot canvas, described by a contemporary in these words: "The Emperor is represented on the field of battle, with all his marshals and masses around him, a troop of cavalry riding up to join the magnificent throng. A regiment of French *cuirassiers* are seen galloping into action, with a flood of light falling on them such as only Meissonier could paint." The artist called this work his pride and joy, and he wept on parting with it.

Stewart, a man who awed Americans, was in turn awed by Continental artists. After paying a duty of $8,000 to get *Friedland: 1807* into the United States, he proudly hung it in his bathroom and wrote Meissonier

> The grand painting each day develops such additional beauty (that) the beholder cannot but feel thrilled with emotion and excitement. . . . I may add that the work is one upon which you may rest your fame with perfect confidence.

The lonely Stewarts had got into the habit of giving Sunday night supper parties for other rich-but-not-social couples like themselves. To these functions came men, with wives, like Moses Taylor, Peter Cooper, Charles P. Daly, Parke Goodwin, Thurlow Weed, and Joseph H. Choate. At six o'clock the guests would begin eating a mammoth meal, topped off by a rare Johannis-berger wine estimated at costing $3 a sip. At nine, the diners moved to the art gallery. Servants brought coffee and in the hushed quietude the men smoked cigars and talked finance and politics, while the women dutifully exchanged small talk.

On the last Sunday in March 1876, Stewart hosted one of these dinners, and during it complained of a chill. Excusing himself, he reappeared in overcoat and hat. Thus protected, he got through the social part of the evening. Next day he had a severe cold which spread to his kidneys and bowels. For two weeks he suffered in his beloved Lace Room. On April 10, 1876 he died, aged seventy-three.

His funeral was worthy of real-life royalty. The Marble Palace, so striking to the eye, had made the city prouder than ever of its Merchant Prince, and as word of his death spread, people converged on the mansion, stopping traffic on both Fifth Avenue and Thirty-fourth Street. On the morning of his funeral 8,000 people crammed the area. His coffin was followed by sixty carriages, and a different crowd stood in respectful silence as his body was lowered into a crypt in the graveyard of St. Mark's in the Bouwerie. There it would rest until completion of the Garden City cathedral.

A. T. Stewart is one of those rare human beings whose experiences after death were more exciting than in life. Two years after burial, his remains were stolen from the St. Mark's graveyard, to be held for ransom. His distracted widow eventually paid the sum of $25,000 for the remains, which were hastily interred in Garden City. But considerable doubt remains as to whether these bones are really those of the Merchant Prince.

3

Twin Mansions

ONE evening during the famous ocean cruise of the Vanderbilt luxury yacht *North Star*, William Henry Vanderbilt, oldest son of the clan, leaned on the rail enjoying a post-prandial cigar. As he puffed and ruminated, his formidable father, the Commodore, suddenly appeared at his elbow.

"Billy," the Commodore snapped, "I wish you would quit that smoking habit of yours. I'll give you ten thousand dollars if you do."

In a controlled voice William Henry replied, "You need not give me money, father. Your wish is sufficient." With these words, he tossed his cigar overboard. The Commodore then reached into his own pocket, pulled out a fine Havana cigar, lit it, and began smoking with the huge relish he derived from the finer things of civilization.

Life with father was a succession of these humiliations, public and private, for William Henry Vanderbilt, who had attained the age of fifty-six when his father died. From the beginning of

William Henry's life, the Commodore had appeared to loathe his eldest son, at first on account of his slight stature and unimpressive appearance, then because of the abject way the boy took parental browbeating. The old tyrant particularly enjoyed ridiculing his son before others, and William Henry's reaction at such times has been recalled as "a falling down of the jaw . . . the peculiar noise of a whine without words."

When William Henry reached manhood, the Commodore crassly allowed him to work as an ill-paid clerk in another rich man's office. The Commodore bestowed no wedding gift when his son married Maria Louisa Kissam—a good match, you will recall. After William Henry got the better of him in the manure deal, rather than being enraged, the old gentleman was delighted. From then on he began letting William Henry take part in family business activities, eventually appointing him vice-president of the numerous companies, among them the New York Central, of which the Commodore was president.

On the Commodore's death William Henry, as oldest son, inherited the convenient sum of $60 million. Slipping ably into the chair of president of the New York Central, the pallid little man cleverly tripled his inheritance by improving railroad service and investing sagely in outside stocks. At home a tender husband and tolerant father of eight children, William Henry was in business as icy cold as his father had been brutal. It was William Henry who, at a moment of railroad crisis, spoke the classic words, "The public be damned!" On another occasion he said, "My only responsibility is to the stockholders." Thus he enunciated the credo of the predatory Robber Barons, both then and now.

While calmly multiplying his fortune, William Henry was becoming known as an art collector. During the cruise of *North Star*, he and his wife had nervously bought a few Italian paintings. Following that, Vanderbilt showed a commendable interest in American artists, purchasing the work of talents like Samuel Colman, S. J. Guy, James Hart, J. F. Cropsey, and J. G. Brown, the so-called "bootblack Raphael," who specialized in newsboys, shoe-shiners, and street urchins. Artist S. J. Guy excelled in painting children and William Henry was sufficiently impressed by his work to allow him to paint the Vanderbilt family grouped in one of the large, comfortable rooms of their residence at 450 Fifth Avenue, at Fortieth Street.

Guy was so pleased with the result that he asked William Henry's permission to hang the family portrait in a show at the National Academy. In those days American art critics were Europe-oriented and downgraded home-grown talents. Critiques of the National Academy show disparaged the Guy portrait of the William Henry Vanderbilt family, with the high-brows professing amusement at the idea of a multimillionaire sitting for a family portrait in his own parlor. Once more in life William Henry felt humiliated, and never again did he buy an American painting.

Instead, he cultivated the friendship of Samuel P. Avery, the most influential art dealer in New York City. These two journeyed to Paris, where Avery introduced Vanderbilt to Meissonier, Rosa Bonheur, Edouard Detaille, and others. These artists of the Barbizon school of French painting had considered Stewart, with his willing payments to Meissonier and others, a unique American phenomenon. But the appearance of William Henry Vanderbilt indicated that the Merchant Prince might be only the first of many.

Thus the French artists became the first to realize that upon this earth had come a group of self-made multimillionaires who believed that the more an object of art cost, the better it must be. In line with this, they were equally convinced that the larger a painting, the more valuable it became. With more than enough resources to follow through on this singular philosophy, they stood prepared to shell out improbable sums of money for contemporary art.

A. T. Stewart, William Henry Vanderbilt, and the numerous Midas-into-Maecenas types who followed them raise a question. Why did these rugged men of millions, who heretofore saw beauty only in the Yankee dollar, suddenly perceive loveliness in European paintings and other art forms? The question is particularly apt because the majority of Splendor Seekers kept on increasing personal wealth, no matter how many monopolies or

millions accrued to them. In addition, several stand on the record, calling it harder to hold onto multimillions than to earn
the first of them.

Still, the achievement of enormous wealth inevitably created
pockets of emptiness in a man's life. One writer saw the American Croesus as all dressed up with no more places to go. As with
lesser men, emptiness could stem from personal lives; perhaps
the bride of yesteryear might grow boring or overpowering; a
second marriage might prove to be a mistake; children turn out
to be disappointing, disgraceful, or want to live far from home.

Casting around for solace from emptiness, no matter what its
source, our Croesus could easily settle on the proud field of
art-collecting, since its prime requisite was money in lordly quantity. Unless a masterpiece turned out to be a non-masterpiece,
art was never fickle like happiness or human beings. Good art
was immutable, bringing pleasure to those able to appreciate it.
Lacking appreciation, pride of possession remained as a substi-
tute. Says one writer, "Pictures . . . shed their radiance, and it
was a lovely, soothing light. When you had visitors you could
bask in the admiration the pictures and sculptures excited, which
was directed toward you, as much as them—the works of art
became children."

Art purchases could also be considered excellent financial investments. Over the years important works had grown prodigi-
ously in value and the Maecenas who invested in paintings could
equate his hobby with money profits. Henry Clay Frick, a Splendor Seeker-to-come, paid inverted tribute to art as he sought to
portray the soundness of the nation's railroads. "Railroads," he
said, "are the Rembrandts of investment."

The acquisition of art also served to satisfy a rampant competitiveness ever-present in the hearts of plutocrats. First came the
heady excitement of besting the rest of humanity in competition
for a painting, followed by the rare satisfaction of owning
something coveted by others. Overnight, the owner of a valuable painting became unique; in this one thing, no other person on earth matched him. Then, the possession of an admired
painting made its owner respectable, not to say celebrated. For

the art critic James Jackson Jarves had just declared, "It has become the mode to have taste."

So we have William Henry Vanderbilt—like the Merchant Prince before him—ingratiating himself with the French contemporary artists who have been described as the soul-less painters. Every bit as greedy for money as the millionaires who secured their works, these artists possessed egos as swollen as their outsize canvases. For the most part, they specialized in paintings of lush, unembellished photographic realism often as large, or larger, than life. There was so little soul in their paintings—and so little integrity in the artists—that they stood ready to custom-paint for a wealthy purchaser; that is, he could tell them what to put in the painting. Artist and patron often haggled over the number of people to appear in a work of art, the number of medals a general should wear, or exactly how cows should browse in a pasture.

Almost to a man, these artists considered themselves the greatest talents the world had ever produced, and believed they ought to be paid accordingly. Still, it must be said in their favor that they worked. When Meissonier undertook to depict Napoleon's retreat from Moscow, he strewed his capacious lawns with flour to simulate a Russian winter, then dressed his servants in French army uniforms and ordered them to stagger through the flour. Himself a small man who slightly resembled Napoleon, Meissonier painted the Emperor by dressing himself in full regalia, standing before a full-length mirror, and reproducing what he saw.

If Napoleon was Meissonier's specialty, his fellow artists also had their favorite subjects. Rosa Bonheur, of course, preferred to paint large-size animals; Felix Ziem was paramount in scenes of Vienna and Constantinople; Edouard Detaille stuck to the Franco-Prussian War and its dramatic episodes; Jehan Georges Vibert favored Greek and Roman baths with male bathers; Anton Mauve was considered the world's greatest delineator of pastoral scenes; Emile van Marcke created the finest cows, using his own sleek herd as inspiration; and Adolphe William Bouguereau was best known for his lush nudes—"they are not

created with chaste intent," William Henry Vanderbilt shud-
dered.

The artists who painted historical scenes often did so much
preliminary research that they sent supplementary comments
along with their paintings. When Jean Léon Gérôme sold his
epic *Reception of the Prince of Condé by Louis XIV* to William Henry,
he appended a brochure describing long months in libraries
preceding the first stroke of his brush.

Before these artists Vanderbilt bowed as respectfully as had
A. T. Stewart. The artists in turn registered delight when it
transpired that Vanderbilt was willing to pay even more than
Stewart had for paintings. Samuel P. Avery now occupied a place
on the Vanderbilt payroll as a well-rewarded art consultant. He
and Vanderbilt made frequent trips overseas to buy or commission works of art. Like Stewart, Vanderbilt became especially
chummy with Meissonier. Whenever William Henry came to
visit, the artist kept him waiting a few minutes, letting him cool
his heels in an anteroom with a pile of unsold canvases. Naturally
Vanderbilt browsed through them and by the time Meissonier
appeared had already picked out several purchases. Once he
paid Meissonier $188,000 for seven such paintings; he gave
$40,000 for the artist's *Arrival at the Château*.

Cold and cryptic in business, Vanderbilt was warm and en-
thusiastic as a connoisseur of contemporary art. "I like pleasing
pictures," he explained once. Childishly proud of his friendship
with Meissonier, he was rendered joyous when the artist offered
to paint his portrait, saying, "I do not often do portraits, Mon-
sieur Vanderbilt, but I will do yours." During the sittings the
artist confided that his own favorite among all his works, *General
Desaiz and the Captured Peasant*, had become the property of an
unfeeling Teuton who refused to allow anyone, including its
creator, to view it. "It is lost to me and to France," Meissonier
moaned.

Setting Samuel P. Avery on the trail, Vanderbilt discovered
that the German owner would sell the painting for $50,000,
provided the sum be paid in cold cash. A few days later a
buoyant Vanderbilt appeared at Meissonier's studio and said,

"My good friend, I want your judgment on a painting I have just bought." Meissonier asked, "Where is it?" "In the next room," Vanderbilt answered. There he unwrapped Meissonier's favorite among his own creations. Says the writer who described this scene, "The effect was electric. The artist threw up his arms, uttered exclamations of delight, danced a jig, got down on his knees before the canvas, sent for his wife, and leaped about as only a mad French artist can."

Yet the Meissonier masterwork was again lost to France and the artist. For after savoring these raptures Vanderbilt had *General Desaiz and the Captured Peasant* crated and dispatched to Fifth Avenue.

Vanderbilt likewise enjoyed the friendship of Rosa Bonheur, though the two needed an interpreter to communicate mutual esteem. Once he commissioned the lady to paint two pictures, to be called *A Flock of Sheep* and *Ready for the Hunt*. "I shall require two years to finish them," the artist declared. Vanderbilt appeared crushed. "Tell her," he instructed the interpreter, "that I must have them in a single year. I am getting to be an old man and wish to enjoy them while I can." The artist chuckled and finished both within a year.

Like A. T. Stewart and other Splendor Seekers yet to come, William Henry liked paintings that told a story. His favorite backgrounds were battlefields, ceremonies of pomp and circumstance, and pastoral scenes. He was utterly opposed to any unseemly exhibition of feminine flesh. "He owned no pictures of an indelicate or questionable nature," Samuel P. Avery attested. "One by Diaz was the only approach to what is called the nude." Yet the discriminating collector who recoiled from painted nudity seemed perfectly content to have life-size statues of naked nymphs in his sculpture collection.

In 1878, the year after his father's death, Vanderbilt flexed his artistic muscles by buying Meissonier's *An Artist and His Wife*; Detaille's *Arrest of an Ambulance, Eastern Part of France, 1871*; and Gérôme's *Reception of the Prince of Condé*. Over the following year he purchased Alma-Tadema's *Down by the River*; Louis Leloir's *Portrait*; Madrazo's *Fête During the Carnival*; and Alfred Stevens'

Ready for the Fancy Ball. In 1880 Meissonier's portrait of Vanderbilt joined the collection, as did *Homeless,* by Anton Seitz; water
colors by Detaille and Vibert; and *Attiring the Bride,* by Jules
Lefebre, a giant canvas measuring sixty-nine by ninety-four feet.

The possession of such masterpieces quickly put Vanderbilt in
a class by himself as an American collector. A. T. Stewart's paintings and statuary had been valued between $750,000 and $1
million. Vanderbilt had already passed the million mark and was
galloping toward $1.5 million. With a fortune advancing toward
$200 million, this made William Henry a very important person-
age indeed. On New York Central business he traveled the
tracks in a majestic $50,000 private railroad car fittingly christ-
ened *The Vanderbilt.* Despite its owner's lack of personal magnetism, the car was painted a sunburst orange, with Niagara Falls
and other scenic features of the Eastern United States gaudily
depicted on its exterior.

Soon William Henry began to feel that his residence at 450
Fifth Avenue, comfortable though it might be, lacked true impressiveness. He had surpassed the lamented Merchant Prince
in both art works and millions. Why, then, should he not live in a
mansion even finer than Stewart's Marble Palace?

Over the protests of his wife, who felt at home in familiar
surroundings, he summoned Samuel P. Avery, together with the
heads of the decorating firm of Herter Brothers, and J. D.
Snook, the city's top builder.

Herter Brothers, with picturesque German-born Christian
Herter in charge of its colorful operations, was the foremost
interior decorating firm in the pristine land. Herter drew on
every country and every period for inspiration, but stood out
especially as the first to employ Oriental motifs in decoration and
to bring such rarities as Chinese porcelains, Persian potteries,
and Japanese art objects to this country; thus he influenced
American taste and revolutionized textile design. The prosperous Herter *atelier* employed a resident architect in the person of
Charles B. Atwood, who stood ready to design buildings for the
firm to decorate indoors.

To these assembled men William Henry revealed his desire

for the finest and costliest private residence in the United States. He had acquired the block front on Fifth Avenue between Fifty-first and Fifty-second Streets on which to build it. He told the group he had set aside $3 million for the entire job.

What Vanderbilt had in mind—as Herter Brothers soon found out—was not one mansion, but two. The first, at 640 Fifth, would be used by himself and his wife, along with the precious, growing art collection. The second mansion, connected with the first by a floor-high passageway, would be divided in two and shared by his married daughters, the Mesdames Sheperd and Sloane. Already two other married Vanderbilt daughters lived on Fifth Avenue—Mrs. William Webb at 680 and Mrs. Hamilton McK. Twombly at 684.

Following Vanderbilt's instructions Charles Atwood of the Herter firm designed what New Yorkers came to call the Twin Mansions. In style they were, if anything, French Renaissance, though once again it was hard to be sure. The original plans called for buildings of black marble streaked with red, but William Henry sharply countermanded this order. The importation of marble would take time; he, William Henry, was feeling his years and wished to occupy his magnificent home as rapidly as possible.

So the buildings were made of easily available brownstone—"the chocolate brown horror of brownstone," a writer has said. In time, Vanderbilt's use of brownstone caused one detractor to speak of the sullen banality of the Twin Mansions; another outspoken fellow referred to Twin Horrors; and a third was reminded of unfortified castles. Yet any humiliation these caustic cracks brought William Henry was erased when the widely read *Harper's Weekly* magazine called his dream quarters the Taj Mahal of New York.

Vanderbilt had not become a major art collector without learning that the citizenry of Europe included numerous art dealers, or agents, who were ambulatory encyclopedias of the art treasures to be found in historic French chateaux, Italian palazzi, and German castles on the Rhine. Aware that the owners of such

fine places were often hard pressed for cash, these agents be-
sieged American millionaires, architects, and art dealers, offering to act as middlemen in procuring treasures of days gone by.
Sometimes the agent already had a rare *objet d'art* in his possession.

With free enterprise vastly admired by contemporary Americans, few wealthy purchasers bothered to ascertain how their
agents behaved while obtaining the art spoils of Europe. Nor was
it ever easy to learn the exact amount of profit made by a glib
middleman. Some of the agents were men of scrupulous hon-
esty, but others were devious, if not dishonest. One of these
agents is said to have spotted an exquisite small fountain in the
courtyard of a nunnery near Nantes. Seeking out the Mother
Superior, he whispered to her that the delicate fountain was
instead a bidet of a special type favored by the courtesans of
Paris. Its presence in a nunnery, he went on, was nothing short
of desecration. The Mother Superior reacted by begging him to
take the offending object with him as he went.

These were the men with whom Samuel P. Avery and his
representatives proposed to deal in finding suitable furnishings
for William Henry's half of the Twin Mansions. For unlike
Stewart, who could largely be satisfied with Victorian furniture,
Vanderbilt wished the proper Medieval and Renaissance pieces
in his rooms. Suits of armor, huge draperies, frescoes, elaborate
chandeliers, candelabra, mighty fireplaces and mantels—all
these and more were to be transported from overseas. Nearly
everything, including the beds, would be wrenched in some
way—bought or stolen, but never borrowed—from a historic
site, crated with infinite care, and carried to New York by boat.
Of the $3 million budget of the Twin Mansions, Avery was ex-
pected to use one-third for the lavish interiors of William
Henry's home. When objects could not be acquired abroad, Herter Brothers were to duplicate them at home.

Again the good people of the metropolis were privileged to
watch as a hole in the ground was transformed into a double
Renaissance mansion on the sidewalks of New York. The process

took only two years, for William Henry saved at least a year by using Connecticut brownstone instead of the imported marble for his Twin Mansions, each of which contained forty-seven rooms. Seven hundred workmen labored to erect the block-length mansions, sixty of them sculptors from Italy imported to carve a conglomeration of cornices, pilasters, columns, entablatures, balusters, arches, and pediments. When the exterior was finished, European mural painters, fresco artists, and wood carvers arrived to beautify the interiors.

Though William Henry had delegated most of the authority to others, he kept a strong finger on the pulse of his project. Passing as much time as possible on the building site, he encouraged the workmen by offering on-the-spot bonuses for extra-hard labor. At the same time, he insisted on being informed by cable of all purchases overseas. Wrote a contemporary, "He took great interest in the work during its progress, and all designs were submitted to him, from the first stone to the last piece of decoration."

At last—the year was 1882—the latest magnificent residence, its wonders rivaling anything overseas, stood ready for occupancy. Like the Stewart mansion, the Vanderbilt homes were box-like and incongruous in urban surroundings, crying out for gardens, hedges, and greensward rolling to the forest where the master hunted boar. Yet the people of New York were fascinated and clustered in groups to feast their eyes on the outside and wonder what life was like within.

The Twin Mansions were three-story, flat-roofed buildings joined by the large passageway. Classical details were modified, so that some saw the style as Neo-Grecian. The Vanderbilt homes were far more richly decorated on the outside than the Stewart mansion, with Renaissance pilasters, intricate frieze work, balconies, and ornate fenestration. Around them ran a low iron ornamental fence with handsome street lamps midway and at each corner.

The fortunate few given a tour of William Henry's Twin Mansions entered a world of triumphant ostentation. Entrance was made through two massive doors which were superb copies by

Barbedienne of Paris of the famous Ghiberti *Gates of Paradise* portals to the Baptistry in Florence. These reproductions formerly graced the palace of the Prince of Donato; Vanderbilt had authorized his agents to spend $20,000 for them.

The grand portals opened into an entrance hall with a bronze and stained-glass ceiling, filled in with mosaics made by Fecchina of Venice. The walls were of light colored Nubian marble surmounted by a frieze of figures in mosaic. Fixed marble seats decorated the room, the floor of which was marble and mosaic. A large malachite vase occupied a prominent place—Vanderbilt and his agents had been alerted to its existence by the American consul at Florence; it had belonged to a czar of Russia.

From this outer vestibule, the awed visitor entered the private entrance hall of William Henry's residence. It was lined with a high wainscotting of marble, with three doors opening out. The first went into a small dressing room for guests; the second into the main hall of the residence; and the third into William Henry's private dressing room. This last had mahogany wainscotting; the space above was of stamped leather; the massive ceiling of mahogany.

The middle hall, or court, rose the full height of the mansion and was surrounded by galleries, tier on tier, leading to various private quarters. Off its marble expansiveness opened a great ballroom, dining halls, and four superbly decorated salons. The hall was lighted by nine large stained-glass windows and surrounded by wainscotting twelve feet high, of carved English oak. Eight square pillars of dark red African marble, with bronze capitals, supported the galleries. Facing the entrance was a huge protruding French fireplace with a large, handsome mantelpiece of red marble and bronze. This bit of decoration rose to the first floor of the gallery and had on each side a life-size female figure in bronze high-relief. The chimneypiece was of massive sculptured marble. Carved oak seats stood on two sides of the hall, and the main staircase rose from the north side, lighted by nine gorgeous stained-glass windows of green and blue made by the American artist John La Farge.

The drawing salon, twenty-five by thirty-one feet, had a ceiling

painted by Gallaud of Paris. The massive frames of its doors
were encrusted with gold, while the woodwork was a mass of
sculpture, gilded and glazed with warm tints. Walls were hung
with pale red velvet, embroidered with foliage, flowers, and
butterflies encircled with cut crystal and precious stones. Gas-
lights were built into eight vases of stained and jeweled glass, and
placed in corners of the room. Other vases, upheld by female
figures in solid silver, stood on pedestals of onyx with bronze
trimmings, while the lights in corners were backed by mirrors to
increase the brilliance. Boiserie adorned the walls. Carpets had
been woven in Europe from special designs. Especially striking,
here and elsewhere, were the magnificent story-tapestries from
the Royal Manufactory at Lille, two of them being *Agamemnon
Preparing to Sacrifice Iphigenia* and *Romulus Directing the Seizure of
the Sabine Wives*. But in this room, as in others, a profusion of
tables, chairs, curio cabinets, statues, pedestals, and vases de-
tracted from the impressiveness of indubitable works of art.

At the north end of the drawing room a door led to the library, which measured twenty-six by seventeen feet. Woodwork
was mahogany and rosewood inlaid with mother of pearl and
brass in an antique Greek pattern. Bookcases, mantels, and
doors were treated in the same manner. A large table stood in
the center of the room, and all the furniture in the room
matched it in wood and design. The ceiling was set with panels of
small square mirrors. In this room stood two statuettes carved
out of solid ivory by Moreau-Vauthier. "They are completely
adapted for parlor meditations," says a description of the Vanderbilt home.

Next to the living room lay a Japanese Parlor worthy of a
Nipponese palace. (In addition, there were Early English and
Grecian Parlors.) The ceiling of the Japanese Parlor was bam-
boo, picked out with red, green, and yellow lacquer work. A
low-toned tapestry, with panels of Japanese uncut velvet in varied designs, covered walls and furniture. A cabinet of Japanese
design extended around the room, offering shelves, cupboards,
and closets. At various points there were bronze panels. A huge

open fireplace warmed this Japanese Room, which was identical in size with the library.

To the west lay a handsome dining room in Renaissance style, measuring twenty-eight by thirty-seven feet. It held an arrangement of glass-faced cases supported by rich consoles and filled with silver, porcelain, and glass. An elliptically arched ceiling was divided into small oblong panels and carved in relief, with fruit and foliage designs carried out in varying tints of gold. The dining table had once served for the banquets of a French marquis. Spaces at each end of the room were filled between wainscot and ceiling with huge paintings by Luminais of hunting and other outdoor scenes. The furniture was English oak, covered in stamped leather with brass ornaments.

William Henry's picture gallery occupied the entire rear of the house. A thirty-five-foot ceiling featured a skylight of opalescent and tinted glass, leaded with quaint designs. A monumental mantelpiece of red African marble and glass mosaic filled one wall of the gallery. Woodwork was black oak, with San Domingo mahogany for caryatids and pilasters. The floor was inlaid with the same mahogany and bordered with a mosaic of Siena marble in Pompeiian style. Walls above the wainscotting were covered with dark red tapestry, the better to set off the art. Over the doors on three sides of the art gallery were balconies connecting with the second story of the house. The gallery had its own special entrance on Fifty-first Street, with a vestibule entirely of marble mosaic work from Venice.

Ascending a brass-banistered staircase to the second floor, the visitor found the family parlor, finished in ebony inlaid with ivory. Walls were covered with a dark-blue silk brocade, and the ceiling divided into small sections, with paintings of children at play.

Mrs. Vanderbilt's bedroom overlooked Fifth Avenue and was enthusiastically described as "the culmination of everything elegant, delicate, and fresh contained in the house." Furnished by Alard of Paris, its walls were of white marble hung with silk, the ceiling covered by the painting *The Awakening of Aurora*, by

Lefebvre. In this work of art, says one account, "every trace of the empire of carnal knowledge has been kept away." Another observer said of Mrs. Vanderbilt's bedroom, "in this elegant room silver toilet services and delicate hangings vie with the masterly painting. Among the fragile glitter of the upholstery, where everything seems to start fresh and crisp from the hands of the artificer, there is one worn object, and only one. It is the little family Bible."

In her husband's adjoining bedroom, a large Turkish rug covered the marble floor, with richly embroidered draperies enveloping windows and doors. The furniture was of polished ebony, artistically inlaid with satinwood; the canopy over the four-poster bed was heavy silk. A few of the owner's most treasured paintings graced the walls. Next door, in the master's dressing room, wainscotting rose eight feet high in glass opalescent tiles of blue, gold, and silver tints. The only pieces of furniture were a well-appointed dressing table and a luxurious barber's chair where a valet shaved and trimmed William Henry every morning.

On the day William Henry took possession of his superb quarters, he suffered a few qualms. Like several of his successors in the mansion sweepstakes, he felt on entering his marble halls as if he had stepped into a mausoleum. "I will die in this place," he grumbled. For a time his depression was so great that he seemed to turn against the family fortune. One day he surprised a business associate by bursting out, "The care of $200 million is too great a load for my brain and back to bear! It is enough to kill a man! There is no pleasure to be got out of it! I have no more real gratification or enjoyment of any sort than my neighbor who is worth half a million!"

William Henry's fear of dying in his extravagant surroundings was well founded; only five years later death visited his sumptuous bedroom. But during those years, it may be said, he made the most of his Twin Mansions. True, William Henry was alternately proud and overwhelmed by the luxury of his home. At times the surpassing decor got him down and he retreated to a corner of the library where a rocking chair from his old farm on Staten Island had been placed. Here he read and rocked. Once he paused long enough to plan an imposing, fortress-like mausoleum on Staten Island, where Vanderbilts could be buried. In large part this came from fear that the bodies of family might be snatched like the remains of A. T. Stewart.

At other times, however, William Henry's pride of possession was obvious and he went out of his way to impress the world with his domestic magnificence. Forgetting his early tribulations, Vanderbilt had turned into a snob. Caring nothing for what he sarcastically called "the *dear* public," he nonetheless wanted his fellow inhabitants of the world of vast wealth to know about his dwelling.

Accordingly, he once more called faithful Samuel P. Avery and instructed him to prepare a gilt-edged volume which in prose, etching, and photograph would forever enshrine the indoor glories of the Vanderbilt residence. With the help of an editor and ghost-writer, Avery produced a book titled *Mr. Vanderbilt's Home and Collection*. The first edition of this work —one of the most elegant books ever printed—was fifteen copies, each so heavy that together their weight was a ton. "A ton of tomes," quipped a wit.

A later critic assayed the Vanderbilt mansion as a glorious hash of styles—French tapestries, Florentine doors, African marbles, English china, Dutch old masters, Japanese knick-knacks. Vanderbilt's ton of tomes took a different view. It viewed the interior as "Completely elegant, artistic, and re-fined. . . . Everything sparkles with flashes of gold and color, with mother of pearl, with marble, with jewel effects in glass, while every surface is covered with ornament."

Naturally, Vanderbilt was proudest of the art gallery that featured his paintings and statuary. Over the door to the gallery hung Alma-Tadema's *Entrance to a Theater*; above the mantelpiece was Detaille's *Wounded Soldiers*. As he rocked in the comfortable corner of his library, William Henry could congratulate himself on being the most important art collector on this side of the Atlantic. In London, only the Sir William Wallace collection compared to his.

Vanderbilt's pride in his art works went so far that he set aside an afternoon for art critics and gentlemen of the press who cared to see his collection. No other Croesus ever did the same. This worked so well that he began to admit groups of so-called art lovers who wrote in advance for permission. However, a few lived up to Vanderbilt's conception of the *dear* public. They stole flowers from the fountained conservatory adjacent to the gallery, and a few tried to slip through forbidden portals to inspect the rest of the mansion. William Henry irritably withdrew the privilege.

While the gallery was open, though, the favored few could gaze upon such gems as the following, which constituted a mere taste of the $1.5 million Vanderbilt collection—*Arrival at the Château, Information,* and *Ordinance,* by Meissonier; *Champigny* and *Ambulance Corps,* by Detaille; *The Sower* and *Water Carrier,* by Millet; *Fountain of Innocence,* by Turner; *After the Chase,* by Sir Edwin Landseer; *Odalisque,* by Sir Frederick Leighton; *Bourget,* by De Neuville; *Two Families,* by Munkácsy; *Sword Dance,* by Gérôme; *A Study from Nature* and *Gorges d'Apremont,* by Rousseau; *Rainbow,* by Jules Breton; *Picture Gallery, Sculpture Gallery,* and *Down by the River,* by Alma-Tadema; *Fête during the Carnival* and *Masqueraders,* by Madrazo; *Arab Fantasia at Algiers,* by Fortuny; *Village Fête,* by Knaus; *Midday,* by Jules Dupré; *Bride of Lammermoor,* by Millais; *Arab Plucking a Thorn from His Foot,* by Bonnat; *King's Favorite,* by Zamacois; *A Dream of Arabian Nights* and *Christening,* by Villegas; *Blindman's Buff* and *The Bathers,* by Diaz; *The Good Sister,* by Bouguereau; *Forbidden Books,* by Vibert; *Game of Chess,* by Leloir; *Cattle Grazing,* by Van Marcke; *Oriental Market Place,* by Muller; *Twilight in Scotland,* by Gustave Doré; *Young Mother,* by Béranger; *The Reaper's Return Home,* by Becker; *Paying the Rent,* by Nicol; *Rubens in His Studio,* by Sir John Gilbert; *Monarch Oak* by Linnell; *Returning from the Fair,* by Bochman; *Hungarian Volunteers,* by Pottenkoffen; *Flemish*

Cabaret, by Madou; and *What Has Mother Bought?*, by Von Bremen.

When asked which of his paintings he liked best, William Henry replied with stunning simplicity, "I like them all."

The fame of the Vanderbilt Twin Mansions spread across the land and visitors to New York placed them high among places of interest. One day a pair of travelers from Pittsburgh hired horse and buggy to tour the metropolis. They were Henry Clay Frick and Andrew Mellon, and both were ardent worshippers at the shrine of the Almighty Dollar. Frick, just turned thirty, had recently made his first million dollars from the sale of coke to the steel industry. Mellon, a few years younger, was the son of the man who had advanced Frick the money to get into coke. These two young men were already close friends, and over the next forty years were destined to work closely together in the field of millions-making. Yet never once did they address one another as anything but "Mr. Frick" and "Mr. Mellon."

The two stopped on Fifth Avenue to give undivided attention to the William Henry Vanderbilt Twin Mansions. "I guess these are really the finest homes in the city," Frick finally commented. Andrew Mellon never liked to commit himself unnecessarily. "I believe they are so considered, Mr. Frick," he answered cautiously.

Frick, his mind inevitably running along money lines, went on, "I wonder how much the upkeep of Mr. Vanderbilt's home would be?" Mellon sat silent, refusing to speculate. Frick did some fast mental arithmetic and said, "I'd say three hundred thousand dollars a year." "It might be," Mellon agreed. "That would be nearly a thousand dollars a day," Frick concluded. Mellon vouchsafed no reply.

Having disposed in characteristic fashion of the thousand-dollar-a-day Vanderbilt mansion, Mr. Frick and Mr. Mellon drove on, each nursing his private thoughts.

4

Four Châteaux
for Fifth Avenue

OVER the next half-century, the name Vanderbilt glowed with increasing radiance. Outdistancing the stolid but deeply entrenched Astors, members of this supernal group proceeded to devote their ever-mounting millions to living in the manner of American royalty—or, as some put it, in feudal style. Whether in New York, Newport, or North Carolina, those bearing the gilt-encrusted cognomen existed in ultra-extravagant style, with a panache unknown on this side of the Atlantic.

This was already apparent in 1882, when the family flaunted no less than four impressive dwellings along a few blocks of Fifth Avenue—the Twin Mansions, plus the townhouse residences of Mrs. Twombly and Mrs. Webb.

There was more to come, for at this time the Vanderbilts were providing two more mansions for admiring eyes, one of them the loveliest ever to grace Fifth Avenue. In years to come eighty opulent dwellings would arise on the Avenue between Fifty-first and Ninety-fifth Streets, but none ever had the lasting réclame accorded the home of William Kissam Vanderbilt, at 660 Fifth, at the corner of Fifty-second Street. Through the years verbal and written praise has been heaped on this urban Francis I château, erected by the second son of William Henry.

Still, the main figure in the creation of this colossal architectural triumph was not a Vanderbilt by birth, but by marriage. Alva Erskine Smith Vanderbilt began life on an Alabama plantation and was brought up in France, where her father took the family to escape the dangers of the Civil War. Chubby of figure, with a face like a Pekinese, Alva returned to this country at age twenty possessing no notable prospects for the future. However, the sparkling of her personality intrigued Consuelo Yznaga, a half-Cuban beauty who had wed Lord Mandeville of England. Lady Mandeville introduced Alva to young William Kissam Vanderbilt, who miraculously asked her hand in marriage. The two were married in 1875 and rode in the Commodore's private train on their Saratoga honeymoon. On the register of the honeymoon hotel, the bridgroom nonchalantly wrote, "William Kissam Vanderbilt, wife, two maids, two dogs, and fifteen horses."

Marriage in those days was a risky toss of the dice. Because of the careful punctilio governing the lives of the privileged classes, engaged couples were seldom together long enough to learn one another's true character. In the words of novelist Edith Wharton, who was born into the Knickerbocracy, "Brides knew nothing and expected everything." The first night of her honeymoon was usually a cloistered girl's initial introduction to the sex experience, and the compatability of numerous marriages began and ended on the nuptial bed. Mrs. Wharton explains, "Brides were plunged overnight into what people called 'the facts of life.' "

Sometimes, however, it was the husband who stood on the receiving end of the marital shocks, and it is possible to call William Kissam Vanderbilt one of them. Not until the happy honeymoon did he realize that the plump girl who had become his wife was a dynamo of determination with a force of will nothing short of fanatical. This worsened with the passage of years. No matter how she behaved before marriage, Alva Smith Vanderbilt developed into a termagant who dominated those around her by every means, including awful temper tantrums.

"Her combative nature rejoiced in conquests," wrote her daughter Consuelo, who, at age seventeen, was forced by her

mother into an undesired marriage with the Duke of Marl-
borough. "It was her habit to impose her views rather then invite
discussion." In a lifetime of winning her own way, Alva trampled
more men than women and eventually decided that females
were superior to males and that God must be a female. Once,
when asked advice by a friend, she urged, "Pray to God. *She* will
help you."

In her early years as a Vanderbilt, the dreams of this awesome
young lady were beamed on one thing: conquest of New York
Society, if possible by wresting the scepter of leadership from the
tight grip of Mrs. Astor. Yet Alva was smart enough to realize
that Vanderbilts could never penetrate the Four Hundred while
the old Commodore was alive. This had been the case with the
Astors, for not until boorish John Jacob Astor removed himself
from the scene did social acceptance come to that money-sodden
dynasty.

When the Commodore finally expired in 1877, Alva needed
only to find a means of ascending the social ladder. She rapidly
derived inspiration from the plans for William Henry's Twin
Mansions, which gave her the idea of building on her own a
mansion so magnificent that Gotham Society would beat a path
to its portals. There are those who believe Alva hatched the
mansion idea first, only to have William Henry plunge ahead of
her. However, he beat her to completion and we must consider
him the originator of the idea. This may have been lucky for
Alva, since it gave her an opportunity to study plans for the
Twin Mansions. The dedicated young woman, already the
mother of two, had the good sense to see that, on the outside at
least, the projected houses were banal and perhaps ugly.

Raised in Paris, Alva had taken enough trips through the
French countryside to know a château could be a thing of
beauty. She decided that her conquest of the Four Hundred
might best be achieved by building herself a really beautiful Fifth
Avenue château.

Alva anticipated no trouble from her husband, since William
Kissam could easily afford the money for his wife's caprice. On
the Commodore's death he had received a sizeable chunk of the
old man's $100 million; on his father's demise added millions

would wend his way. Meanwhile, he was a highly paid officer of the New York Central Railroad.

In addition, William Kissam Vanderbilt was one of those husbands who valued domestic harmony at any cost. He never got much of it from Alva, who among other things tried to turn his offspring against him. Mainly to buy peace in the household, William Kissam obligingly agreed to part with approximately $3 million for a family residence. The location Alva picked was the block north of her father-in-law's Twin Mansions. Her single dwelling would fill the northwest corner of Fifth Avenue at Fifty-second Street.

Alva's bourgeoning ambitions were next crowned with the good fortune that often befalls the bold and the brave. Her quest for an architect led her to the *atelier* of Richard Morris Hunt, fifty-three years of age in 1880. Like Alva Vanderbilt, Hunt was an American who had grown up in France. He was the first American to study architecture at the world famous Ecole des Beaux Arts and had been known as the handsomest Yankee in Paris.

Returning to this country, Hunt was not only the best-trained architect in the United States, but he was owner of the finest domestic architectural library. Settling in Paris-like Greenwich Village, he turned out to be a first-class teacher of students who clustered around him in the Tenth Street Studio Building. Among other commissions, Hunt designed the first apartment house in New York; the tall Tribune building on Park Row; and the base of the Statue of Liberty. At the same time he developed a philosophic attitude toward his various employers and once told his students, "The first thing you've got to remember is that it's your client's money you are spending. Your business is to do the best you can while following his wishes. If he wants you to build a house upside down standing on its chimney, it is up to you to do so, and still get the best results possible."

Hunt had not yet found himself in his native land. Posterity would rate him as an architect with a glorious yet reminiscent imagination, but until 1880 he had failed to apply it. Yet when Alva Vanderbilt darkened his door—or he hers—Hunt's career suddenly slid into focus. Wrote a biographer, "It was as if some angel had descended . . . and whispered the word with which he was to immortalize himself, namely—Adaptation."

According to legend, Alva outlined to Hunt her dreams of a Fifth Avenue château, ending, "You can choose any style you like, Norman, Italian, or Spanish. I don't care what it is, so long as it's medieval."

This does not sound like Alva Vanderbilt; nothing in her life indicates she would treat a serious matter so airily. Like other anecdotes about her efforts during the construction of the mansion, this sounds like the fabrication of a jealous rival. During her lifetime, Alva occupied personal mansions of Francis I and Louis XIV, and stately homes built in Colonial, Gothic, and Georgian styles in such localities as New York, Newport, and Sands Point, Long Island. She took enough interest in their development to be accepted as a member of the American Institute of Architects. The court jester of Society, Harry Lehr, once quipped that Alva liked nothing better than to find herself knee deep in mortar. Years later, when she was a guest at Blair Castle in Scotland, the centuries-old home of the Duke of Atholl, Alva lifted up her nose and said, "It's not correct. My castle at Sands Point is far more authentic."

So it hardly seems possible that Alva sat by doing nothing while her beautiful château was built. While construction was being carried on, Richard Morris Hunt took trips abroad, scouring southern Europe for tapestries, doorways, chandeliers, wainscotting, stained-glass windows, flooring, fireplaces, marquetry chairs and tables, and suits of armor. One treasure he proudly bore home was Rembrandt's *Turkish Chief*; another was an alabaster bathtub, which Alva grabbed for herself.

Alva's daughter Consuelo says her mother went abroad as often as Hunt in quest of furnishings from Paris dealers and historic sites. She also sat herself down one day and designed a Vanderbilt coat of arms involving three acorns. "Because great oaks from little acorns grow," she explained graciously. The acorn design was spread lavishly over the exterior of her mansion. Throughout Alva seems to have treated Richard Morris Hunt with more courtesy than she accorded her husband. If at times his lady employer acted in an overbearing manner, Hunt did not seem to care. "She's a wonder," he said. "It's as much as one man's brain can do to keep up with her."

In preparation for his job, Hunt re-examined and revalued the foremost châteaux of the French Renaissance. As he did this, the architect evolved his idea of Adaptability, which can otherwise be described as irregularity or informal eclecticism. Up to that point the Stewart and Twin Mansions, as well as a few public buildings, had borrowed from various classical styles, but had done so in regular fashion; that is, the buildings were formal, box-like, conventional. Hunt began to think of utilizing past styles in an informal manner, creating irregular silhouettes with the cream of past glories.

Accordingly, he sketched for Alva a mansion loosely employing the most graceful features of the Château de Blois in Touraine and the castle at Bourges of Jacques Coeur, a self-made Croesus of the fifteenth century. The projected mansion was a joyous amalgam of balconies, bay windows, bow windows, dormers, high-tilted roof with pinnacles, gables, and an eye-catching conical spire above the front entrance. Areas of richly carved design—arabesques of cherubs, acanthus leaves, and the Vanderbilt acorns—contrasted with handsome wall surfaces. A deeply recessed balcony on the second floor, oriel windows, high turrets, and picturesque steep roof with chimneys and decorative crestings reflected Blois and Coeur, with occasional touches of the equally beautiful châteaux at Chenonceaux and Azay-le-Rideau. All this blended perfectly, producing a latter-day château with the true ambiance of centuries gone by.

Hunt understood that, unlike males who ordained mansions, his female patron did not want a building to stand forever as a monument, nor did she particularly wish a comfortable place to live. Alva craved a social weapon, a residence with design so stunning that no one would refuse her invitations. Hunt obliged. The Vanderbilt mansion turned out to be as lovely as its instigators hoped. In heartfelt tribute, one writer called it a singing marriage between the two noble châteaux from which it had been adapted.

Instead of standing solidly, like its Fifth Avenue predecessors, the Alva mansion had a graceful sweep promising delights

within. One who admired the mansion—surprisingly—was
Charles Follen McKim, of the fledgling architectural firm
McKim, Mead, and White, who confessed that whenever possible he walked up Fifth Avenue at night before going to bed and
stood across the street feasting his eyes on the Vanderbilt
château. Of this work by a rival architect, he stated, "I can sleep
better at night, knowing it's there."

Alva's singing-marriage château was of aristocratic gray limestone and stood four stories high, with a blue-slate roof. Set back
slightly from the sidewalk, it was entered by wide steps of glistening marble leading to an impressive iron-grill entrance. At either
side of the portals two bas-relief watchdogs stood guard. The
structure, architects said, was a notable example of verticality, or
pyramidization; that is, the human eye instinctively traveled
from bottom to top in viewing it, rather than side to side. The
whole was topped by several irregular, steep mansard roofs
crowned by high copper crestings, with chimneys of multiple
shapes.

Around the roof were culverin towers and battlements from
which medieval archers could be imagined shooting arrows at
Fifth Avenue strollers. Pinnacles and gables rimmed the roof
and eye-catching medieval spires rose above the Fifth Avenue
front. No two areas of the exterior appeared the same in the
profusion of balconies, dormers, arched windows, and frieze
work. Here was an indubitable bit of Renaissance France on a
Manhattan corner, and everyone seemed to approve except the
iconoclastic Chicago architect Louis Sullivan. After viewing it, he
inquired, "Must you wait until a man in a top hat comes out of it
before you begin to laugh?"

The portals of Alva's château led into a majestic reception hall,
with a floor of checkered marble and ceiling of paneled oak.
Above a high wainscotting of carved Caen stone hung rich
Italian tapestries. Ahead and to the right stood a grand staircase
of white marble which rose three floors against a background of
stained-glass recalling Milan Cathedral. It was said that this
noble staircase was wide enough for a regiment of cavalry to
mount without tightening ranks, but to growing Consuelo Vanderbilt, it became a thing of nightly terror. "I can still re-

member," she writes, "how long and terrifying was that dark and endless sweep of stairway as, with acute sensations of fear, I climbed to my room every night, leaving below the light and its comforting rays."

Most of the decoration was by Herter Brothers, though Alard of Paris did the Regence Salon, a Francis I chamber off the vestibule where Alva planned to receive her guests on the nights the Vanderbilts gave a dinner or ball. Naturally, the hostess would station herself beneath her full-length portrait by Raymond de Madrazo, an artist whose best-known work was *After the Ball*. The salon further boasted three Gobelin tapestries a century old but still of amazing color and freshness. The ceiling, painted by Paul Beaudry, showed the marriage of Cupid and Psyche.

Also on the first floor was a mammoth dining room; on dancing nights the sliding doors between it and a large Louis XV salon could be opened to create a huge ballroom. At the ends of the baronial banquet hall stood twin Renaissance fireplaces of stone and oak. One end culminated in a stained-glass window of monumental proportions, picturing Francis I and Henry VIII, in the midst of colorful courtiers, meeting on the Field of the Cloth of Gold. Floor, wainscotting, and high ceiling were of polished oak, transported piecemeal from a historic château in France. The Renaissance fireplaces had also been lifted from their original settings.

Along the sides of the room more stained-glass windows by Oudinot added bright color. Elaborate crystal and wrought-iron chandeliers lighted the hall. Fifteen feet up from the floor was a balcony big enough to hold twenty musicians on dancing nights. The three Vanderbilt children would crouch on this balcony on dinner-party evenings, when the long table below was covered by damask cloth, gold service, fine crystal and china, and red roses in glorious profusion.

Adjoining the dining room was a so-called breakfast nook adorned with Flemish tapestries; here Rembrandt's *Turkish Chief* had come to rest. Nearby a white drawing room featured Boucher tapestries, paintings, delicate French chairs and tables, and numerous *objets d'art;* its priceless piece was a beautiful *secretaire* and commode, with bronzes chiseled by Gouthière, once the property of Marie Antoinette. The family living room, a paneled Renaissance salon, occupied the front of the house, overlooking Fifth Avenue. Nearby was a carved-wood Grinling Gibbons Room.

On the second floor were various state bedrooms, each boasting heavy draperies, tapestries, and mighty canopied four-poster beds worthy of royal palaces. Alva's boudoir was considered the most luxurious room in the house. Among much else it was walled with squares of plate glass mirrors touching one another; on them were painted blossoming cherry trees that seemed to rise from the floor. In the bathroom, with its alabaster tub, fixtures were of solid gold and plumbing the most modern.

It is hard to imagine this expensive urban château containing rooms that could be called small and dreary, yet Consuelo Vanderbilt uses these words to describe the third-floor quarters of William Kissam Vanderbilt, whose millions made the whole edifice possible.

This same third floor was dominated by a gymnasium or play-room two stories high, its area so large that the children and their cousins roller skated and rode bicycles without inhibition. On ball nights the gymnasium, decorated by orchids, roses, and clinging vines, was transformed into the gorgeous bower where guests enjoyed the post-midnight supper prepared and served by Vanderbilt chefs and servants, with an assist from the staff of the famed restaurant Delmonico's.

The William Kissam Vanderbilt mansion radiated a medieval atmosphere of romance, intrigue, and potential sorrow. In the years that followed this branch of the family turned its marble halls into a backdrop for drama. The chief romance touching it was a rancid one, involving acts of mother-to-daughter cruelty worthy of the Dark Ages; before that, the air was poisoned by marital discord, as Alva and William Kissam edged toward the first major divorce of American Society.

Where intrigue was concerned, however, the lovely château more than lived up to its aura. Because of the mansion—and it alone—the Vanderbilts became top members of the snobbish group known as the Four Hundred. Alva's overall plan in building the mansion was, of course, to establish herself amidst so much opulence and luxury that the Knickerbocracy would demand to see it and (incidentally) her. This would automatically place her inside the platinum ring of Society, for those who accepted her hospitality out of curiosity were obliged by good manners to invite her back to their own homes.

Accordingly, she announced plans for a gala costume ball on the night of March 26, 1883. Alva picked that date because it came just after Easter, with Gotham Society parched for diversion following the drawn-out rigors of Lent. She displayed self-confidence—even arrogance—by scheduling her ball for a Monday night, a time of the week sacred to at-homes given by Mrs. William Astor, formidable leader of the Four Hundred.

Despite her outward confidence Alva was nervously aware that the success of her ball depended heavily on Mrs. Astor. If Caroline Schermerhorn Astor, escorted by major domo Ward McAllister, appeared at the ball, her presence would automatically ensure the attendance of the cream of New York Society. But if Mrs. Astor doggedly remained at home, presiding over her own gathering, the best people would stay away from the Vanderbilt ball.

Nor did it seem very likely at first that Mrs. Astor would attend. On every previous occasion she had snubbed Vanderbilts, young and old. To her intimates she characterized the Vanderbilt fortune as vulgar railroad money and called their Renaissance mansions *nouveaux riches* blights on the Avenue.

The story of Alva Vanderbilt's conquest of Caroline Astor is an oft-told saga of Gotham Society. The chubby, determined lady did it by means of Carrie Astor, Mrs. Astor's youngest and favorite daughter. To provide entertainment for the Vanderbilt ball, various High Society groups had begun rehearsing quadrilles like the Hobby Horse and the Mother Goose, the latter conceived in the fertile mind of Ward McAllister. One of the young persons involved with her girlfriends in a Star Quadrille was Carrie Astor. Alva professed to learn this only a few days before the ball, reacting with outrage. "Why, I have never met this young lady or her mother," she exclaimed indignantly. "I cannot possibly entertain her in my home!"

Carrie Astor's sobs of disappointment softened her mother's heart and the reigning queen of the Four Hundred hastily deposited her calling card at the door of the Vanderbilt mansion, indicating receptivity to a ball invitation. On the magic night Mrs. Astor appeared costumed as a lady of the Venetian court, adorned with a $200,000 sampling of her million-dollar jewel collection.

Thus Alva Vanderbilt's ball added up to triumph. Outstanding, perhaps, was the mansion itself, since it offered a dream-setting for an opulent costume ball of days gone by. Thoughts of such gaudy occasions had no doubt spurred the imaginations of the original architects of Blois and Bourges.

That night, 1,200 people—a far cry from Mrs. Astor's ballroom and its paltry 400—arrived at 10:30 or after, to cross the sidewalk under a striped awning and over a carpet of Vanderbilt maroon, past the bas-relief watchdogs, and through the portals of the mansion. A large crowd of outside onlookers, mostly women and girls, gasped at the costumes of those alighting from spanking horse-drawn carriages.

In the reception hall, footmen in powdered wigs and knee breeches relieved gentlemen of coats and directed ladies upstairs to a state bedroom where maids in French peasant dress attended milady's needs. Since the mansion resembled a sixteenth-century château, most of the assembled guests had chosen to wear costumes of the contemporary French court, or similar courts in Italy, England, Germany, Austria, and even Russia. Several young girls came as Joan of Arc, while engaged couples and young marrieds opted for Romeo and Juliet. Among middle-aged ladies, Madame Pompadour won favor, while mature men chose Cardinal Richelieu. A few males appeared as monks, several with bare feet; ladies were abbesses. Men were knights, courtiers, princes, hussars, gondoliers, or court jesters. There was a smattering of Villonesque troubadours and a handful of tattered streetgirls. No one, a cynic noted, came as Napoleon or the Marquis de Sade.

When ladies returned from the upper regions, the couples joined the reception line leading to host and hostess. Approaching Alva, they identified themselves to a footman, who announced the names loudly. This was necessary in part because Alva did not know all her guests, but also because so many were costumed beyond recognition. While dawdling on the receiving line, guests were free to compare Alva in person with her Madrazo portrait, under which she stood. One critical fellow thought the painting did not do justice to its subject. "She is small," he mused, "with a French cast of countenance, very pretty and distinguée." The Madrazo portrait failed to capture this.

For the ultimate event of her life to date, Alva had arrayed herself as a Venetian Renaissance countess, following a painting by Alexis Cabanel. On her curls perched a wide, upturned Milan bonnet studded with jewels whose glow further brightened a radiant face. From under the fetching cap, ringlets of hair tumbled to bare shoulders. A low cut shoulder-strap bodice was of blue satin covered with gold embroidery, square-cut at the neck, with flowing sleeves of transparent gold tissue. From the center of her bodice, a double-strand pearl necklace looped to the midriff, then rose to a shoulder-strap anchor. Her brocade skirt, puffed at the hips, was of white and yellow with shadings from deepest orange to lightest canary, and highlighted in white. On it figures of flowers and leaves were outlined in gold, white, and iridescent beads. A light blue satin train, elaborately embroidered and lined in Roman red, draped her feet.

By her side stood William Kissam Vanderbilt attired in yellow silk tights, yellow and black trunks, yellow doublet, and black velvet cloak embroidered with gold—a replica of a portrait of the Duc de Guise that hung in his own collection. The Duc de Guise, incidentally, was murdered in the Château de Blois.

At Alva's other side stood the matchmaking Lady Mandeville in a dress copied from Van Dyck's portrait of Princess de Croy, black velvet with puff sleeves and stand-up collar of Venetian lace, crowned by a Van Dyck hat and Venetian plumes. Nearby stood William Henry Vanderbilt in severe black and white evening attire; he was the only guest not in costume. His wife was garbed as a lady-in-waiting to Marie Antoinette.

After exchanging words with hostess and host, people advanced to a ballroom which, in addition to its usual massive chandeliers, was illuminated by special calcium lights that contributed a silvery glow to the proceedings. Impressions of magnificence induced by the surroundings were increased by the stained-glass window showing the meeting of Francis I and Henry VIII. Set high above the assemblage, it gave the illusion of another fancy dress ball in another ballroom.

The Hobby Horse Quadrille began promptly at 11:30, with musicians in the balcony playing violins, violoncellos, double basses, horns, trombones, and kettledrums. In this imitation steeplechase, dancers on human horses performed twists and turns with great dexterity. The feet of the human horses were hidden by multihued hangings and several of the bent-over men tripped on these, hurling riders to the hard, polished floor. Yet no one was hurt and the Hobby Horse sparked a night of fun and gaiety.

Next came the Mother Goose Quadrille, brainchild of McAllister, in which dancers dressed like Mary, Mary Quite Contrary and other folk of nursery rhymes. This was followed by the Dresden China Quadrille, and after it the Star Quadrille, among its performers Carrie Astor, happy as could be. Also dancing was Miss Edith Carow, destined to be First Lady of the Land as Mrs. Theodore Roosevelt. Society's empress, Mrs. Astor, beamed with maternal pride as her youngest daughter cavorted on the floor. Last came the Opera Bouffe, danced by sixteen young marrieds trained by Alva's sister, Mrs. Frederico Yznaga. This was deemed eccentric rather than pretty, but neatly done.

So concluded the entertainment part of the evening, allowing guests to take over the dance floor themselves for waltzes, gavottes, and the currently popular Ticklish Water Polka. Or they could proceed upstairs to the third floor where the gymnasium had been turned into a spectacular garden of roses, evergreens, and orchids, the last costing $2 apiece. Guests could dine buffet style or sit down at a table for an eight-course meal which included eight different wines of ambrosial vintage.

More interesting than dancing or eating was looking at the costumes. All the Vanderbilts were handsomely garbed. Of the daughters, Mrs. Elliott F. Sheperd was a marquise with a train of Nile-green satin; Mrs. Seward Webb, a hornet with antennae of diamonds; Mrs. W. D. Sloane, Bo-Peep with jeweled poppies and diamond-studded crook; and Mrs. Hamilton McK. Twombly, a Lady of the Dutch Court, in a brocade of embroidered pink roses and leaves of gold and silver, with a Watteau back.

Mrs. Astor's Venetian-lady gown of dark velvet was embroidered with gold roses and other designs in pearls. Inside her long, flowing sleeves glittered surprising jewels. Her hair, left loose, was covered by a cap fastened with plumes and *aigrettes* of diamonds. Ropes of diamonds and pearls girdled her neck.

Ward McAllister appeared as Count de la Mole, lover of Marguerite de Valois, in a suit of purple velvet slashed with scarlet silk. Doublet and hose were so intricate that he had to climb into them from a stepladder with the aid of two manservants, a process that took an hour.

Mrs. Paran Stevens, known as the Mme. Sans Gene of New York Society, was Queen Elizabeth; Mrs. Bradley Martin, who ten years later gave her own celebrated ball, was Mary Stuart in ruby velvet embroidered with gold, a blouse of silver and white brocaded with satin ornaments and a network of pearls. Mr. Bradley Martin was Louis XIV. The male costumes at the Vanderbilt Ball inspired a joke that kept Society chuckling for years. "I'm Appius Claudius," one guest supposedly said to another. "Oh, are you?" came the reply. "I'm uncomfortable as Richard the Lion-Hearted."

One of the most admired gowns adorned Mrs. Chauncey M. Depew, who came as Ondine in a dress of sea-green satin with velvet moons caught up in clusters of water lilies and long grasses. Her hair, powdered with silver dust, was coiled under a cap of white tulle, spangled with silver stars and ornamented by a diamond pin. Her jewels included a large diamond lizard and a turtle, a diamond star necklace, and pins and bracelets representing dew drops.

A few guests showed unusual imagination. Miss Amy La Farge, attired as a huntress, wore a splendid tiger skin lined with red satin; her hands clutched a bow and a quiver of arrows hung on her back; on her hair perched an unlikely crescent of diamonds. Senator Wagstaff was Daniel Boone in a suit of leather, with leggings, moccasins, and coonskin cap with protruding porculine quills; he carried a rifle and Bowie knife in his belt. A male member of the Oelrichs family was a Sioux Indian chief. Mrs. Arthur Welman was Puss, her ornate hairdo topped by the face of a stuffed kitten; lest anyone fail to understand this, the word Pussy was spelled out in rhinestones on her neckband. Mrs. Buchanan Winthrop, as Pride, was a peacock.

Chauncey M. Depew contrasted with his wife as Father Knickerbocker in rich broadcloth and diamond shoe-buckles. Isaac Iselin, as a Polish general, wore a tilted fur shako and gleaming leather hip boots, together with realistic spurs. Mrs. Theron Strong was Goddess of Ice, with diamond icicles pendant.

Older folk began leaving the party at 3:00 A.M., but others remained. Supposedly the festivities were to end at 4:00, but fun and frivolity reached such heights that the dancing went on until 6:00.

At one point during the night, Alva Vanderbilt and Mrs. Astor, both dressed as Venetian noblewomen, were observed in deep conversation. The two appeared to like one another as much as was possible for an established Society matron in her middle years and an aspiring lady who had just turned thirty. At this precise moment, Alva dropped her idea of ousting Mrs. Astor as Gotham's social leader. She liked her too much.

Mrs. Astor showed approval in a more concrete way. Returning home in the dawn's early light, she paused to add the name Vanderbilt to the list of guests for her exclusive annual ball. This was exactly what Alva had wanted. By using her husband's millions and her own wits, she had overnight risen from parvenu status to top drawer New York Society. Without her, the Vanderbilts might have gone on forever as a clan rich but not social. From then on, however, the public told tales of a mythical personage called Mrs. Astorbilt.

Also present at the epoch-making Vanderbilt Ball was Cornelius Vanderbilt II, oldest son of William Henry and the one who would inherit the major part of a $200 million fortune on William Henry's demise.

For the affair Cornelius II, who had inherited the Commodore's tall handsomeness, garbed himself as Louis XVI, in fawn-colored brocade trimmed with *point de Espagne* lace and a waistcoat of olive hue with pointings of real silver; with this he wore a diamond-hilted sword. His wife had gone off on her own tangent to dress as Electric Light, in white satin trimmed with jewels and a high-rise diamond headdress.

Few who knew Cornelius Vanderbilt II were surprised that he stepped forth in the raiment of a monarch. For Corneel—as the family called him—was ever-conscious of the importance of being a Vanderbilt. Whereas his two brothers, William Kissam and George Washington, were occasionally lighthearted, Corneel lived with the full weight of riches on his shoulders. The world-at-large might believe wealth lightened the problems of living, but this Vanderbilt knew better: Being a millionaire was tough work. Of him, a contemporary wrote, "Mr. Vanderbilt has no fads or hobbies, and is a man of industry and strong domestic habits."

Bypassing the call of higher learning, Cornelius as a youth went to work in an accounting and banking firm outside the family, thus preparing himself for the management of an eventual fortune. While still in his teens, his grandfather offered him a trip abroad; Cornelius refused on the grounds that vacations were an indulgence. It is hardly surprising that this sober-sided man met his wife while they both taught Sunday school at St. Bartholomew's. She was Alice Gwynne, daughter of a wealthy Cincinnati family, and from the time she took her wedding vows she matched her husband in awareness of the value of Vanderbilts.

With the death of his father, in 1885, Cornelius became the hard-working chairman of the board of the New York Central, at the same time grasping the reins of numerous other Vanderbilt enterprises. A business associate evaluated him in this way—

> Cornelius is the brightest of all the Vanderbilts. He is not so sharp as his grandfather, nor so shrewd as his father, but in mental equipoise he is their superior. He is more phlegmatic than either, never allows his passion to sway him, is always courteous, considerate, and gentle. . . . he is never heard to use a harsh or impure word and is known for his blameless, upright life.

With his stern dignity, Cornelius realized his prominence as head of a family which had among its many obligations that of showing other millionaires how to spend money. On the night of Alva's ball, Cornelius was serenely aware, in his regal attire, that a glorious mansion of his own was rising a few blocks uptown. His site was on Fifth Avenue and Fifty-seventh Street, with an imposing entrance on the side street. Officially his address was 1 West Fifty-seventh, but his huge domicile encompassed 742–46 Fifth Avenue.

Since his father had secured the architectural services of Herter Brothers, and Alva had employed Richard Morris Hunt, Cornelius had been obliged to hire George Browne Post, smartest of Hunt's pupils at the Greenwich Village *atelier*. From him Cornelius demanded a domicile so elaborate that Post labored from 1880–1882 on the plans alone. Then a residence larger than Alva's—though not yet as big as the Twin Mansions—began to appear on the northwest corner of Fifty-seventh Street.

Corneel had set aside the sum of $2–3 million for his new abode. Rising four stories on a high basement—five stories in all—it was of red pressed brick that contrasted strikingly with ornately carved Bedford limestone trim. This time horizontality got emphasis, as strongly developed floor lines ringed the structure. Irregularity ran rampant, with far more classical detail visible than on Alva's singing marriage. Corneel's stately mansion fairly bristled with gabled dormers, picturesque chimneys, turrets, carved stone cornices, balconies, recessed and bay windows. A large sloping roof of brick and tile topped the edifice.

Like Alva's mansion, this was a French château transplanted to New York and some said it derived from the Château de Blois, while others called it Henri IV. Corneel and his architect knew better. Successfully or not, they had labored with Fontainbleau in mind and finally a critic obliged them by calling the latest Vanderbilt mansion "a reminiscence of Fontainbleau." Those in search of further words to praise Corneel's mansion could only call it more impressive but less interesting than Alva's.

So within an area of six blocks the Vanderbilts had built four Renaissance-oriented mansions and could be said, with an assist from A. T. Stewart, to have begun a neo-Babylonian era of living among the Very Rich. Probably never before—and certainly not since—had a single family dominated so large a stretch of the foremost boulevard of a metropolis. For in addition to the mansions, the Vanderbilt domain also encompassed those impressive residences of Mrs. Hamilton McK. Twombly and Mr. Seward Webb, daughters of William Henry.

Taking a Sunday stroll to look at the Vanderbilt homes became a popular diversion among citizens of the growing city and one lady privileged to see the mansions both inside and out was reported as stating, "Any dreams of splendor by the passerby are more than surpassed by the revelations inside." However, another New Yorker took a European houseguest to view the mansions. He was unimpressed, saying, "Wouldn't it be nice if they were surrounded by moats."

Years passed, and amidst his Fifty-seventh Street magnificence Cornelius Vanderbilt II grew uncomfortably aware that other multimillionaires were following his family pattern a trifle too closely. Land on Fifth Avenue below Fifty-ninth Street was hard to come by, in large part because of the Vanderbilts' own construction. But millionaires from New York and elsewhere had suddenly begun building on the Avenue above Fifty-ninth, an area until recently known as Squatters' Sovereignty, since it was covered with the lopsided shacks of down-and-outers. This property was now being gobbled up, with fine homes arising on the east side of the Avenue, facing Central Park.

The skills of Richard Morris Hunt, the most celebrated architect in town because of the beauty of Alva's chateau, were conspicuously at work here. At Sixty-first Street, Hunt had created for Elbridge T. Gerry one of his mansions of picturesque irregularity, inspired by the Louis XII wing of the Château de Blois. Working with his son, Hunt had remained an architect indulgent to the demands of his money-drenched employers. Under Gerry's guidance he produced a pink château, vast and ornate, which caused a critic to comment, "He eschewed the classic for the rococo and the result revealed a degree of ornateness and sumptuousness unsurpassed." Featuring a high, pointed roof, the Gerry mansion also possessed a medieval tower, the whole called by another critic "a nostalgic repertoire of transitional Renaissance motifs."

At Sixty-eighth Street, the inspired Hunt evolved for Henry G. Marquand an early Renaissance dwelling with overtones of Gothic, displaying even more towers, balconies, turrets, spires, and other colorful embellishments than decorated the Cornelius Vanderbilt mansion.

All this gave Cornelius food for thought. At first he assuaged his ego by commissioning Hunt to build The Breakers, then and forever the finest (if coldest) mansion in Newport, Rhode Island, Society's favorite summer colony. But this was not enough. Powerful pride in family next impelled him to summon George Browne Post and order him to more than double the size of his Fifth Avenue mansion by extending it back to Fifty-eighth Street, with a grander portal there. Not only would this result in the largest mansion in the city, but it would also offer the best conceivable view, looking as it did over Grand Army Plaza and off into Central Park. To the far left stood the original Plaza Hotel; the Plaza familiar to our world did not rise until 1907.

In order to achieve his grandiose dream, Cornelius needed to buy and demolish the fine brownstones between the rear of his mansion and Fifty-eighth Street, as well as pay the city $190,000 for a parcel of land facing Grand Army Plaza—all this territory, including the original half of the Vanderbilt mansion is covered today by the Bergdorf Goodman specialty store. These fresh plans would bring the overall cost of the Cornelius mansion to more than $5 million. Explaining to friends his reasons for expansion, Cornelius modestly declared, "I want to dominate the Plaza." More likely he meant Fifth Avenue.

This time the populace was denied the pleasure of watching a mansion grow. Sober-sided Cornelius was the oldest son of the man who disdained the common people and in one generation the family mind had not altered. Cornelius instructed architect Post to erect a high shell around the construction site, to keep the curious from peering inside. At the same time Cornelius was so anxious to complete his mansion that he paid the workmen extra salary—there was nothing like overtime then—to labor into the night. To make this possible, huge bonfires were lit inside the shell and an eerie orange glow illuminated the region of Grand Army Plaza.

Finally, in the spring of 1893, the Cornelius Vanderbilt mansion was ready. The protective shell came down and before the eyes of New Yorkers appeared a mansion that, impressive before, had doubled in splendor. Saluting it, a newspaper rhapsodized, "The Vanderbilts have come nobly forward to show the world how millionaires live."

Like the Fifty-seventh Street half of the mansion, the new wing was built of red brick with facings of gray limestone. To augment his reminiscence of Fontainbleau, architect Post had devised a giant potpourri of styles, a structure of bastard beauty borrowing not only from Fontainbleau, but from the French château style of the sixteenth and seventeenth centuries along with touches of Victorian modern. A solid, pointed Gothic tower at the Fifty-eighth Street corner (Richard Morris Hunt was called in to consult on this) dominated the building. Instead of a single mansard roof, the elongated mansion appeared to have dozens rising in peaks and gables, with a forest of lightning rods atop. Dormer windows were in abundance, and everywhere lay examples of an architect's unbridled imagination. In all, the mansion was huge, magnificent, overpowering. Cornelius Vanderbilt had gained his wish: He dominated the Plaza—and indeed the Avenue and the city as well, for no more spectacular mansion ever rose afterward.

Inevitably there were those who thought this Vanderbilt mansion too dominant. Critics of the building noted that, though a combination of two structures, the result somehow resembled three—"aggregated rather than built together, a strong central roof might have brought the whole into alliance." Another said that the original mansion on Fifty-seventh Street should have been demolished, enabling the architect to start from scratch!

Indoors, the Vanderbilt mansion had a stunning total of 137 rooms, with an army of thirty servants to take care of them. These servants were required to rise at 6:00 A.M. and do most of their work before 9:00 A.M., at which time the family appeared to begin the day without the sight of sordid matters like house-cleaning.

One aspect of the hybrid mansion won everyone's admiration. This was the Fifty-eighth Street entrance, known as the "state" entry and used only for galas, weddings, and funerals. Here was a design of nobility and beauty—a huge iron fence around an area the size of a pocket-park. Within it lay a circular driveway leading to and from a magnificent *porte cochére*. On festive nights this entrance, lighted by lamps on all sides, was a dramatic sight. Said *Valentine's Manual*, "Visitors lucky enough to be on this spot during a social function will never forget the procession of smart equipages, drawn by blooded horses, and manned by liveried footmen and grooms, discharging passengers, each of them a Society member of high standing."

Lucky guests traversed the Vanderbilt maroon carpet to a reception hall considered more impressive than the Supreme Court of the United States. Measuring forty by fifty feet, with a ceiling fifty feet high, it was made entirely of Caen stone, in the manner of Blois. To the left lay a mahogany paneled library with large windows looking out on Fifth Avenue. Adjoining this was a small Louis XV salon and next to it a Watercolor Room. By joining the ballrooms of his first and second houses, Cornelius had achieved an expanse of immense proportions. His solid oak dining room was one of those legendary places where 200 guests could sit down to dine from gold plate. A meal for this number could be whipped up on a few hours' notice.

Harper's Weekly dusted off the words "palatiality" and "sumptuosity" to describe this Vanderbilt mansion. The magazine pointed out that life in such stately halls was akin to dwelling in a museum. The writer then compared Fifth Avenue's many mansions to the White House and said they were less for comfortable living then a background for social functions—" designed for the exercise of ceremonious hospitality."

Confirmation of this was later relayed by a young lady who married a Vanderbilt scion and lived for a time in the Corneel mansion. She found the awesome quarters chilly and uncomfortable. For one thing the windows were set in disconcerting places, since in those days the facade had to be beautiful no matter where windows appeared—Stanford White became the first American architect able to locate windows in the proper spot for interior use as well as exterior appearance.

Though the Vanderbilt mansion radiated "sumptuosity"—the young lady proceeded—the bedrooms were small with tiny adjoining bathrooms in which the bathtubs were chilly tin encased in wood. The Cornelius Vanderbilts had not employed a decorator for the interior of the mansion. Rather they seemed to have tried a few experts, then ended up by doing most of it to please themselves. The result was room after room of routine French or Victorian taste. Gilt panels of birds and fruit were everywhere, along with ponderous red velvet hangings and paintings—"family portraits and badly painted cows and unnatural trees."

One room loathed by the rest of the family was doted on by Mrs. Vanderbilt, who had ripened into a formidable dowager. This was the so-called Persian Room on the first floor, replete with Turkish corners with striped awnings held aloft by scimitars, red satin pillows providing the only seats.

Great care had been lavished on creating Cornelius' master bedroom on the second floor overlooking Grand Army Plaza. But as he peered out the window following his first night of slumber the humorless man found a sight that drove him berserk.

In Grand Army Plaza, the city fathers had recently placed a fountain depicting a nude girl bathing in a pool. Corneel got an unobstructed view of the maiden's naked back from his bedroom window. To him, the sight was indecent, immoral, and obscene. The fulminating Croesus immediately contacted City Hall, demanding that the offending statue be removed. For once the weight of wealth failed to count, and the authorities laughed. So one of the richest men in the world, having spent millions to dominate the Plaza, found the Plaza dominating *him*. Rather than view the statue each morning, he angrily moved to another bedroom and stayed there.

"The old boy couldn't stand the 'rear' view," quipped the family member who passed this story along to posterity.

5

The $50 Million Club

THE multimillion-dollar homes of the Vanderbilts stood on Fifth Avenue below Fifty-ninth Street, while those of other families of wealth rosè on the Avenue above. All at once there were so many mansions a-building on Fifth Avenue between Fifty-ninth and Ninetieth Streets that a newspaper coined the name Millionaires' Row for that two-mile stretch of boulevard.

Another interested party took pencil in hand to estimate that a basic fortune of $50 million was required to build a mansion in any way comparable to the Vanderbilts. This was reminiscent of a story involving J. P. Morgan, proud owner of a series of increasingly handsome yachts christened *Corsair*. When a fellow Wall Streeter consulted him on the sums of money involved in owning and operating a yacht, Morgan grumped, "If you have to ask, you can't afford it."

It was the same with mansions. Those who needed to consider cost had no right to enter the mansion sweepstakes—though, as we shall see, a few considered themselves members of the hyper-exclusive $50 Million Club but were mistaken in this euphoric view.

Aside from suffering delusions of grandeur, another acceptable way existed to achieve an exalted mansion. This was to purchase a fine Fifth Avenue residence—of which a few were available between Fiftieth and Fifty-ninth, or a block east on Madison Avenue—then gut the interior and have it redecorated in Byzantine splendor.

Quite a few families did this, and it did not necessarily indicate a paucity of ready cash. Rather, it showed a lack of desire to go through the rigors of mansion building, preliminary planning followed by endless waiting for completion. One more possibility for evading headaches was to inhabit a handsome mansion already built and have it redecorated by Herter Brothers or the Tiffany Studio, formed in 1878 by Louis Comfort Tiffany, brilliant son of the city's foremost jeweler.

Such was the policy followed by the Mesdames Robert and Ogden Goelet, sisters-in-law and social rivals locked in deadly combat over who should stand before the world as *the* Mrs. Goelet. In the drawing for boxes at the Metropolitan Opera, Mrs. Ogden had been fortunate enough to get Box Number One. Mrs. Robert, forced to be content with Box Twenty-four, had evened matters by putting a brass plate on the door that simply said *Mrs. Goelet.*

These ladies and their Goelet husbands provide a primer-like example of the way the Knickerbocracy grew and flourished. Back in the early 1700s Peter Goelet, maker of musical instruments, began buying real estate. Perhaps because of this interest, he married a girl who inherited extensive holdings in what became the Fourteenth Street area of Manhattan. His son Peter continued the family enterprise, acquiring much land in the Forty-second Street area where Grand Central Station stands today. This second Peter waxed so rich that his two sons inherited $50 million apiece.

So both Goelet families had enough money to build Vanderbilt-style mansions, but opted for redoing the interiors of their own fashionable homes. The husbands faded into the background as the two socially ambitious ladies labored feverishly to out-do one another in the glories of decoration. Mrs. Robert jammed her home with elegances in the French tradition—pink, blue, and gilt rooms, furniture of the various Louis periods, and a connoisseur's collection of sedan chairs. Her sister-in-law favored the Italianate school of decoration, including suits of armor. The interiors, each splendid in its fashion, still failed to settle the issue of who was *the* Mrs. Goelet.

Another choosing the path of redecoration was the cool, calm, and collected Darius Ogden Mills. This Splendor Seeker paid $175,000 for a residence opposite St. Patrick's Cathedral and gave Herter Brothers *carte blanche* to redecorate the interior in the most lavish style possible. Then he left for the Pacific Coast on business.

On his return Mills found himself amidst surroundings a Shah of Persia might have envied, with richly carved woodwork, gorgeously picturesque ceilings, and beautifully inlaid furniture. The Wall Street banker Henry Clews, who wrote a thick book of reminiscences, reports that Mills also discovered himself on the receiving end of a bill for $450,000. At first enraged by the magnitude of the sum, he was soon assuaged by the fact that, for a brief moment at least, his stood as the most glorious interior along Fifth Avenue.

As opposed to the Goelets, Darius Ogden Mills was a specimen of the plutocrats just beginning to invade New York. Smooth rather than uncouth, he was not exactly a Barefoot Millionaire, yet in boyhood his shoes had been exceedingly thin of sole. Born in 1825 to an impecunious family in Westchester County, on the doorstep of New York City, he had been forced to seek work at age sixteen. He had done so in Buffalo, where a relative found him a job in a bank. Five years later the clever smoothie was chief teller, getting a percentage of yearly profits.

However, banking was too slow a road to riches for this icy young man. In 1848, Mills began listening to the siren song of the California Gold Rush. He did not consider becoming a rough and ready prospector; rather, he saw himself as banker and financial adviser to those who struck it rich.

Ever prudent, he traveled to the Coast with a load of pistols and other commodities to be disposed of at enormous profit in the gold fields. Setting up as banker in the Mother Lode town of Columbia, he soon advanced to the Gold Bank of Sacramento, dealing in gold dust, bullion, and financing panners of gold. As head of the Bank of California in San Francisco, he dominated the Golden West's most important source of money. He and his bank acquired railroads, mines, ranches, timberland, and water rights. Mills bought a 1,500-acre rancho as his own estate, and became the first millionaire west of the Mississippi to luxuriate in a private railroad car. His fortunes soared as the bank gained control of the fabled Comstock Lode in Nevada.

Yet Mills was an Easterner at heart. From the Pacific, he had invested heavily in Vanderbilt-run railroads and even secured ownership of the Mergenthaler Linotype Company, with headquarters in New York. In 1880, he moved to Manhattan, to function as a director of banks, railways, and industrial concerns. This change of locale in no way hindered his money-making; probably he was accumulating more millions than ever before.

However, a few plutocrats did choose to challenge the Vanderbilts on the top level of mansioneering. First and foremost among them was Henry Villard, who decreed a mansion that to the naked eye looked larger than Twin Mansions or Alva's château. Even as these two were under construction, ground was broken a block away, on Madison Avenue between Fiftieth and Fifty-first Streets, for the urban palace of this newest of Splendor Seekers.

But was he a true Robber Baron? At least three indubitable members of the breed—Jay Gould, J. P. Morgan, and Charles Crocker of San Francisco—stand on the record as believing it easier to make millions than to keep them. J. P. Morgan spoke for all when he told one of the Vanderbilt children, "Even a fool can make a million dollars, but it takes a sage to hold onto it." The Splendor Seeker who built the first keeping-up-with-the-Vanderbilts mansion made his fortune—on paper, a billion dollars—faster than anyone else in the rugged game, but was destined to lose it. In his book *The Robber Barons*, Matthew Josephson writes, "In those who led the procession, dishonesty, chicane, vulgarity, and a fierce passion for lucre were united." Villard's character lacked this necessary distillation.

But in his prime, Henry Villard was saluted by Wall Street as a modern Monte Cristo. Tall, solid, strong of feature, visage decorated by a fine down-turned mustache, he was a curious example of a decent, scrupulously honest man encumbered—you might say—by the glib tongue and winning personality of a sideshow spieler. Capable of conjuring up mighty schemes, Villard was uncannily able to make others believe his dreams would come true.

A few distinctions still cling to Henry Villard. First, his mansion on Madison Avenue behind St. Patrick's Cathedral remains standing today, the most central of the handful remaining in an unsentimental metropolis. Second, his urban palace brought the firm of McKim, Mead, and White—the last-named Stanford White—into the mansion building sphere. Lastly, he stands out as one of the few Splendor Seekers who by background rated the status of gentleman.

Born Ferdinand Heinrich Gustav Hilgard, in Bavaria, he was the liberal-minded son of an aristocratic family whose views enraged his Establishment father. At age nineteen the daring young man fled to America. Fearful that a stern parent might send agents to bring him home, he anglicized his name to Henry Villard and set about losing himself in the Middle West. Rapidly mastering English, he gained attention by his kinetic personality and gift of gab. For a time he sold books door to door, then real estate lots. Deciding on journalism as his career, he edited a smalltown newspaper and served as Midwest correspondent of the New York *Staats-Zeitung.*

In this capacity, he covered the Lincoln-Douglas debates and became close to Abraham Lincoln. His reportage attracted the attention of Horace Greeley and during the Civil War Villard served as adventurous war correspondent for Greeley's New

York *Tribune.* Following the war, he won further attention by marrying Helen Frances Garrison, only daughter of Abolitionist William Lloyd Garrison. Described as a dainty aristocrat in appearance, Helen Frances had inherited the forceful energy of her doughty parent.

How to explain the change in Henry Villard, over fifteen years, from intrepid war correspondent to wizard of financial manipulation? It is difficult and the man himself offers small aid. In time he wrote three heavy volumes of memoirs in which he referred to himself as "Mr. Villard" and used true Victorian reticence about the major events of his life. The book tells that, as a newly married man, he lived in Boston to be near the Garrison family. There he worked for the American Social Science Association which somehow introduced him to the mysteries of corporate and public finance. After surviving a stroke, he took his pregnant wife to Germany for a visit. In Heidelberg the dynamic fellow, not yet forty years old, was feted as an outstanding journalist and traveler. At one function he lent sympathetic ear to a group of German holders of defaulted Oregon & California Railroad bonds. Departing Germany, he promised to investigate their problem on his return to the United States.

In 1874, he left wife and baby in Boston to begin the long journey to Oregon. There his first view of the Great Northwest proved nothing short of cataclysmic; the beauty of the majestic land drained by the Columbia River set his emotions aflame. The Northwest acted like a massive dose of adrenalin on him, and Henry Villard instantly began to think the thoughts of an empire builder.

At this moment in history empire building was something quite feasible and the man who controlled transportation in any given area could become the emperor. The rails of the Northern Pacific Railroad, projected as the country's second transcontinental span, reached only to Bismarck in the Dakota Territory. Oregon's own railroads—Oregon Central and Oregon & California—were in poor financial shape, in need of a strong hand to pull them together. Conditions were better in the shipping field, where the Oregon Steamship Company operated at a profit. A delighted Villard found that, despite its prosperity, the steamship line could be bought for $3 million.

He quickly set about raising every dollar he could beg, borrow, or pledge, but his best efforts resulted in only $30,000. To his perfervid mind, anything had begun to seem possible. Using the $30,000 to obtain a sixty-day option on the steamship line, he raced back to New York—this, in itself, an accomplishment at the time. Using his magnetic personality to the utmost, he persuaded a Wall Street bank to execute a mortgage against the shipping line—"an amazing bit of financial legerdemain," this has been called. Proceeds from the mortgage, plus bond sales, brought him the $3 million needed to acquire Oregon Steamship. Under his management, the value of the company rose to $10 million. Writes Villard in his memoirs, "This astonishing increase naturally raised Mr. Villard to a commanding position on Wall Street."

With his steamship profits, Villard next bought the two railroads in Oregon and others elsewhere, issuing stocks with high, quick dividends. Shortly, he had issued $21 million in stocks, some paying dividends as high as $200. According to an admiring Henry Clews, this made Villard the topmost stock-waterer in the seamy field of railroad finance. (Another has pointed out that the Robber Barons invented a new type of arithmetic, in which two and two no longer equaled four, but six, eight, or ten.) The empire builder's aim was to extend one of his Oregon railroads south along the bank of the Columbia River, a move which would not only enrich him, but keep the Northern Pacific from becoming transcontinental.

In this effort to thwart the Northern Pacific, Villard found himself pitted against original master manipulators like J. P. Morgan, Jay Gould, and Collis P. Huntington, the railroad king of California. Villard learned that these men had arranged the sale of $40 million in Northern Pacific first-mortgage bonds to a powerful banking syndicate headed by Drexel, Morgan, and Company. The largest such transaction so far in history, it assured Northern Pacific enough money to build rapidly through to the Pacific.

In Villard's manic mind, only one action seemed possible: He himself must gain control of Northern Pacific. Already he had made secret purchases of its stock and once again the empire builder rushed to New York to execute a maneuver that has been saluted as Napoleonic.

Assembling a group of wealthy men who had profited greatly from Northwest investments, Villard confided that in his mind reposed a plan with so vast a profit-potential that details could not be divulged. Using his hypnotic powers of persuasion, he asked the men to demonstrate faith in him by investing heavily in an unknown scheme. "The very mystery of the affair caused a rush of subscriptions," one writer says. Speedily Villard raised $8 million for use as he saw fit. This transaction, known as "the blind pool," remains one of the dramatic moments in railroad finance.

Yet $8 million was still not enough to gain control of Northern Pacific. Once more—in the summer of 1881—Villard convened his faithful investors and this time held nothing back in revealing the monumental plan. Again he aroused high enthusiasm with the assembled men who subscribed an additional $12 million to Oregon & Transcontinental, a holding company that promptly issued $30 million in stock to those who had so far provided support to the extent of $20 million. In September, after what had been called sensational maneuvers on the market, Villard got control of Northern Pacific. Proclaiming himself president, he amended its charter to permit "mining, shipping, land-jobbing, town building, and the claiming of land needed for such operations." He then issued orders for fast completion of the transcontinental Northern Pacific. Of this multiplicity of operations, a contemporary wrote—

> There is probably no instance in the whole history of railway manipulation in which a man has presented to the world, and with such amazing success, such a specious appearance of possessing solid capital where so little existed in reality.

He began in 1879 with nothing and succeeded in the course of a year in accumulating by adroit methods . . . $3,500,000 of assets in railroad securities. With this as a basis of operation, in five years he managed to obtain temporary control of property aggregating in value one billion.

Few men in the annals of civilization have been as busy as Henry Villard during his heyday as King of the Great Northwest. Every detail in the vast area considered a personal fiefdom seemed to involve him. When summoned to New York, he dashed across the continent aboard record-breaking trains that stopped only to change locomotives every 200 miles. One of his bubbling schemes was to dispatch hundreds of agents overseas to persuade Germans, Russians, Scandinavians, and others to emigrate to Washington and Oregon. As a result, thousands of covered wagons loaded with hopeful settlers wended a slow way across the prairies. To promote the Northwest further, Villard issued brochures and publicity material worthy of a later day. And there was more, ever more! The subdivisions of a single chapter in his memoirs indicate the fury of his activities—

Fast trip across the Continent; organizes Terminal Company at Portland; builds Portland Hotel; supports and endows the State University and saves Territorial University of Washington; eastward overland journey; transcontinental exploration under R. Pumpelly; forms Terminal Company at St. Paul and organizes St. Paul & Northern Pacific Railroad Company; builds branch line to Canadian border; publishes history of Northern Pacific.

In the midst of this turmoil Villard had time to take two exceptional actions totally uninvolved with the Northwest. As a newspaperman and war correspondent, he had often dreamed of owning journals reflecting his idealistic political beliefs developed as a fiery youth and still cherished as a grown man. With his initial millions, Villard bought the New York *Post,* a liberal daily reputedly founded by Alexander Hamilton, along with the equally liberal magazine *The Nation.* Having done so, he appointed a trio of editors for the *Post* (one was Carl Schurz) and placed the esteemed E. L. Godkin in charge of *The Nation.*

Simultaneously he promised never to interfere with the editorial policies of either publication. Villard was a man who kept his word whenever possible, and in this instance he succeeded. The *Post* occasionally carried his by-line atop articles on travel, but he never exerted pressure on the policies of his newspaper or magazine.

Villard's other important step came in the spring of 1881, a few months before his Wall Street blind pool. He held a consultation with the members of the fledgling architectural firm of McKim, Mead, and White, in existence only two years. Stanford White, who became its most famous member, was only twenty-eight years old. One of Helen Garrison Villard's seven brothers had married McKim's sister, and McKim had already drawn plans for the Hotel Portland, in Oregon. McKim had also charted the reconstruction and enlargement of Villard's country estate Thorwood, a 100-acre hilltop at Dobbs Ferry, New York. This job included six beautiful living rooms, but not enough bathrooms, and a California redwood hall. Stanford White had designed the library at Thorwood.

Villard informed the architects that he had bought a block-front facing Madison Avenue between Fiftieth and Fifty-first Streets directly behind the newly completed St. Patrick's Cathedral. Here the empire builder wished to erect a mansion that would, in its way, outdo the Vanderbilts. Villard did not want to live on the grandiose scale of William Henry, but he did desire a building that would appear bigger than the Twin Mansions. Thus he conceived of no less than six mini-mansions merged together to seem like one. He himself would live in one of these residences, with the others sold to friends or compatible folk of wealth. If nothing else, Villard was outlining the first cooperative dwelling in the country.

The Villard mansion would be unusual in another aspect. The owner had noted how the Stewart marble palace and the Twin Mansions utilized nearly every inch of available land. As an intelligent and far-sighted man, he realized that buildings built this way would result in a city cramped and airless. Therefore he stipulated that his complex have plenty of air space—it would be the first of the so-called elbow room mansions.

The man who had done most of his traveling in America was receptive to the advice of his architects about harking back to the European past for inspiration. Charles Follen McKim had studied architecture at the Ecole des Beaux Arts in Paris, where the classical was stressed, and Stanford White had taken walking tours through southern Europe, rapturously sketching its architectural glories. Both McKim and White—and, to a lesser extent, the engineering-minded William R. Mead—considered the noble structures of the past adaptable to sumptuous living in the town and country mansions of the American rich. Himself a Renaissance man in character, White was inclined to favor the Italian Renaissance style, with touches of the Baroque; McKim tended toward the Greco-Roman. Both men loved color and in the profession the firm was irreverently called McKim, White and Gold.

However, the work of these men could never be termed mere copying or plagiarism of older masters. Like Hunt and other fashionable architects of the era, they functioned as eclectics making full use of the best in the many patterns of the past. Admiring, even adoring, the Renaissance, they worked within this adoration when designing old-world mansions to suit the demands of new-world millionaires. In the words of Aline Saarinen, "The eclectic architects of the time were using the vocabulary of the Gothic and the Renaissance to make, at its best, a new style."

Having commissioned this distinctive building, Henry Villard resumed his frenetic empire building. He was in the Great Northwest as plans were drawn for a U-shaped Madison Avenue mansion built around an open courtyard, or court of honor. Villard's own residence would be the southern, or Fiftieth Street, wing of the building. Just who in the McKim office designed the handsome edifice has become a moot point. History gives Stanford White credit—as it does for so many impressive buildings in New York. This is true to the extent that White may have been the first in the office to sketch a three-sided mansion, with en-

1. *Alexander T. Stewart, contemporary sketch.*

2. *The fabulous Marble Palace of department store owner Alexander T. Stewart. Standing at the corner of Fifth Avenue and Thirty-fourth Street, it commenced the neo-Babylonian era of mansion building in New York as other multimillionaires, especially the Vanderbilts, tried to surpass its splendor.*

3. The few privileged to enter the Stewart mansion were greeted by a ghostly gallery of some of the most famous statues of the time.

NEW YORK CITY.—MR. WILLIAM H. VANDERBILT'S ART GALLERY, IN HIS FIFTH AVENUE MANSION.—THE PRESS RECEPTION OF DECEMBER 21ST.

FROM SKETCHES BY A STAFF ARTIST.—SEE PAGE 310.

4. William Henry Vanderbilt was so proud of his million-dollar-plus art collection that he invited gentlemen of the press to view it. No other Splendor Seeker ever did the same. Here is a contemporary re-creation of the event.

5. *William Henry Vanderbilt House.*

6. *William Henry Vanderbilt's drawing room, with Gallaud murals and other embellishments, was done in crimson and red. The objet d'art in the foreground is a statuette of Cupid in a plate glass case, the glass made "as transparent as possible." Other encased statues stood atop tables in the splendid room.*

8. *The magnificent staircase in th W. K. Vanderbilt mansion we created after designs by Richar Morris Hunt, though it looked as lifted from a Renaissance châtea abroad, as were many others alor Millionaires' Row.*

7. *The William Kissam Vanderbilt mansion was considered a thing of beauty by writers then and now. Designed by Richard Morris Hunt, it was the first of the "irregular" type—that is, it was not boxlike but borrowed the best features of the Château de Blois in Touraine and the home of Jacques Coeur in Bourges. Left, a side view of the mansion.*

9. *Alva Vanderbilt, wife of William Kissam, provided the real energy and inspiration for the most beautiful mansion on the Avenue. Above, she is garbed as a lady of the Venetian court for the ball that christened her mansion in 1883.*

10. The huge mansion of Cornelius Vanderbilt II lacked the graceful beauty of William K.'s, but was larger and occupied one of the finest sites in the city, at Fifth Avenue and Fifty-eighth Street overlooking Grand Army Plaza. The Bergdorf Goodman store stands there today.

11. Cornelius Vanderbilt III forfeited an eldest-son inheritance of some $40 million to marry Grace Wilson (right), youngest of the "marrying Wilson" family. Despite this sacrifice (or perhaps because of it), the union turned out unhappy. However, Grace Wilson Vanderbilt became the American social leader of the twentieth century.

12. *THE* Mrs. *Astor.*

13. *The hub of Society shifted in 1896 as Mrs. William Astor moved from an imposing brownstone at Thirty-fourth Street to this colossal mansion at Sixty-fifth. Some newspapers said her new residence was "more meaningful" than the White House. "To tread her marble floors was to know social success," one writer has said.*

14. *One of the priceless tapestries in the Italianate purlieus of the William Collins Whitney mansion. A French Renaissance Gobelin, it featured a young Bacchus with vine leaves in his hair and a flowing fountain of wine below. Eleven feet high and eight wide, it was, of course, worked in glorious color.*

15. *Pittsburgh steelmaster Andrew Carnegie, tiny of body but outsize in mind and greed, spent the last years of his life giving away a fortune of more than $300 million. His block-size mansion at Fifth Avenue and Ninetieth Street is one of the few remaining in the city.*

16. *Charles Tyson Yerkes, onetime Chicago Traction King, erected a Fifth Avenue pleasure dome but passed little time within its marble walls. Unlike other denizens of Millionaires' Row, his life was an open book with many lurid pages.*

17. Charles Schwab's mansion on Riverside Drive derived from the famed château of Chenonceaux. With a river at his door and block-size grounds for gardens, Schwab possessed the ideal setting for grandeur.

18. Schwab's art gallery filled a wing of his mansion. Multimillionaires had good taste, and his collection included old masters as well as modern works like Turner's Rickets *and* Blue Lights.

HARPER'S WEEKLY

VOL. XLVI. New York, Saturday, August 2, 1902—Illustrated Section NO. 2380

AMERICANS OF TO-MORROW

19. Charles Schwab, personable and popular, made his mint as boy wonder of the steel business. He was the only Croesus alive musical enough to play his personal $100,000 pipe organ.

20. William Andrews Clark came out of the West determined to live in the most ostentatious mansion on Millionaires' Row. He did, after serving a term as a senator from Montana.

21. *The Clark mansion took seven years to build and earned the name "Clark's Folly" from an amused citizenry. Above, it stands close to completion. Architects were outraged at the steeple or spire crowning the building.*

22. *The first, or state, floor of the mansion known as "Clark's Folly." Picture galleries and Music Room to the north could be thrown together to make a colossal ballroom. Main Court, at right, was open-air. On the ground, or street, floor below lay another art gallery named the Faience Room, also Billiard and Smoking rooms.*

Counterclockwise:

23. *The entrance hall and grand staircase of the Clark mansion—the stonework is of ivory-tinted Maryland marble, the ceiling of oak overlaid with gold leaf.*
24. *The Grand Salon of the Clark mansion—the decorations of this room were*

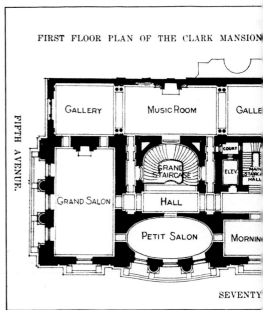

FIRST FLOOR PLAN OF THE CLARK MANSION

FIFTH AVENUE.

GALLERY

MUSIC ROOM

GALLE

COURT

GRAND STAIRCASE

ELEV

MAIN STAIRCA HALL

GRAND SALON

HALL

PETIT SALON

MORNIN

SEVENTY

THE CARRIAGE GATEWAY

A DORMER WINDOW

brought practically complete from an old French château. The windows on the left overlook Fifth Avenue.

25. *Some details of the Clark mansion—in the upper engraving is shown the great dormer window facing Seventy-seventh Street, with statuary modeled by Philip Martiny—below are the great bronze gates of the carriage driveway.*

26. *The Main Dining Room of the Clark mansion, with the great mantel of carved stone—the ceiling is of carved oak, gilded.*

27. *The Reception Room of the Clark mansion, opening out of the main corridor on the ground floor.*

28. *The Main Court of the Clark mansion, looking into the vestibule under the great picture gallery—the Faience Gallery is on the right.*

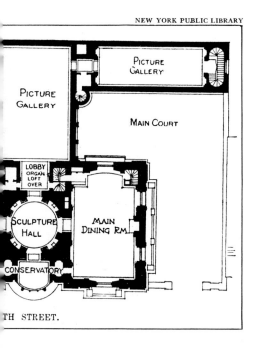

See Page 29

THE FIRST COTILLION OF THE CENTURY

Given by Hon. W. C. Whitney, January 4, 1901

29. *The social history of the twentieth century hung in limbo until January 4, 1901, when the Honorable William Collins Whitney gave a house-warming ball in the Fifth Avenue mansion richly redecorated for him by Stanford White. With this event, the social whirl of the new century officially began. Whitney, wearing pince-nez, appears in the center of this* Harper's *Magazine by A. I. Keller.*

30. *Stanford White was murdered by the husband of Evelyn Nesbit in the worst scandal of the time. Charles Dana Gibson drew the girl as "The Eternal Question."*

trances on the courtyard. Moreover, the finished job appeared to bear the imprint of White's strong personality.

Nonetheless, the lore of American architecture indicates that the Villard complex was actually designed by Joseph M. Wells, a lesser figure in the firm. Supposedly Wells took over because White was overburdened by other commissions. Wells insisted on beginning from scratch, tossing out White's preliminary work. The fact that Henry Villard was agreeable to Italianate style brought special pleasure to Wells, for he revered Bramante, the Roman architect of the High Renaissance, a cousin and mentor of the painter Raphael. Of Joseph Wells it was said, 'The works of Bramante are his Bible." Wells himself wrote, "Italian architecture is great and grand and dignified."

So equipped, Wells set out to create the Villard mansion, using the Palazzo della Cancelleria and the Palazzo Farnese, both in Rome, as inspiration. Despite his worship of Bramante, Wells' completed work was no slavish copy of his models. Proof lies in the fact that the Villard mansion, with supposed roots in Rome, emerged with an unmistakable aura of Florence.

The fact that the building was U-shaped, with a courtyard opening on Madison Avenue, gave it dignity and repose. Everything about the complex was massive, with little attempt at decoration. The two large wings, one of them Villard's home, jutted out along the side streets, with entrances in the courtyard. The middle mansions, set deep in the court, were entered through a beautiful arcade of five arches. Windows on the first and third floors were arched, those on the second sunk in panels. Small attic windows were square. Unobtrusive balconies sat over the impressive doorways to the wing-mansions. Some thought the iron work of the gate and the wrought iron guard bars over the ground floor windows gave the feel of a citadel. Others called it an air of monastic mystery.

For all its striking qualities, the finished mansion proved a disappointment to a few observers, who deemed it more grand than beautiful. In large part, this was because the Florentine palazzo was constructed of dull American brownstone. Transported from nearby Belleville, New Jersey, the brown blocks were set atop one another and topped off by brownstone cornices. An inconspicuous, slightly tilted roof, with chimneys emerging, topped the building.

The Villard mansion cost $1 million and took three years to build. Villard's south-end residence was completed with spectacular speed in a little more than a year. When the exterior of this wing was completed, the moment had come for interior decoration. Here Stanford White did indeed take over, personally designing halls, dining room, and probably more. No doubt because of the gloomy exterior, White chose a cheerful reddish-brown and light yellow for the interior color theme. In the marble reception hall, floors, walls, and columns were strikingly inlaid with wood; the ceiling mosaic-work was fashioned by America's Maitland Armstrong. From the hall, a marble staircase twelve feet wide rose to the second floor. Embellishing it was a wall clock created by sculptor Augustus St. Gaudens.

Drawing rooms on both sides of the main-floor hall were of mahogany, the predominating color White's cheery brown-yellow. On the hall leading to a music room White lavished enormous care. "Aladdin's lamp never revealed a passage more magnificent," says one tribute to his efforts. It was done entirely in mosaic, the material yellow Italian marble, the floor small pieces of chaillon marble in intricate designs. Spanning the hall were three semicircular arches of Siena marble, again with sculpture by St. Gaudens. The hall did full justice to the music room, for here was a diminutive theater, saluted as a stunning example of the architect's art.

On the first floor, dining room and breakfast room could be thrown together to create a large banquet hall or ballroom. Carved wood replaced marble here—English wood overlaid with mahogany. Rooms were lighted at night by spectacular cut-glass chandeliers and given dignity by huge hanging tapestries and sweeping window draperies. The cost of decoration, not including furniture, came to $50,000 for the reception room and hall; $26,000 for the dining room; and $20,000 for the bijou of a music room.

With this assignment, White may have begun his famous annual trips to Europe from which he returned laden with paintings, furniture, carved doors and doorways, rugs, tapestries, frescoes, mantelpieces, boiserie, brocades, and velvets. A later client dubbed him "Mr. King of Europe," declaring that half the agents and antiquarians of London, Paris, and Rome thrived on his bounty. On these expeditions, White chartered a large sailing ship and left it at a place like Leghorn while he rampaged over the Continent buying miraculous works of arts and decoration. With the boat crammed, he got aboard and sailed home like a latter-day Ulysses returning with the treasures of Troy.

As the mansion rose, Henry Villard's fortunes slid downward. Unlike Commodore Vanderbilt, who mastered the rudiments of steamboating before putting money into steam, the empire builder knew little of the in-depth construction and operation of railroads. He had ordered completion of the transcontinental Northern Pacific with the utmost speed, but with haste came carelessness. One day Villard learned that his trusted engineers had made a grievous miscalculation—the estimated cost of finishing the road was short by $14 million. Having borrowed so much money already, and watered so many shares of stock, Villard was in no position to raise more. He was, in short, ruined.

The King of the Great Northwest kept this dire secret locked in his heart on September 8, 1883, as eastern and western sections of the Northern Pacific ceremoniously joined at Gold Creek, in the Dakota Territory. The event took place before the eyes of ex-President Grant, Secretary of State Evarts, assorted diplomats and English titles, Chief Iron Bull, Villard relatives from Germany, and Mrs. Villard and her children, along with a crowd of railroad workers, cowboys, and Indians. A thousand feet of track had been left unlaid to give the crowd a demonstration of the way the work had been done. The last stretch was put down to the accompaniment of gun volleys from the military, music from military bands, and loud cheers from the crowd. Villard personally hammered down the final, golden spike.

The empire builder had been able to complete his transcontinental railroad by the simple expedient of non-payment of bills. But after the triumph, he could no longer put off the moment of truth. Making one more fast cross-country journey to Wall Street, he desperately tried to save his toppling empire. This time his electric magnetism failed to work. In his own words, "Mr. Villard learned then the lesson. . . . that the throng of people which follows with alacrity the man who leads them to profits, will desert him just as quickly when he ceases to be a money-maker for them."

In January 1884, he resigned from Northern Pacific and most other Northwest enterprises, while retaining control of the New York *Post* and *Nation*. Some of his companies went bankrupt, with the funds of thousands of investors evaporating overnight. Northern Pacific tottered dangerously, but failed to fall. Returning to New York, Villard found himself penniless; he could not afford to take his family to a hotel. Fortunately, he had awaiting him—for free—the splendidly decorated wing of the Madison Avenue mansion that had been his conception.

It is hardly a surprise that during his initial months in this noble abode, Villard suffered a kind of breakdown—nervous prostration, he called it. Physically and mentally shattered, he fought to control his mind and regain that soaring self-confidence.

The process was rendered difficult by jeering crowds that congregated daily outside the mansion. The rest of the block-long edifice was still under construction, and to New Yorkers of the time—as well as to the millions who have looked at the mansion and courtyard since—it seemed like one giant residence. It infuriated the public that a man whose companies were bankrupt should be enjoying a large, luxurious palace. "The railroad is wrecked, but look at what the president has built for himself!" people were reported as yelling. Then they began hurling insult and invective at the curtained windows above them.

Villard was able to raise ready cash by selling the mini-mansions in his complex to members of the Four Hundred with names like Fahnestock, Adams, Holmes, and Michaelis. All six residences were completed by 1885; in time, two were combined into one, so that six mansions became five. Villard lived in his wing for a year, a period his son Oswald Garrison Villard recalled as nightmarish. Then the ex-empire builder abandoned metropolitan luxury for Thorwood. Of himself and family, he wrote, "They bade farewell to their city residence without regret."

Those who ponder the rise and fall of Henry Villard usually say that he lacked the rapaciousness to hold his fortune, much less build an empire. The same was never true of the aforementioned Darius Ogden Mills, still proud of the sumptuous decor of his mansion on the Fifth Avenue side of St. Patrick's. In 1888—four years after Villard abandoned his quarters—Mills' daughter married Whitelaw Reid, the calculating fellow (only twelve years younger than his father-in-law) who succeeded Horace Greeley as publisher of the New York *Tribune,* most influential newspaper in the country.

Henry Villard had become prosperous enough to take his family abroad. Among other things, he was representing Thomas Alva Edison in Europe. There he received a cable from Whitelaw Reid offering $400,000 for the southern wing of the Madison Avenue complex. Villard accepted with alacrity, for he had hardly set foot in the urban palazzo since quitting it for Thorwood. Darius Ogden Mills figures here because of the general belief that he presented the $400,000 purchase money to his daughter and her husband as a wedding gift. Or that Elizabeth Mills Reid bought the mansion out of funds settled on her by her parent.

Whatever the case, the block-long building once loosely called the Villard mansion now became known as the Whitelaw Reid mansion. This remained the case until 1970, when whispers were heard that the Madison Avenue palazzo, occupied mainly by the Catholic Archdiocese of New York, might be torn down. The various civic groups that rose to preserve it reverted to the original name Villard mansion.

As for Henry Villard, he slowly regained prosperity and in 1890 was able to write, "Mr. Villard was again the possessor of wealth." Most of the newfound funds stemmed from his inspired promotion here and abroad of the Edison electric light. For a time he served on the board of the Northern Pacific, but his stay there was short and unhappy. After that he lived contentedly at Thorwood. He died in 1900.

Despite a striking appearance, as well as high incongruity on the island of Manhattan, the Villard mansions never attracted exceptional attention in print. Newspapers seldom mentioned the complex and its superb courtyard when recounting the wonders of the big city; illustrated weeklies like *Harper's* and *Frank Leslie's* failed to carry pictures to the hinterlands. Such strange neglect might be the result of the drab brownstone exterior, or the cloud hanging temporarily over the head of Henry Villard, or the fact that the separate-but-together mansions were on Madison Avenue rather than fabulous Fifth.

Another reason might be that the Villard houses were overshadowed by the surpassing beauty of Alva Vanderbilt's château. Or that, except for Whitelaw Reid, no person of great prominence lived in the Villard complex. It must be noted, though, that the eyes of the Four Hundred once swung in horror to the Villard homes as the oldest son of one of its Social Register families married a girl who lived by leasing herself as bed partner to Splendor Seekers and other males of towering wealth for a reputed $10,000 a night.

Society's reaction to top-echelon scandal has often been perverse and in this instance the arbiters of Society appear to have deemed the girl a most unusual damsel, as well as a rarely beautiful one. In any case, the Four Hundred accepted the sensational union with no more then shocked whispers, leaving the odd couple to live out long, compatible lives together.

An additional cause for disregard of the Villard (or Reid) mansions was the growing profusion of distracting extravagances and elegances, of which the great American public heard tantalizing tidbits. The moneybags families of Manhattan were spending vast millions not only on Fifth Avenue domiciles, but on private railroad cars, oceangoing yachts, superlative summer residences, and eventually pioneering motor cars.

While Alva Vanderbilt determinedly erected her Château de Blois on the Avenue, husband William Kissam was pleasuring himself by construction of a 285-foot yacht costing $500,000, which when launched became the finest private craft afloat. Of course the traditional Vanderbilt name for yachts was *North Star,* but William Kissam devotedly christened his *Alva.* Yet it was during a round-the-world cruise on this oceangoing gem that his marriage to the real-life Alva blew up.

When one multimillionaire launched the finest yacht afloat, others in the exalted yachting echelon naturally felt challenged to outdo him. J. P. Morgan commissioned a succession of *Corsairs,* each for a time surpassing its competitors. William Astor, husband of the queen of the Four Hundred, possessed two yachts. His favorite was *Nourmahal,* a word said to mean "Light of the Harem." With his wife dominating Fifth Avenue, William Astor lived up to his yacht's name by taking long, gay cruises with sporty male friends and girls from musical comedies and (some said) the better brothels.

Centimillionaires demanded that their yachts be decorated by the type of skillful hands that did their lavish homes, and Stanford White designed the interior of at least one oceangoing palace. The same was true of the private railroad cars whereby these men outdid one another in palatiality. Here the rococo interiors were expertly created masterpieces of compressed elegance and extravagance, with shiny oak bars, regal beds, upholstered chairs, jewel safes, wine bins, card tables, and intricate chandeliers cushioning the hardships of rail travel. Did the public wonder what it was like to ride in a private railroad car? Mrs. August Belmont offered enlightenment by reporting, "A private car is not an acquired taste—one takes to it at once."

The Immensely Rich did much traveling—and why not, since it was accomplished with quintessential ease. Fifth Avenue families made frequent trips to Europe, usually taking even the

youngest children along, not so much out of affection as to ac-
custom them to the terrain as early as possible. To escape the
heat of summer the Four Hundred scattered to places like Bar
Harbor, the White Mountains, the Jersey Shore, or Far Rocka-
way. But the crème-de-la-crème of the snobbish set customarily
journeyed to Newport, Rhode Island, making the trip by family
yacht or private railroad car.

In Newport families like the Vanderbilts and Goelets had
begun duplicating or exceeding Fifth Avenue mansions. At first,
large shingled summer residences euphemistically known as
"cottages" were the Newport vogue. Mrs. Robert Goelet hired
Stanford White to design the finest of these, naming it South-
side. Ever-determined to outdo her sister-in-law Mrs. Ogden
Goelet utilized Richard Morris Hunt to design Ochre Court, a
limestone mansion worthy of any Fifth Avenue corner.

With this, stone mansions became the mode at Newport, most
of them designed by the indefatigable Hunt. For Alva Vanderbilt he had done Marble House, inspired by the Grand Trianon
in the park of Versailles. The mansion boasted a hall and stairway of yellow marble, together with a dining room of red marble
that, according to one guest, gleamed like fire.

After Alva divorced William Kissam Vanderbilt and married
Oliver H. P. Belmont, she became mistress of Belcourt, her new
husband's mansion. By the terms of her divorce from Vanderbilt, she still retained ownership of Marble House. As owner of
two great Newport mansions, she straightaway began expensive
revisions that brought their combined worth close to $10 million.
Alva did not appear upset by the fact that her horse-loving husband had his luxurious stable on the Belcourt ground floor,
in order to be close to his beloved equines even when asleep.

For Cornelius Vanderbilt II, lord of the largest mansion on
Fifth Avenue, Hunt provided The Breakers, mightiest of all
Newport residences, cited for its "frigid dignity." The entrenched personnel of the Four Hundred resisted changing any
accepted nomenclature and, in what must be the understate-
ment of all time, these marble halls of Newport were still called
"cottages."

6

Eight Rembrandts in a Single Room

ONE day in the late 1880s, Collis P. Huntington, majority stockholder in the Central Pacific and Southern Pacific Railroads, and therefore Railroad King of the West, stood on the corner of Fifth Avenue and Fifty-seventh Street glumly regarding the mansion of Cornelius Vanderbilt II who was, of course, the Railroad King of the East.

Cornelius had not yet expanded his looming residence to Fifty-eighth Street, but it was still big and impressive enough to kindle fires of envy in Huntington's breast. Supposedly he muttered to himself, "No Railroad King of the East is gonna outdo the Railroad King of the West." The next morning he purchased the plot of land diagonally opposite Cornelius (where Tiffany's stands today) and started the wheels turning for his own overpowering mansion.

No longer was it necessary to speculate about the psychological motivations of millionaires like Huntington who, in the manner of many North American potentates, decreed rococo palaces in Manhattan.

Suddenly the forces driving men of wealth to erect and inhabit urban mansions were simple to decipher. Foremost, of course, was the ingrained urge to excel fellow millionaires, as well as impress a nation of pecuniary inferiors by a show of monumental extravagance. "They came to the place where they could best display their wealth and advertised their arrival in the most obvious manner," Charles A. Beard would write. As possessors of a God-given gift for accumulating money they wished to broadcast their ability to live in the lordly manner of the Vanderbilts. Involved were such characteristics as pride, envy, insecurity, and a desire to lord it over the rest of humanity.

Moreover, the nature of these men was to thrust forward, leaving one successful operation behind while cunningly contriving its successor. So it is not surprising to find that, having achieved money-making empires, hungry eyes lit on New York, a city of more hotels, theaters, art galleries, luxury shops, and general diversions than any other. For the lord and master, this included proximity to Wall Street, where the Croesus with multimillions from mine or monopoly could use his practiced guile and ruthlessness to make another fortune as a financier.

Important, too, was the eternal hope of breaking into the sacred confines of the Four Hundred. In an era before the enchantments of motion pictures, radio, and television, the Four Hundred star-crossed folk invited to Mrs. Astor's annual ball existed as celebrities of the day, names known to the public and activities chronicled as closely as possible in the daily press.

The Splendor Seekers, along with wives and children, believed their single-generation fortunes were big enough to ensure them entry into this top-notch group. "One of the baubles many of them set their minds on buying . . . was social prominence," writes Andy Logan in *The Man Who Robbed the Robber Barons.* The first influx of out-of-town millionaires struck the metropolis immediately after the Civil War, and the Knickerbocracy resisted by remaining icily aloof to the brash newcomers.

Yet the newcomers, relishing a flavorsome city, stayed on anyway, to be joined by others who launched fresh onslaughts on Society. In the meantime, the *nouveau riche* entertained one another and posed before the world as a society based on riches rather than blueness of blood. True Society dubbed them Climbers, Shoddies, and Bouncers. Edith Wharton referred to them as the New People, but perhaps the snootiest designation came from the socialite Frederick Townsend Martin who called them the Suddenly Rich.

By attempting to enter High Society, the Suddenly Rich were flashing signals to the rest of the country that America had become a plutocracy, and they were its plutocrats. They came to New York by way of the gold regions of California, the oil fields and steel mills of Pennsylvania, the silver mines of Nevada, or less dramatically from barbed-wire or shoe factories, or the sanctums of corporations where monopolies in sugar, flour, public transit, coal, and even undertakers' coffins were devised and executed to the tune of uncountable millions.

In the financial and industrial jungle of the time, these men and their families were surviving as the fittest, and the best way to proclaim this fact was to emulate or surpass the Social Rich by a show of Renaissance palaces, private art collections, personal railroad cars, and oceangoing yachts. If they lacked the education or taste necessary to be discriminating, they had a simple yardstick with which to measure: if something cost a lot, it must be good. To build Fifth Avenue mansions might require a basic fortune of $50 million, but what could be more impressive than belonging to this Fifty Million Club, with an ornate mansion as a billboard announcing membership?

In the years between the end of the Civil War and the Wilson administration, the multimillionaire was revered as a hero by the majority of the American people. Inherent in this respectful admiration was the cozy belief that men of massive wealth got to the top by methods rough and tough, but essentially honest. The accepted image of the Amassers of Fortune was of an outsize type, equipped by Almighty God with more energy and acumen than the rest of mankind. Admittedly vicious in business, he was supposed to be contrastingly gruff, hearty, and likable in repose. If one met a rising tycoon, his overbearing manners might be hard to take, but underneath the bluff exterior beat an artery of gold.

This was far from the truth. Robber Barons may have had more drive than the average man, but when examined closely the breed loses charm. Deviousness, ambition, and a deep-rooted slyness seem to have been essential attributes. A man who dealt with them often characterized the breed as essentially insecure, viewing the world as a hostile place. Born crafty, with preternatural energy, they acquired various sorts of special learning while growing up and forged ahead by a credo that said, "Self-interest first, last, and always—and crush anyone in the path."

Such men mainly possessed a God-given gift for mortal accomplishment and nothing delighted them more than demonstrating the fact. Once, banker James Stillman asked railroader E. H. Harriman what interested him most in life. Replied Harriman, "I guess it is to be told that some big thing can't possibly be done, then to jump in with both feet and goddam well do it."

Of the nefarious breed, Collis P. Huntington, Railroad King of the West, was a prime example. This man was the dynamo-personality behind the remarkable success of the so-called Big Four millionaires of California, the others encompassed by this designation being Leland Stanford, Mark Hopkins, and Charles Crocker.

His fellow members of the Big Four had been content to remain on the Pacific Coast and dominate California, but Huntington preferred the East and so far forgot himself as to disparage the sunny climate of the state that made him rich and famous. The famed California sunshine, he often complained, was suitable only for sissies.

Huntington's partiality for the East was hardly unusual. An amazing proportion of the nation's self-made millionaires came from upstate New York and New England. Huntington was one of them, and among others were J. P. Morgan, Jay Gould, Darius O. Mills, Russell Sage, Jim Fisk, and (surprisingly) the other members of California's Big Four.

Born the fifth of nine children to a hard-working tinker in Harwinton, Connecticut, Huntington's formal education ended at age fourteen when he went to work on a neighboring farm for $7 a week, plus room and board. Through life Huntington was a man who lusted for lucre, but enjoyed saving it more—he was,

you might say, a passionate saver. After a few years as a hired
hand he had saved enough dollars to move with an older brother
to Oneonta, New York, where the pair opened a general store.
Huntington always cherished this town and later named his private railroad cars *Oneonta I* and *Oneonta II.*

Young Collis P., big of bulk even then, was a restless soul.
While his brother tended store, he piloted horse and buggy
around the countryside selling watches and other items. Ever a
glib and forceful salesman, he was later hailed as the trader
supreme. Huntington had reached age thirty when the country
began harking to the sound of wealth from the California gold
rush. With his Oneonta savings, he headed West and set up a
miners' supply depot with Mark Hopkins as partner. By making
money and hoarding it lovingly, he soon became a man of considerable means.

Huntington's unceasing drive to make and keep money made
him one of the least popular men in California. Later historians
rated him as the epitome of the callous financier of the era, but
contemporaries were blunter. One associate called him scrupulously dishonest; another said he had no more soul than a shark;
a newspaper branded him ruthless as a crocodile. "I'll never be
known for the money I've given away," he once told a reporter.
To another he admitted, "You can't follow me through life by
the quarters I've dropped."

Fortune really arrived after he decided to finance a railroad
across the Sierra Nevada mountains to meet the transcontinental
rails on the other side. Railroading never seemed an adventurous or glamorous game to Huntington; the Iron Horse was just
another means of making dollars to be saved. Gathering the
others of the Big Four around him, he established the Central
Pacific Railroad. Soon he was one of the richest individuals in the
state.

The restlessness that marked him as a young man remained
with him as an adult. While others of the Big Four stayed West,
he made frequent forays to New York and Washington. In the
nation's capital he handed out bribes of $200–500,000 to con-
gressmen who did him favors. "I am fearful this damnation
Congress will ruin me," he moaned after turning over one large

sum. Such wholesale bribery was not only for the interests of the
Big Four, but for himself as well. By 1880, the year he turned
sixty, Collis P. Huntington may have controlled more miles of
railroad track then any man alive; he also owned steamship lines,
coal mines, timber forests, real estate around Los Angeles, and a
shipyard at Newport News. His personal fortune was estimated
at $70 million, but no one could really be sure.

Huntington grew partial to living in New York, although he
kept a fine residence in San Francisco. His shadowy wife died in
1883 and a year later the tight-fisted Midas unexpectedly wed
thirty-five-year-old Arabella Duval Worsham, née Yarrington, in
a ceremony performed by Henry Ward Beecher. Arabella's
origins may have been shrouded in mystery, but the second Mrs.
Huntington was no adventuress in quest of a millionaire mate.
Presumably with money from her first husband, she had bought
real estate around Fifth Avenue in the West Fifties. William
Henry Vanderbilt had purchased some of her property to assure
further privacy in the Twin Mansions. John D. Rockefeller had
taken more of it for his New York residence on West Fifty-
fourth Street, just off of Fifth. When Huntington met her, Mrs.
Worsham had earned $300,000 by her own efforts, an astound-
ing achievement for a woman in those days.

Arabella was no miser; she liked her money to show. Before
the merry widow came into his life, Huntington boasted that he
spent no more than an annual $200 on clothing and creature
comforts. Arabella Huntington changed this. She bought him a
wardrobe and took him to Europe. There the Barefoot Millionaire endeared himself to Parisians by disparaging the Eiffel
Tower, saying American engineers could do a far better job of
work.

The second Mrs. Huntington dreamed of social triumphs.
Since Collis P. had made his millions in the West, she decided to
begin there and sent out invitations to dinner parties in their
large San Francisco home. But Huntington was still the most
hated man on the Coast, and social leaders found reasons to stay
home.

Having been snubbed by San Francisco's upper crust, Arabella
turned her eyes eastward. The Huntingtons had established

themselves in a fine residence on Fifty-first Street behind the Twin Mansions, the area where she had excelled as a real estate entrepreneur. Again she mailed invitations to dinner parties, but members of the Four Hundred could say—with truth—that they had never met the Huntingtons socially. A moist-eyed Arabella waited on party nights for guests who never appeared to eat her food.

Still nursing social hopes, she joined enthusiastically with her husband in planning the mansion on Fifth Avenue supposed to rival the sumptuosity of Cornelius Vanderbilt's. Yet to watchers the Huntington mansion that slowly arose proved disappointing. Though far from an aristocrat by birth, Huntington had some-where along the line picked up a haughty contempt for his fel-low man. He openly spoke of working people as his inferiors, and in the case of his mansion showed contempt for the world. The interior of his $2 million dwelling might have boasted a domed court, a sweeping marble staircase, and stunning col-umns of marble and onyx, but the exterior was of a heavy dun-colored brick resembling a storage warehouse or a prison. Still, the Huntington home enjoyed one distinction: While other Fifth Avenue mansions built so far seemed like châteaux or palazzi, this resembled an Anglo-Saxon castle. Inevitably, it became known to New Yorkers as Huntington's Castle.

Into his castle Huntington poured an additional $2 million for decoration. Under the supervision of bright-eyed Arabella the mansion so drearily affronting on the outside became a riot of color within. Arabella used bright reds, yellows, blues, and even oranges in draperies, rugs, upholstery, and tapestries, along with ceilings of shiny gilt. The center of it all was a crimson brocade drawing room of dazzling color. Collis P. easily contained his enthusiasm for the vivid decor and complained that the French Louis chairs his wife had scattered throughout the premises were too delicate for a man of his bulk. Easychairs were almost unknown in those days, but Huntington found a furniture-maker who provided him with an upholstered chair not only comfortable, but capable of being raised, lowered, and swung around by levers.

Like William Henry Vanderbilt, Huntington felt a chill at the back of his neck on officially taking possession of his mansion. In the manner of William Henry, he saw himself destined to die amidst the mausoleum-like marble of his new surroundings. So began a struggle of wills between husband and wife, with Huntington trying to stay away from the mansion and Arabella intent on remaining there. Huntington bought a camp-like estate at Raquette Lake in the Adirondacks and it became his favorite haunt. He also built himself a $250,000 mausoleum in Woodlawn Cemetery. If the man who once spent only $200 annually on his needs seemed to be disposing of money at a prodigal rate, he was simultaneously practicing small economies. Where the Astors and Vanderbilts paid sums like $25,000 a year to French chefs, Huntington imported a Chinese cook from San Francisco, gave him a minuscule wage, and cheerfully devoured his food.

Socially, the Huntingtons fared well in their castle. Alva Vanderbilt, having catapulted herself into social prominence, had been dismayed to discover no further boxes available at the Academy of Music on Fourteenth Street, the only fashionable opera house in town. Thereupon she set about raising funds for a rival Metropolitan Opera House uptown, but found her friends of the Four Hundred cautious about contributing. Alva was a Robber Baron in her feminine way, and considered that her own ends justified any means. Accordingly, she obtained large donations from Barefoot Millionaires like Huntington, Darius Ogden Mills, Jay Gould, and others Society had vowed to shun forever. This was one of the important surrenders in the annals of Gotham Society for, after contributing, each multimillionaire rated a box in the Diamond Horseshoe of the grand new opera house.

One more event aided the Huntingtons. Twenty years before, Collis P. had adopted Clara Prentice, daughter of his first wife's deceased sister. This girl had grown up to be a colorless character, but with the arrival of good-time Arabella in the family circle, Clara Huntington (as she called herself) began to think of fun. At age twenty-eight, she demanded a trip to Europe and, accompanied by a proper chaperone, finally set off. In London she met Prince Francis von Hatzfeldt de Wildenberg, the handsome, impoverished nephew of the German ambassador to

Great Britain. After Clara began a grand tour of Europe, the Prince borrowed money, kissed his Parisian mistress a final farewell, and followed her.

Next Clara wrote home that she intended to marry the German princeling. Collis and Arabella made haste overseas to prevent the match to a suitor who sounded like a fortune hunter. They were disconcerted to learn that, though poor, he possessed impeccable credentials. Collis P. took in stride the obvious fact that the Prince expected a large financial settlement from a father-in-law. The four returned to New York, where Huntington shelled out for an expensive church wedding. This was the first real union of a New York–based family of wealth to a foreign title and the press went wild over it. Newspapers reported that Huntington had settled $10 million on the Prince, but more likely it was only $2.5 million.

With a box at the opera and a Princess in the family, the Huntingtons seemed in a perfect spot for social climbing and if the Prince and Princess Hatzfeldt had elected to live in New York the gates of the Four Hundred would have opened wide for them. But the newlyweds crassly preferred London and settled there after the wedding, not even returning for family funerals. To Collis P. this brought no sorrow, for in his mid-seventies this man was no longer in a mood to take advantage of social opportunities. Though married to a charming but aggressive female, the dynamo of the Big Four never let her dominate him. In his old age he felt no need for socializing and flatly refused to go through the required motions.

Instead, he chose to step forward as a connoisseur of art. It is hard to imagine this heavy-handed Midas as a Maecenas, but in the traditional manner of A. T. Stewart and William Henry Vanderbilt, he began investing in enough art work to become a figure in the art world. Using European agents, he bought a Rembrandt and a Vermeer, but closer to his heart were works of the Barbizon School and French salons. The man who took the bribery of senators as a matter of course was oddly superstitious, and liked to pay $26,300 for paintings. For this sum he purchased *The Game Lost*, by Meissonier, a barracks-room scene less than a foot square; Gérôme's *Moliere Breakfasting with Louis XIV at Versailles*; and similar paintings. On his death, the collection was valued at $500,000.

By far the favorite painting of this man of crocodile ruthlessness was Jehan Georges Vibert's *The Missionary's Tale*, presently hanging in the Metropolitan Museum of Art as *The Missionary's Adventure*. To the crusty Huntington this work seemed a meaningful allegory of life. Using the levers of his armchair to adjust himself properly, he liked to study it for long periods. Once he was so carried away by its message that he rang for the butler and demanded pencil and paper. Then he scribbled his feelings about the picture for posterity—

> There are seven figures in it—the cardinals of the different orders of their religion. There is an old missionary that has just returned; he is showing his scars, where his hands are cut all over; he is telling a story to these cardinals; they are dressed in luxury. One of them is playing with a dog; one is asleep; there is only one looking at him with that kind of expression saying what a fool you are that you should go out and suffer for the human race when there are such good times at home. . . . *I lose the picture in the story when I look at it. I sometimes sit half an hour looking at that picture.*

Collis P. Huntington got small thanks from New Yorkers for preferring their city to San Francisco; for providing the gilded spectacle of his adopted daughter's wedding to a Prince; for building a $4 million mansion on Fifth Avenue; for erecting a mausoleum in Woodlawn Cemetery for his mortal remains to rest. In return for such beneficence, a local wrote disparagingly of him, "He is a rough Western sample of the *nouveaux riches* flocking to this city and domiciling themselves in pretentious and ostentatious dwellings."

But there was no point in disparaging Huntington's type, for the multimillionaires and their families were on the move, and Fifth Avenue was their preferred destination. Moreover, they were a group well equipped. Wrote Frederick Townsend Martin, a diligent chronicler of Society, "I remember very well the great march of the Suddenly Rich. . . . Very distinctly it comes back to me with what shock the fact came home to the sons and daughters of what pleased to call itself the Aristocracy . . . that

here marched an army better provisioned, better armed with
wealth, than any other army that had ever assaulted the citadel
of Society."

Novelist Edith Wharton, who grew up in the bosom of the
Knickerbocracy, was another who noted the arrival of this well-
provisioned army. She saw them as strange weeds pushing up
between ordered rows of social vegetables. But like certain
others she was not unhappy over their arrival. For one thing,
they brought rich material for her fiction. For another, the New
People lightened a social stuffiness that had become intolerable
to many, especially the young. Life within the confines of the
Four Hundred had grown so rigid that ladies stored away their
latest Paris gowns from Worth and Paquin to be worn the next
season, lest the wearer be considered overly ostentatious; in Boston the gowns were put away for two years. August Belmont, the
European man of mystery who brought a Parisian flair to
Gotham Society, caused a sensation by insisting that his well-
born American wife don her gowns at once.

It is melancholy to report that in this determined opposition to the Suddenly Rich, Gotham Society was first betrayed by
its own children. This had happened before. Back in colonial
days, the top-drawer Dutch had vowed to remain eternally aloof
from the English who took over the city in 1664. But the children of the Dutch had soon found the English attractive and
intriguing. Amidst muttering among the elders, the two groups
began to intermarry, making the Knickerbocracy a mixture of
Dutch and English.

No less than Edith Wharton, others among the young people
of the Aristocracy were bored by Society and greeted the advent
of the New People with approval. Some rich newcomers had
pretty daughters or handsome sons; at any rate, these outlanders
proudly wore their gowns immediately after purchase and their
balls and parties promised gaiety.

Still, the New People do not deserve full credit for diluting
Society. History is inclined to indicate that rough types like Collis
P. Huntington initially played the extravagant game of keeping
up with the Vanderbilts. Actually, the Aristocracy was first.
"Never talk about money, and think about it as little as possible,"

was a nugget of advice offered by Edith Wharton's mother. Supposedly this was the code of the Knickerbocracy. Yet many of Manhattan's best families had fortunes of $50 million or more and so great was the call of ostentation that they quickly entered the mansion sweepstakes. In the end, the forty-block stretch of Fifth Avenue known as Millionaires' Row became a jumble of homes of the Suddenly Rich and the Established Rich.

No sooner had the Vanderbilts started to inhabit mansions than the socially prominent Mrs. Herman "Tessie" Oelrichs built herself a mansion at Fifth Avenue and Fifty-seventh Street, officially 1 East Fifty-seventh. Some observers thought it looked like a Paris hotel, but it was nonetheless striking.

Others of the aristocracy built above Fifty-ninth Street. J. Hooker Hammersley, with roots deep in the Knickerbocracy, was constructing a baroque palace. At 810 Fifth Avenue, Hamilton Fish, Secretary of State under President Grant, had commissioned an outsize mansion. Mrs. Henry Phipps ordered a block-size mansion at Fifth Avenue and Eighty-fifth; it was so big it looked like an apartment house. Augustus Van Horne Stuyvesant, ninth in line from Peter, occupied a six-story château at Seventy-ninth Street with two spinster sisters and a battery of servants.

Yet the *nouveaux riches* always managed to perform most strikingly. Among them was Isaac Vail Brokaw who, like A. T. Stewart, made his millions in uncomplicated trade. Brokaw Brothers, Clothiers, provided the means, and the enterprise had made the necessary millions for this canny money-grubber. An uncouth fellow, Brokaw called Society "Sassiety" and knew that, like Stewart, he was forever barred from its ranks because he ran a store.

Still, Isaac was shrewd enough to know what he wanted in the way of a mansion. Somewhere he had learned that a few Fifth Avenue mansions had been criticized for deriving from too many sources. So he ordered the architects Stone and Rose to base their designs on a single source. They chose Chenonceaux, the picturesque château overhanging the River Cher in Loire once given to Diane de Poitiers by Francis I. The three-story

Brokaw mansion that decorated Fifth Avenue and Seventy-ninth Street was the purest on the Avenue.

One who got inside reported, "It is a masonry house, with very thick walls, very high ceilings, a monumental staircase, and large rooms." Artisans brought over from Italy had done most of the mosaic work, wood carving, and frescoes, but Isaac Vail Brokaw also knew about the European dealers who provided furnishings from authentic sources. No less than the Vanderbilts he had agents hopping around the Continent buying Louis XV chairs, richly decorated tables, hallowed beds, tapestries, and other spoils.

His great hall was paneled in yellow marble, with a huge projecting fireplace and mantelpiece, and a high ceiling intricately patterned with gold leaf. The twisted columns supporting the arch of his grand staircase had golden capitals. At the rear were stained-glass windows of plump, allegorical lasses representing *Abuntiata, Hospitalitas, Concordia,* and *Recreatia.* Elsewhere twin drawing rooms were separated by a graceful archway, each room lighted by a magnificent crystal chandelier and ostentatiously furnished in French gilt and ormolu. Nearby an oval library led to a rectangular drawing room tastefully paneled in dark oak.

Brokaw's château did not completely fill a corner plot; like Villard he had decreed an elbow-room mansion. This also allowed him to show, once again, that he had done his artistic homework. "I've seen pictures of them châteaux," he told his architects, "and they all seem to have a ditch around 'em. Now dig one of them for me right now."

Isaac wanted a moat—and a moat he got! He also had a drawbridge that was raised at night, since Isaac Brokaw was a millionaire who lived in fear of thieves and prowlers. "There's more robbers in this here town," he was wont to say, "than all those King Looies had to put up with."

So Isaac had his moat—something no other multimillionaire in the city ever possessed. It lay there, anachronistic and protective, until the night an inebriated gent in a light buggy attempted to round the corner of Seventy-ninth Street at top speed. He lost control, and horse, buggy, and driver plunged into Isaac's moat.

New Yorkers laughed, a sound Isaac Brokaw did not enjoy. He ordered the moat filled up and forgotten.

A millionaire of far different plumage was Henry Osborne Havemeyer. Like his contemporaries among the Astor family, he belonged to a German line that achieved immediate prosperity in New York. The basis of the Astor fortune was the fur trade, but the Havemeyers had gone into sugar refining and founded what had become the largest firm in the country. William F. Havemeyer, Henry's uncle, was a three-time Mayor of New York City, while Henry's father realized several million dollars from the family business. Henry O. Havemeyer advanced from cradle to grave without a single moment of financial worry.

Yet on assuming command of Havemeyer sugar interests, this young man fought tooth and nail to turn his millions into multimillions; no Barefoot Millionaire labored as vigorously or callously. "He wanted millions where his father and uncle were content with thousands," a contemporary commented. Havemeyer's obsession was to sweep his sugar business competition into a giant trust with himself in charge. He was assisted in this by the changeover in 1887 from sugar cane to beetroot in sugar manufacture.

Henry Osborne Havemeyer became Sugar King of the East, while Claus Spreckels reigned as Sugar King of the West. Havemeyer's American Sugar Refining Company, capitalized at $75 million, made profits of $25 million in two years; in fifteen the amount was $150 million. Naturally, the public vastly admired this stolid, laconic, phlegmatic, and secretive tycoon. "Mr. Havemeyer was dauntless where increased profits were concerned," an associate wrote. In gaining octopus-like control of one of life's necessities, Havemeyer devised numerous angles called inspired by other greedy monopolists. Of his slick tricks of the trade, an aide cautiously commented, "It may be that some of Mr. Havemeyer's methods savored too much of Wall Street and too little of legitimate and natural business expansion."

Yet there was a surprising side to this moon-faced Teuton. As a young man he had journeyed to the Philadelphia Centennial

Exposition of 1876, and for the first time viewed exhibits of exotic art from China and Japan. He had grown up in overstuffed Victorian surroundings, and the sight of this vivid art from the East set him afire. He began buying Oriental lacquer boxes, silks, Samurai swords, and carved ivories. Sometimes he bought in bulk, as if ordering for the family sugar business. "He acquired things because they appealed to him," Aline Saarinen has written. "He knew what he liked and finicky scholarship annoyed him."

Havemeyer had attained age thirty-six when his first wife died. Shortly thereafter he married her niece, a girl who had lived in Paris and formed a friendship with the American painter Mary Cassatt. Under the tutelege of this expatriate artist, the young lady hesitantly paid $100 for a Degas, a purchase that came in the nick of time for that starving artist, who stood on the verge of abandoning his career because of poverty.

When Havemeyer married for the second time, he was diligently adding to his Oriental collection and also buying at auction items like Persian lusterware and Cypriote glass. His wife and Mary Cassatt determined to turn his strong collecting instincts toward paintings. At first Havemeyer favored works of the living French artists. Then he progressed to Rembrandts, buying no less than eight of them.

By 1889 the Havemeyers—she had kept on collecting, too —owned so many paintings and Oriental *objets d'art* that a mansion became a necessity. The Sugar King built his on the corner of Fifth Avenue and Sixty-sixth Street, from plans by architect Charles Haight. It turned out to be a low-slung "horizontality" mansion, with a bulging oval corner at Fifth Avenue that somewhat resembled the Frank Lloyd Wright Guggenheim Museum of a later day. With domes instead of mansard roofs, the Havemeyer manse looked like a feudal castle of granite, with minimal embellishment and rough, uninviting walls. A stately, arched entrance was at 1 East Sixty-sixth Street.

Unlike the Astors, the Havemeyer family had never cared about Society or tried to claim a place in the Four Hundred. Yet because of their interest in art, Henry O. and his young wife visited the best mansions, with the sharp-eyed Mrs. Havemeyer noting that these examples of the city's neo-Babylonian era had a terrible sameness, with massive marble entrance halls, Renaissance tapestries, and delicate French furniture.

So the Havemeyers turned to the Tiffany Studio for a different type of decor. Founded by Louis Comfort Tiffany, who had an exotic mansion of his own at Madison Avenue and Seventy-second Street, the studio specialized in the brightly original and custom-made. It not only created what has come to be called Tiffany glass, but built furniture and lighting fixtures, cast ornamental bronze, hammered wrought iron, hand blocked wall papers, and dyed textiles and rugs. Louis Comfort Tiffany derived his inspiration from bizarre Byzantine chapels and colorful palaces of doges. Working mainly in medieval style, he blended East and West to create what have been called neo-Byzantine effects.

Exactly this sort of inspiration went into the Havemeyer mansion, though it might not have been immediately apparent to visitors. The white mosaic entrance hall resembled the Byzantine chapels of Ravenna, with ten columns and (yes!) a tinkling fountain; the stairway rising from this hall derived from a doge's palace. Elsewhere, however, Tiffany Studios had catered to Havemeyer's interest on Oriental art. Chinese embroideries were used lavishly throughout. The walls of the music room were covered with Oriental designs, and on blue and gold Chinese rugs stood richly carved Chinese furniture rubbed with gold leaf and varnish to give the look of ivory. Furniture and woodwork in the library were based on Viking designs and Celtic motifs, but here too the aura was Oriental.

The ceiling—called "sensational, resplendent, and lustrous" by one writer—was a mosaic design of multicolored Japanese silks, all bought by Havemeyer many years before. The whole ceiling resembled a rainbow, outlined with heavy braid and framed with panels of gold carved moldings. Here, in this single room, Havemeyer hung his eight Rembrandts.

Still prodded by his wife and Mary Cassatt, Havemeyer was raising his artistic sights by adding Courbet, Manet, Degas, and Cézanne to his collection. Mrs. Havemeyer purchased as well, and one day a friend inquired why she did not collect diamonds and pearls instead. "I prefer to have something painted by a man than something made by an oyster," she answered tartly. Both Havemeyers believed nudes improper in a household with three growing children. When Havemeyer bought Courbet's *Woman with a Parrot*, featuring a seductive, red-headed, bare beauty, he sent it straight to the Metropolitan Museum of Art, to which he had willed most of his great collection.

Taciturn and unresponsive before the public, Havemeyer was a warmer person at home, surrounded by loving wife and children. He worked so hard as a rapacious monopolist that underlings could not picture him as an art lover. "He was a man of business first and last," one of them said. Yet he had become an eminent art collector, one of the select American men of millions who bought for love rather than status or investment.

To this impregnable man came a stroke of fortune that carved him a niche in the history of world art. It's hard to believe, but at the turn of the century the work of the great Spanish artists was largely unknown to the rest of the world. On a first visit to the Prado, the Havemeyers saw before their incredulous eyes the glories of Goya, El Greco, Velásquez, and more. As the first foreign Croesus to appreciate them, Henry O. Havemeyer practically had his pick of Spanish masterpieces and wound up (for example) with no fewer than twelve majestic Goyas, obtained at bargain-basement prices.

It was a collector's dream—he had virtually opened the market for Goyas and El Grecos in the United States! Of his purchases it has recently been said, "The Havemeyers' Spanish paintings remain unsurpassed."

7

The White City

THE whispers began in the year 1893—Mrs. William Astor, the lately widowed dowager-leader of the Four Hundred, planned to abandon her commodious but unstylish brownstone at the corner of Fifth Avenue and Thirty-fourth Street to take a more suitable place as Society's queen in a sumptuous mansion on Millionaires' Row.

At first the rumors were hard to credit. Mrs. Astor had been friendly with the Vanderbilts for the past ten years, inviting them to her frequent balls, dinner parties, and at-homes, while enjoying their hospitality in return. Yet on occasion she still indicated a belief that mansion-building on the ostentatious scale of the Vanderbilts and others was in poor taste.

This lady was not a flavorsome talker like J. P. Morgan, who described the Fifth Avenue mansions as "architectural monstrosities corrupting the landscape." Nor was she intellectual enough to refer to them as "palatial plagiarisms," in the manner of avant-garde artists. But her opinion was essentially the same: She did not believe that grandiose mansions belonged on Fifth Avenue.

Yet the rumors turned out to be true—the towering social leader had indeed summoned Richard Morris Hunt and told him of her intention to build a pretentious double residence for herself and her son John Jacob Astor, who had recently wed beauteous Ava Willing of Philadelphia. Hunt sketched out a magnificent Francis I château that would take at least three years to erect and furnish. Thus Mrs. Astor would not be able to move until 1895 at the earliest.

In defense of Mrs. Astor's aristocratic tastes it must be said that the determined dowager was not changing her living style of her own volition. Rather, she had been forced into it by the actions of nephew-by-marriage William Waldorf Astor, who had inherited the second of a pair of identical Astor residences on the land occupied today by the Empire State Building. With the death in 1892 of Mrs. Astor's husband, young William Waldorf had decided that his regal aunt ought to fade gracefully into widowhood, allowing Mrs. William Waldorf Astor to become *the* Mrs. Astor of Gotham Society.

The still vigorous Mrs. Astor had no intention of allowing herself to retire. In a short, bitter struggle she trounced her nephew, in large part because his wife did not desire to don the weighty tiara of social leader. Fiendishly vindictive in defeat, William Waldorf Astor moved his family to England, starting a famous Astor branch there. His final stipulation before departing America was that his brownstone at Fifth Avenue and Thirty-third Street be torn down to make room for a hotel—yes, a hotel!—named the Waldorf.

This, he believed, would drive his aunt out of her own home, and he was proved correct. The thought of living next door to a hostelry was too much for Caroline Astor and she sold her own property for a joint hotel to be called the Astoria.

Richard Morris Hunt did not let his lady down in the matter of her mansion. At the north corner of Fifth Avenue and Sixty-fifth Street, he provided a massive white marble edifice that, to the eyes of many, outdid even the White House in Washington in overall magnificence. Cleverly designed to look like a single château, it was actually two residences, a house divided to make almost identical quarters for Mrs. Astor and her son, whose life with the former Ava Willing had turned into what has been called "a marriage to fill the heart with compassion and horror."

Mrs. Astor's urban domain stood forth as another palace less like a home than a museum. It was entered through an impressive entrance comprising a series of indoor bronze gates described as super-wrought. The atrium, or entrance hall, seemed as large as a small church; it was hung with tapestries from Belgium depicting such scenes as *The Visit of Cyrus to the Defeated Croesus*. Each state room of the house was of a different period. Mrs. Astor's reception room was rococo in white and gilt, filled with knick-knacks and decorated by a peacock-tail rug.

By rolling back the large sliding doors that cut the mansion in two, a great gold-and-white ballroom which held 1,500 people could be created. If nothing else, this wrote *finis* to the Four Hundred. Even with the sliding doors shut, Mrs. Astor's half of the ballroom could hold more than 500 people. Plainly the Four Hundred was passé.

But the impressive ballroom conceived for her by Richard Morris Hunt had already been vitiated by the lady herself, for she had seen fit to festoon its walls with the paintings of the Astor collection, which featured outsize scenes of the Franco-Prussian War and was known as one of the least inspired in the city. These works of dubious art were hung from floor to ceiling—"sky-ed" was the word for the process. "No matter how big the paintings might be, they looked like postage stamps on those great walls," a lady has recalled.

The Astor mansion was a true combination of the impressive and banal. With its paintings, tapestries, dignified colonnades, painted ceilings, and Sèvres porcelains, it was an outstanding example of a residence to be admired rather than enjoyed. At the same time its powerful decor included hideosities of the Victorian age. Among them were the bronze group, *The Equestriennes*; the marble-based bronze sculpture *The Children's Masquerade*; and busts of Shakespeare and Wagner on pedestals. Along with these came marble discus throwers, polar bear rugs, tiger skins, and mounted bear cubs. A pair of tapestry panels, in reds, blues, greens, and browns, showed a cherubic boy and girl at innocent play. In the first they are sailing a tiny boat in a stream; in the other the girl listens as the boy plays a cornemuse, or horn.

It is indicative of the life of the majestically rich that Mrs. Astor gave a dinner-dance only two days after taking possession of her Millionaires' Row mansion. In matters like moving a home, the queen of Society and others like her felt no responsibility whatsoever for supervision of moving men or arrangement of furniture. So great was the power of wealth that changing homes seemed like moving from one grand hotel to another. All Mrs. Astor's decoration and furniture selection had been done for her by Richard Morris Hunt. Everything else was the responsibility of her own legion of male and female servants.

Every signal was "go" as Mrs. Astor majestically crossed her new threshold on January 30, 1896. On February 1, she opened the wrought-iron gates for a gala in honor of her niece, May Van Alen. The dinner, it might be noted, was served by male servants in court livery—dark green coats of plush, knee breeches and black silk stockings, vests of bright red whipcord, with gold buckles and buttons, the latter stamped with the Astor coat of arms.

Mrs. Astor had decreed that the kitchens in her new abode be as large as the state dining room, and the meal offered guests on this night shows why—

CHAUD

Consommé à la Princesse
Croquettes de volaille St. Cloud
Térapene
Filet de boeuf aux champignons
Canard Canvas-back Rôti
Salade de laitue et céleri

FROID

Galantine de perdreau aux truffes
Chaud-froid de caille à la Richelieu
Aspic de pâté de fois gras en bellevue
Pâté de gibier à la St. Hubert
Salade de volaille   *Sandwiches assorti*

ENTREMETS SUCRES
Glaces fantasies
Biscuit Glacé   Biscuit Tortoni   Gelée Macédoine
Charlotte Parisienne   Gâteaux Assortis
Marrons Glacés   Fruits glacés
Fruits   Café
Champagne   Claret Cup
Apollinaris   Limonade

The presence of Mrs. William Astor at the corner of Fifth Avenue and Sixty-fifth Street put an end to carping about the incongruity of Old World châteaux decorating the foremost throughfare of the New World. The mansion of this vaunted social leader, its magnificence shared by her son and his wife, acted as the capstone of Millionaires' Row. The few who had dared to mock the mansions on Fifth began to keep their peace.

Instead, the places of those who had ridiculed were taken by those who admired the occupants of Fifth Avenue mansions as American royalty. *Collier's* magazine declared, "If all these people had titles consistent with their wealth, not a man would rank below a prince, nor a lady less than duchess." Exclaimed the visiting Frenchman Paul Bourget, "This succession of luxurious mansions proclaims a mad abundance of wealth!"

The worship of the Aristocratic and Self-Made Rich on Fifth Avenue had already reached such proportions that even those privileged to consort with them became objects of national envy and admiration. It is safe to say, for example, that every architect in America took pride in the fact that Richard Morris Hunt had been accepted as a social equal by the haughty Vanderbilts. Not only had Hunt been entrusted with design of that family's spectacular homes, but he was invited to Vanderbilt balls and was to catch his fatal cold at an outdoor Vanderbilt wedding.

Those involved in architecture realized that, no less than self-made millionaires, the Fifth Avenue architects employed by them required unique talents. Back in the days when architecture first gained recognition as a profession, people jokingly said, "An architect is a businessman with a slight artistic leaning." In our era Wayne Andrews has written, "Though all great architects have been poets, the very greatest have had to double as salesmen in order to survive."

The architect who catered to multimillionaire clients needed rare qualities of charm, tact, persuasion, and culture. He also required intestinal fortitude when (like Stanford White) the costs of a mansion ran $100,000 over his estimate. Because of their compatability with super-rich clients, the Fifth Avenue group stood forth as the topmost American architects. Furthermore, they had become arbiters of taste in top-money ranks.

While Hunt stuck close to his Vanderbilts, members of the McKim, Mead, and White firm dealt with various other possessors of millions. Senior partner Charles Follen McKim got along so well with the filthy rich as to earn the nicknames "Charles the Charmer" and "Blarney Charley." Son of a thee-and-thou Quaker family, McKim, like Hunt, had studied at the Ecole des Beaux Arts in Paris. A bulky, bald man, with a heavy face and thick mustache, he appears a stolid fellow in photographs, but actually was a buoyant personality. This is the more remarkable because his first young wife abandoned him after two years, causing a shocking scandal in those upright days; his second bride died a year after the wedding. McKim never tried matrimony again.

As a personality, McKim suffered by association with the tremendously colorful Stanford White, a man famous in life and notorious in death. White was a Renaissance man in his own right. Redheaded, white-skinned, resembling a Visigoth, he stood six-foot-three, a prodigious height at that time. He won the admiration of clients as well as the world by a gusto and versatility that allowed him to design mansions and public buildings, to decorate the interiors, create pedestals for statues, necklaces for ladies, covers for books and magazines, and more. "A gay pagan," he was called by one lady who knew him. She added: "He seems to tingle with potential energy—there is something meteoric about his exits and entrances."

Nowhere did admiration of the Fifth Avenue architects manifest itself more than in the ranks of the profession in Chicago, a city whose only certified mansion was the battlemented, turreted Gothic castle of the Potter Palmers. There was not a single classic edifice in Chicago, a metropolis of which a contemporary magazine reported, "Work is her play." Instead, Chicago's architectural achievement lay in development of the skyscraper.

The first of these tall, utilitarian buildings had been the Montauk, designed by the local firm of Daniel Burnham and John Root. Others followed, but emphasis on business structures seemingly caused Chicago to be downgraded by the Splendor Seekers, a fact bewailed by Daniel Burnham as he cried out, "Does anyone grown rich in the mines, the forests, or the plains of this country come here to live, or even linger for the sake of pleasure? Does he not pass through the city, remaining only so long as he is compelled to, so that we get the benefit neither of his money nor of his presence among us?"

The pioneering Eastern architect H. H. Richardson had devised Chicago's seven-story block-size Marshall Field department store, with the local firm of Dankmar Adler and Louis Sullivan contributing the Auditorium, a combined theater-hotel-offices so striking that President Harrison, attending the grand opening, leaned over to whisper, "New York abdicates, eh?"

Yet these triumphs had brought no real architectural aura to the Windy City, though the designing talents of the town tried hard. Said the articulate Burnham to Sullivan, "My idea is to work up a big business, to handle big things, to deal with big businessmen." Again the energetic Burnham, who spoke like a primer of go-getterism, advised, "Make no little plans. They have no magic to stir men's blood. Make big plans—aim high in hope and work!"

Still, Chicago had its robust pioneering spirit and in 1890, to the amazement of the country, the city managed to purloin from New York the honor of being site of the World's Columbian Exposition. The ninth World's Fair in history, this was to signal the 400th anniversary of the landing of Christopher Columbus. An immediate question arose as to whether the Fair should occur in 1892 or the year following. Summer weather was necessary for success, but Columbus had not landed until late October 1492. Nit-pickers believed it unseemly to hold the Fair before that time, so a compromise was effected. Formal ceremonies were held on October 30, 1892, with the Exposition opening its gates the following April.

The entire world had watched the 1889–1890 competition for this Fair before a congressional committee. In far-off Britain, Rudyard Kipling noted that two Yankee cities were "ya-hooing and hi-yi-ing at one another" over the honor. Oscar Wilde's new play referred to "an Exhibition, is it not, in that place that has the curious name?" He went on to have a character say, "In America, they have no ruins and no curiosities." At which another snaps, "What nonsense! They have their mothers and their manners!"

New York had expected to win the Fair easily, but the vigorous confidence of Chicagoans proved invincible. The sum of $5 million had been raised by public subscription, and a similar amount from sale of bonds. That much ahead, Chicago received designation as site of the World's Fair of 1893, at a projected cost of $17.8 million. Of this, $7,295,000 was to be spent for magnificent buildings, constructed under the supervision of Chicago's own Burnham and Root.

This resounding victory did nothing to abate the midwestern city's inherent inferiority feelings about New York. One cause lay in highly publicized remarks made by Ward McAllister, major domo of New York Society. McAllister thought Chicagoans pleasant people but crude, and often said so. The fact that Chicago's best families had ballrooms on the top floors of residences struck McAllister as quaint. His barrage of captious comment kept Chicagoans feeling like second-class citizens, and nothing showed the depth of this more than maneuvers over the upcoming World's Fair.

Chicago's first overture toward the East was aimed at Frederick Law Olmsted, landscape designer of Central Park, requesting that he visit the Windy City to select the grounds for the Fair. Olmsted chose the 600 acres of Jackson Park, a sandy waste which he promised to transform into a lovely vista of canals, lagoons, and landscaped islands.

A far more revealing move came as architects Burnham and Root humbly journeyed to New York in the late summer of 1890. Using the offices of McKim, Mead, and White as headquarters, they began a series of meetings calculated to persuade the grandiose Fifth Avenue architects to play a vital part in designing the structures of the midwest Fair.

At first the Gothamites were indifferent to the golden opportunity and had to be dined, wined, and proselytized. Root then fell sick and died, leaving total authority in the hands of Burnham, a man prone to apologize for the cultural weaknesses of his home town. By stressing the global importance of the Fair, Burnham finally succeeded in inoculating Charles Follen McKim with a strong dose of enthusiasm. Once the project captured his interest, says a McKim biographer, "it became the sort of problem in which his mind and soul delighted."

McKim's soaring enthusiasm infected Richard Morris Hunt, now badly crippled by rheumatism, and George Browne Post, the Hunt pupil who designed the Cornelius Vanderbilt mansion facing Grand Army Plaza. Charles B. Atwood, another New Yorker, was designated chief draftsman, or resident architect, of the Fair; he, of course, designed the Vanderbilt Twin Mansions for Herter Brothers. Augustus St. Gaudens, sculptor and cherished associate of the Manhattanites, became chief of sculpture, with Francis D. Millet head of decoration.

Thus, in effect, Burnham handed over the Chicago World's Fair to New York. True, firms from Boston and Kansas City also took part, as did the Chicagoans Louis Sullivan and Henry Ives Cobb, the latter the designer of the picturesque Potter Palmer manse. But with Richard Morris Hunt serving as chairman of the designing group and McKim its most energetic member, the New York influence promised to be overwhelming.

With little difficulty, McKim persuaded Burnham, Hunt, and the rest to join him in a grandiose artistic concept whereby the chief buildings of an American World's Fair would reflect the classical architecture of Greece and the early Renaissance. Specifically, McKim visualized huge, low, richly designed buildings arrayed around a Court of Honor and surrounded by Olmsted's landscaped lagoons, pools, islands, fountains, shrubbery, and waterways.

This World's Fair of 1893 was to be a transitory festival, torn down at the end of a single season. So McKim saw his great edifices built on steel frameworks only and covered by a white, plaster-like substance known as "staff," favored in Mediterranean countries. Official buildings would be uniform in color and cornice line, to create what came to be admiringly known as the White City.

To Burnham, the size and orderliness of McKim's concept represented grandeur, and he was resoundingly in favor. Of Hunt and McKim, he burbled, "Where these two lead, all others will follow." In Chicago, he said to young Frank Lloyd Wright, then a draftsman in the Adler and Sullivan office, "I can see all America constructed along the lines of the Fair, in noble, classical, dignified style."

Over the next two years McKim made twenty-three trips to Chicago to protect his conception and oversee his own work, for in addition to a massive Agricultural Building he was doing the smaller New York State Building, patterned after the Villa Medici in Rome, with casts of Barberini lions at each entrance. Returning from one trip, he informed Richard Morris Hunt, "The visit was a revelation of progress in every direction and, above all, of the wisdom of the classic policy. The scale of the whole thing becomes more and more tremendous as the work proceeds, and is as imposing as such an area girded around by a single order of architecture sixty feet high can make it."

Except for the Chicagoans Sullivan and Cobb, the architects, decorators, mural painters, sculptors, and other artisans involved in the White City formed a mutual admiration society of men intoxicated by the task and the freedom allowed their talents; each seemed to stand in rapturous awe of his job. At the first Chicago meeting one rose to declare, "Oh, gentlemen, this is a dream! I hope the dream can be realized!" At the same gathering Augustus St. Gaudens whispered into Hunt's ear, "Look here, old fellow, do you realize this is the greatest meeting of artists since the fifteenth century?"

Yet problems arose. At another session the preliminary sketches of projects offered by Hunt, McKim, and Post turned out to be so ambitious that even the designers themselves saw the necessity for scaling down. McKim, who seemed so balanced, proved capable of sudden changes of mind and fits of temperament. At one early point, he insisted on altering the perspective

of his $680,000 Agricultural Building. Later, with the Fair
nearly done and the workmen exhausted, he grimly insisted that
an attic story be added. As he argued his case, the other talents
chanted "Charles, we have no money." But McKim got his way.

The World's Columbian Exposition of 1893 opened on
schedule and won acclaim from the beginning. The White City
turned out to be a noble spectacle, with palace after palace
reflected in the lovely Olmsted lagoons. Glimpsing the spectacle
for the first time poet Richard Watson Gilder scribbled the
poetic lines—

> Say not, "Greece is no more."
> Greece flowers anew, and all its temples soar.

Dominant on the Court of Honor was Richard Morris Hunt's
octagonal Administration Building, its golden dome highlighted
by the surrounding White City. With large square pavillions at
either end, and St. Gaudens' strong statue of Columbus at its
main entrance, the Administration Building set the classical tone
of the Fair. Also facing the emerald-tinted waters of the Main
Basin were the Agricultural, Mining and Electric, and Manufactures and Liberal Arts Buildings, each with banners flying by day
and illuminated by searchlights at night. The Manufactures and
Liberal Arts Building, designed by Manhattan's George Browne
Post, was hailed as the largest structure ever built by man.

McKim's heavily ornamented Agricultural Building was
topped on a broad dome by St. Gaudens' beautiful sculpture
of the nude huntress Diana, removed from the Madison Square
Garden in New York as too large rather than too naked, as the
world liked to believe. Below, the wide building featured a
heavenly host of eighty-three sculptured Philip Martiny angels,
along with other statuary groups. For the pediment Larkin
G. Mead, brother of McKim's partner, had provided a lively
depiction involving a young Bacchus playing a flute, happy
satyr with cymbals, gay bacchante, stunning Flora, handsome
Jason, and reclining Gaea, as well as Mercury and Proserpine,
each of them life-size.

In all 28 million Americans attended this World's Fair, which has been credited as being the first time the population of the country turned out for an unrestrained good time. On a special Chicago Day, turnstiles clicked 713,000 times—"Never since Xerxes have there been so many people shoulder to shoulder," a newspaper gloated.

It was truly a World's Fair, for beyond the Court of Honor spread the pavillions of foreign countries, American states, industries, and corporations. Native architects had been used to design most foreign and state buildings, bringing verisimilitude to the fairgounds. The United States Government offered a large rendering of the battleship *Illinois*, sunk in iron, as one exhibit. Germany sent a huge Krupp cannon, while Spain presented a graceful Pavillion of Queen Isabella. The Convent of La Rabida contained Columbus memorabilia, and in one basin floated replicas of the *Nina*, *Pinta,* and *Santa Maria*. The ornate Electric Building featured an outsize statue of Benjamin Franklin flying his kite, while the Women's Building, Italian Renaissance in style with balconies and loggias, had been designed by two female architects. Smaller exhibition halls ran from Paper to Pottery to Perfume.

Statuary abounded as never before, with single figures and sculptured groups profuse on, in, around, and atop buildings. There were renderings that told stories, like Dickens and Little Nell, or the Escaped Slave. Others were more-than-life-size Presidents, statesmen, pioneers, red Indians, lions, and livestock. On a trip to Italy, McKim had ordered the Farnese *Hercules and Bull* group cast in iron and sent to the Fair, requiring twenty-six boxes for the bulls alone—these two occupied their own area of greensward. The profligacy of statuary reminded the literary of Thackeray's lines on a previous World's Fair—

> There's statues bright
> Of marble white,
> Of silver and of copper;
> And some in zinc,
> And some, I think,
> That isn't even proper.

At the far end of the Main Basin stood the Daniel Chester French figure of a ninety-foot male, on a pedestal, clad in golden robes with arms outstretched to offer Liberty to the oppressed of the world. At the east end, directly in front of the Administration Building, appeared the most admired work of art at the Fair. This was Frederick MacMonnies' allegorical *Columbian Fountain*, informally dubbed the *Girl in the Chair* by the hordes who gaped at it.

Supposedly following a design sketched by Columbus himself, this MacMonnies fountain showed a slim, bare-breasted nymph perched high on a throne-like chair aboard a craft resembling a mastless *Nina* or *Pinta*. Four maidens on each side rowed the ship; they represented Arts and Sciences. A figure of Fame posed at the bow, proclaiming the greatness of Columbia, the girl in the chair. At the tiller sat Father Time. St. Gaudens, a rival sculptor, called MacMonnies' work "the most beautiful conception of a fountain in our times, west of the Carpathian mountains . . . the glorification of youth, cheerfulness, and the American spirit."

Not everything was formal, however. Visitors could take gondola or boat rides in the lagoons, or stroll through a Wooded Isle. By night the stars could be scrutinized through a massive telescope, provided by Charles T. Yerkes, the Chicago Traction King. A Midway Plaisance Mile offered Irish and Javanese villages, a Street of Cairo, a Turkish Music Hall, an Original Vienna Bakery, and a Japanese temple Hoo-Dan. The high ferris wheel brought to this Fair the gay spirit the Eiffel Tower had given the Paris Exposition of 1867. Thrills could be found at Hagenbeck's Trained Animals and the tent of the strongman Sandow the Great, managed by Florenz Ziegfeld Jr. Female loveliness took over at the World's Congress of Beauty—"40 Ladies from 40 Countries." Sex had its moment with Little Egypt, the daring hoochie-koochie dancer. Charles Eliot Norton called the whole a "superb and appropriate symbol of our great nation . . . in its refinements, cheek by jowl with vulgarities, in its order and its confusion, in its heterogeneousness and in its unity."

Yet architecture remained paramount, with the White City a continuously inspiring sight to millions—"a dream of loveliness," one breathed. As architect in residence, Charles B. Atwood personally designed over sixty buildings, together with numerous ornamental features; it is hardly surprising that in mind and body he was never again the same.

Atwood's Fine Arts Building was considered the artistic peak of the Fair, "unequaled since the Parthenon," thought St. Gaudens. Here was one of the few solidly built structures at the Fair, since full protection had to be given to the art masterpieces displayed within. Its exterior was Ionic, freely adapted from the Temple of Erectheum in Athens. The many annexes were connected to the main part by colonnades sculpted with friezes after the Parthenon; the same motif was visible in a grand entrance loggia.

On the attic story, statues in full relief stood against pilasters, again representing Arts and Sciences. Between them stood busts of masters of art, while atop the dome of the main hall rose a great free figure after the *Winged Victory of Samothrace*. Naturally, this building too was white. By night, its cornice line was lighted by candelabra of flambeaux from which leaped "great bulky, ragged masses of fire."

Within the Fine Arts Building (a writer said) tons of sculpture and acres of paintings were to be seen, among them Italian, Flemish, and French masterpieces. Of these, 126 came from the collections of Americans like Cornelius Vanderbilt, Henry O. Havemeyer, Charles T. Yerkes, and William H. Crocker. An irreverent observer noted that these ultra-rich men seemed to prefer paintings of the poor, since many of the heroic canvases loaned by the millionaires dealt with peasants, honest working-men, or downtrodden city dwellers. Pastoral scenes with large animals came next.

Those attending the Fair appeared to appreciate the lush paintings telling a simple story, for reproductions of Hovenden's folksy *Breaking the Home Ties* soon found a place in millions of American homes. Thumann's *Psyche*, a girl peering at her likeness in a pool, became the White Rock Girl of tender memory.

Millet's *Man with the Hoe*, based on the Edwin Markham poem, aroused the first stirrings of art consciousness in a girl-child from San Francisco named Gertrude Stein. Also visible were a few nudes—"precise, enameled, salaciously naked"—that brought protests from church groups. Amidst this wild profusion, American artists like Winslow Homer, Thomas Eakins, John Singer Sargent, and James McNeill Whistler were easy to overlook.

Of the main buildings at the Fair only those designed by Louis Sullivan and Henry Ives Cobb of Chicago departed from McKim's overall classical pattern; as a result the word "disobedient" has been applied to them by a writer. Cobb's irregular Fisheries Building derived loosely from the Spanish Renaissance. But Sullivan's Transportation Building stood alone in relying on color for effect. A riot of vivid plaster, it was considered by purists to be discordant in the surrounding symphony of white. For his flamboyant edifice, Sullivan had designed a grand oblong entrance framing five receding half-circles covered with gold leaf, set off by arabesques in orange, red, and yellow stucco. The public loved this and dubbed it the Golden Doorway.

During the Fair the mutual admiration among the talents involved continued unabated. Largely through the efforts of McKim, Daniel Burnham received honorary degrees of Master of Arts from Harvard, Yale, and Columbia for his administrative work in the architectural area of the Fair. In New York, he was tendered a much publicized Burnham Banquet, with Richard Morris Hunt presiding and celebrities like William Dean Howells, Mark Twain, and Henry Villard mingling with McKim, Post, Atwood, St. Gaudens, MacMonnies, and other contributors to the Fair.

Still, a few faulted the Columbian Exposition, downgrading McKim's concept as un-American in its dependence on the classical past. Declared art critic Montgomery Schuyler, "Arcadian architecture is one thing and American architecture another; men cannot bring back the mastodons nor we those times." Totally in accord were the European visitors who had hoped to find originality of design in the United States.

As sheer theater, though, the White City was highly effective, as even its detractors admitted. But was it a true reflection of a nation so in debt to Christopher Columbus? Only the facades of the buildings by Sullivan and Cobb conveyed any innate feeling of the exhibits within—exhibits that bespoke the robust dawn of a machine age. Other facades were intended only for scenic effect, seemingly conceived by minds lacking faith in a native architecture and oblivious to American spirit and technology. The White City, though a lovely sight, represented architecture divorced from reality.

One of those lamenting was Louis Sullivan, who believed that form must follow function in architecture. Said he, "The damage wrought by the World's Fair will last for half a century. . . . It has penetrated deep into the constitution of the American mind, effecting there lesions significant of dementia."

He proved right as across the country city halls, post offices, and public buildings (though not too many homes) emulated the World's Fair of 1893. Yet Sullivan failed to perceive a silver lining imbedded here—that the orderly arrangement of monumental buildings and landscaped settings around the Court of Honor caused Americans to think for the first time of city planning.

Oblivious to this, Sullivan, whose career suffered as a result of the Fair, continued the gloomy observer. "Architecture has been a plaything long enough," he said. "I am tired of this farce."

While McKim devoted attention—though not all of it—to Chicago, his pyrotechnic partner Stanford White had become that rarest of men: an architect better known to the world than his clients. Standing tall on high, stork-like legs, this plunging, forceful, life-loving Renaissance man appeared before the public as a familiar personality. Where other prominent men labored to remain shadowy, White could often be seen hastening along the sidewalks of New York, his bristly, crew-cut red hair seeming to form a halo around his head. It was as if a stiff wind blew perpetually at his back, as he raced from one construction site to another. His figure commanded attention everywhere, and a

contemporary has recalled how White's magnetism caused heads
to turn even as he slipped quietly into a box during a performance at the Metropolitan Opera.

The multimillionaire who dubbed White "Mr. King of
Europe" might better have said "Mr. King of New York," for he
was one of the best known and most admired figures in a town
whose population was edging toward 2 million. Forty years old
in 1893, White began working at age eighteen in the office of the
American master H. H. Richardson, where McKim also labored.
Both young men showed a proficiency at designing the
domestic-style bungalows known as shingle-cottages, though a
few were large enough for Newport. These dwellings were excellent for the country, but what of the city, where the ambitious
young White especially aspired to work? This was settled by a
trip to France, where a walking tour with McKim and St.
Gaudens showed him chateaux whose magnificence of style
might be adapted to a metropolis.

Returning home, he joined the newly established McKim firm
and the partners eagerly watched as the Vanderbilt Twin Mansions rose on Fifth Avenue. These did not inspire them greatly,
but the Richard Morris Hunt sampling of the Château de Blois
done for Alva Vanderbilt did. McKim, Mead, and White had
found a highroad to success.

McKim first called attention to the firm by designing the Newport Casino. White followed with the remarkable Tiffany mansion at Madison Avenue and Seventy-second Street. This resembled an immense medieval chalet transported to city streets, its
interior a wonderland of brilliant color and ingenious decor devised by White and Louis Comfort Tiffany, the designer son of
the owner.

The Villard mansion was completed a year later, and White
seemed to get credit for it as well, though he had done only the
interior. Even then the charisma of this red-headed marvel was
so pervasive that most jobs done by McKim, Mead, and White
were attributed to him. This has continued into the present day,
with White getting credit for too many of the buildings of the
past still standing in Manhattan. "There is a tendency," writes

Aline Saarinen, "to credit everything done in the period to his hand."

As McKim influenced the Chicago World's Fair, so Stanford White (his partners at his side) worked to transform New York from a city of dull brownstone residences and boxlike office buildings—what Edith Wharton called "a cramped, horizontal gridiron of a town without towers, porticos, fountains, or perspectives, hidebound in its deadly uniformity of mean ugliness."

He dreamed of a city of classical beauty, and to this end tirelessly designed churches, gentlemen's clubs, mansions, hotels, banks, office buildings, monuments, and mausoleums —more work, it has been said, than any other busy architect could do in a lifetime. Yet White, moving and thinking at hurricane speed, did it in less than his normal span.

White did not seem to care much about the poor of the city, except for artistic friends who went broke, nor did his name appear in connection with any of the reform movements of the day. Possibly he was a bit of a snob. Yet as a working architect he ranged democratically over the city, designing Strivers' Row in Harlem, the Hall of Fame in the Bronx, and fountains in Brooklyn.

In years of stupendous activity, he also left a mark on localities like Washington, Newport, Niagara Falls, and Charlottesville, where he restored the Jefferson Rotunda of the University of Virginia, destroyed by fire. In addition, he made those annual (or more) trips to Europe, assisting in the plundering of art treasures from châteaux and palazzi. Reputedly the people of New York could tell when a Stanford White project neared completion by the number of ships jammed with art objects anchored in the Hudson.

People gossiped about Mr. King of New York, and it made him seem even more human. White not only lived contentedly with his wife in a fine residence on Gramercy Park, but maintained a bachelor apartment in the Tower of the Madison Square Garden, an edifice he designed. "You must remember," said social arbiter E. Berry Wall, "that Broadway only cuts across Fifth Avenue, but does not run parallel." White failed to agree.

After laboring on Fifth Avenue by day, he plunged at night into the delights of the Great White Way, taking full advantage of the prevailing double-standard that let a husband play while his wife sat home. Sophisticated New Yorkers, seeing the lights of White's Tower apartment gleaming late at night, wondered what sort of revels might be in progress.

White worshiped beauty in every form, and nothing seemed lovelier to him than a young girl just growing out of her teens: the type of post-nymphet so divinely sculptured by his friend MacMonnies. These girl-children were most visible in Broadway musical shows, and White and other men about town devised ingenious methods of meeting and seducing them. It was beauty of body that attracted White—the female form divine. "Don't ever grow old, don't ever get fat," he beseeched Evelyn Nesbit, the teenage chorus girl who eventually caused his downfall.

White, of course, designed the Washington Square Arch, still standing at the foot of Fifth Avenue, with figures of George Washington as warrior and citizen peering uptown. Like all White's work, the Washington Arch has an aura of deep repose with a simultaneous lightness of mood and feeling.

But in his own day White's masterwork was always the Madison Square Garden, opposite the northeast end of Madison Square, then the city's hub. Both dominating and delighting the metropolis, the Garden was an amazingly spirited creation for a midtown area. Of light terra cotta and buff brick, looking faintly Moorish in the heart of the big city, the bright edifice seemed to breathe life into its surroundings.

The Madison Square Garden stood forth as the largest building in the country, and perhaps the world, devoted entirely to amusement. Those entering its main Madison Avenue entrance progressed through a lobby and grand hall to an arena, or amphitheater, capable of seating 5,000 people with the arena in use and 9,000 with the center space filled with chairs, as for political oratory. Half the roof was a movable skylight which, when opened, made the crowd below feel as if it were sitting in the open air. The square, flat-roofed, block-size building housing the arena also contained a silk-walled, yellow and cream theater for plays and musical comedies; a cafe for drinks and refreshment; a white and gold concert hall with two balconies; an assembly or banquet hall, complete with kitchens; and a roof garden for post-performance fun.

Still, the feature that made the Madison Square remarkable was the tower lifting 332 feet from the ground in the center of the Twenty-sixth Street side of the building. Patterned after the Giralda Tower in Seville, it rose square and solid for 249 feet, then broke into a series of open cupolas decreasing in size. Atop the last was a nude statue of the goddess Diana, bow and arrow raised. Smaller than the original Diana who landed in Chicago, this one poised so perfectly on the ball of one foot as to respond to every whim of the wind.

An elevator ran to the top of the solid part of the tower, where sightseers got out to climb a winding stairway leading to Diana's toes. The square section of the tower held apartments that could be used for living quarters or business. From engines and dynamos in the cellar came the power to light 6,800 incandescent electric lights, several hundred of them used to illuminate the outside of the Garden at night, highlighting the tower and its lissom Diana.

The cupolas crowning the tower were Moorish in design, as were five others spaced along the colonnade ringing the front half of the building at a height of sixty-eight feet from the ground. Sidewalks below the colonnades were covered by a picturesque arcade, reminiscent of the Rue de Rivoli. The entire Madison Square Garden radiated a simplicity of design, an absence of trifling detail, that brought beauty, brightness, and serenity.

One writer believed the Garden epitomized the very pulsebeat of Gay Nineties New York—"its gaieties, its carouse and pageants." Certainly the four walls and tower provided a pleasure trove for rich and poor alike. The rich had the theater and restaurants, as well as a smart horse show that opened every social season, with dog, flower, and fashion shows to follow. The rest of the population enjoyed the political speeches in the arena, as well as championship prizefights, wrestling, track meets, six-day bike races, Sousa Band concerts, Buffalo Bill's Wild West Show, and the Barnum and Bailey Circus.

White basked in the glory reflected by his glorious brainchild and it is deeply ironic that in 1906 he was killed during a performance at its roof garden. The work of McKim, Mead, and White is often beclouded, for the three partners not only made constructive suggestions about each other's work, but also employed skilled architects like Joseph Wells and a host of young men in training.

Sometimes it is hard to tell who was really responsible for some of the firm's work, but there is no doubt whatsoever about the Madison Square Garden, for which the fee received was $75,000. When a friend undertook to flatter McKim by complimenting him on the fine job done by the firm on the Garden, the senior partner stopped him abruptly. "White," he snapped.

Richard Morris Hunt died in 1896, leaving behind him the most flavorsome of Fifth Avenue mansions. Some say Hunt designed for men rather than man, as an architect should, but the output of his fifteen years of top creativity was still inspired and prodigious. In his last years, though burdened by rheumatism, he did Mrs. Astor's double mansion; the incredible George Washington Vanderbilt estate at Asheville, North Carolina, largest baronial estate in the United States; and the facade of the Metropolitan Museum of Art, to which McKim, Mead, and White added the wings.

After Hunt died, it might be expected that McKim, Mead, and White would get almost every commission from millionaires or municipalities. Yet architecture is competitive, even for titans. The fees of the McKim firm may have been high, and whereas some clients may have been attracted by their fame, others were put off by it. Often it was necessary to submit preliminary sketches and estimates in competition with other architects, and, incredible as it may seem, the efforts of McKim, Mead, and White occasionally seemed inferior to the work of others. For instance, Stanford White labored long over plans for a new Grand Central Station and produced a majestic building with a tower resembling the Madison Square Garden. Perhaps for that reason it failed to win the competition.

So millionaires were free to pick other architects, and many on Millionaires' Row did. Other outstanding talents of the era were Carrère and Hastings, who created the New York Public Library at Forty-second Street, Horace Trumbauer, Cass Canfield, Whitney Warren, and Henry J. Hardenbergh, the last-named known for the Waldorf Astoria and Plaza Hotels, not to mention the Dakota Apartments on Central Park West, so named because they seemed as remote from the fashionable East Side as Dakota did from the rest of the country.

Yet Richard Morris Hunt and Stanford White best represent this Golden Age of American architecture. Hunt has been immortalized by a monument at Fifth Avenue and Seventieth Street, erected in his honor by art and architecture societies of the city. Stanford White, foully murdered by the jealous husband of Evelyn Nesbit, received no monuments from his peers, but his fame has continued alive in print. Russell Towner, author of the recently published book *The Elegant Auctioneers*, calls him "The master hand in the adornment of that rhapsodic era . . . his skill and knowledge were a Baedeker."

Of the firm McKim, Mead, and White, Aline Saarinen writes, "These three became the master designers for the sumptuous pageant. They designed the buildings; they supervised the furnishings; they set the tone for a way of life."

8

Grandee of Graft

ACCORDING to cherished legend, William Collins Whitney, always cited as the most civilized of the splendor-seeking breed, made up his mind to accumulate $50 million as fast as possible. He then planned to quit the rapacious world of get-rich-fast finance and continue his life in sybaritic style. For the sum of $50 million, you will recall, was the basic amount deemed necessary for the building of a Fifth Avenue mansion and otherwise enjoying the best of possible worlds, as opposed to merely the good life.

It's a provocative story, with just enough truth to assure durability. William Collins Whitney did wind down his money-grabbing at the $50 million mark. Or, to be more exact, by age fifty-two he had amassed $40 million and knew that investment in high-level stocks like Standard Oil would automatically provide the rest—the first $40 million was obviously the hardest! But Fate also played its part in the life of this suave Midas who chose to pass the last decade of his life amidst manorial homes, art masterpieces, gala balls, private railroad cars, and, above all, horseflesh.

Few human beings have won so many encomia as this man Whitney, who was born in Conway, New Hampshire, of a family high in New England pedigree but less exalted in worldly goods. His rich, full life in finance, politics and Society earned him universal praise. Books, newspapers, and recalled conversations pay tribute to his manly beauty, financial skill, business acumen, political shrewdness, magnetic talk, social grace, and irresistible charm. Mention is made of an upright carriage and buoyant step adding up to "a tall, handsome grace that is the despair of men and the admiration of women." All-around knowledge brought him "a careless air of culture."

Thoughts of Whitney caused a few contemporaries to wax epigrammatic. "It is hard to say whether he is the more amiable or the more able," one quipped. Said another, "Gaiety is his loaf of bread and jug of wine." Less soulful folk saw him as a "magnifico," an "intellectual giant," and "brilliant, polished, suave." A male friend found him "the most charming companion in the world." Another thought, "Mediocrity in Whitney is unthinkable." Finally, his loving wife saluted "the goodliest man that ever was."

The only ones who cast jaundiced glances at this paragon were (understandably) those he bested in the realm of high finance and certain of his college classmates who had expected a supremely gifted youth to scale the heights as President of the United States or, at least, Justice of the Supreme Court.

But as Whitney devoted himself at first to money-making and then to Lucullan living these friends of his early days became disillusioned. One viewed him realistically enough to say: "He has a big-domed head, not very broad but long and high, and wears an aristocratic pince-nez over strange blue-gray eyes that are very cold, very steady, and utterly fearless; his mind is an unresting engine, his ambition inordinate."

Another actually wrote to Whitney, "It has made me heartsick to see you apparently contented to give your great mind alone to money-getting and horse racing." One man made rueful note of the fact that Whitney no longer seemed friendly to his college chums after entering the pursuit of pleasure. In a celebrated put-down, Henry Adams wrote that Whitney had "thrown away the usual objects of . . . ambition like the ashes of smoked cigarettes; and turned to other amusements, satiated every taste, gorged every appetite; won every object that New York offered, and, not yet satisfied, had carried his field of activity abroad, until New York no longer knew what most to envy, his horses or his houses."

Those who accused Whitney of worshiping false gods nursed special bitterness because he began his career so bravely. After four years as an exceptional student at Yale, he attended Harvard Law School. Then, like a Galahad, he arrived in New York in 1864. The young man's interests were varied, with the law dominant; he aspired to handle every type of case. But he was also interested in Democratic Party politics and the accumulation of money. At this time only his dreams of riches let him down. Pristine investments in Wall Street were unhappy and for the moment he abandoned finance.

It is hardly surprising that so personable and keen-minded a young man quickly attracted the attention of Samuel J. Tilden, leader of the reform forces battling to break the stranglehold of the Tweed Ring on New York City. When in time the reformers emerged victorious, Whitney stood high in their ranks.

Politicians and public became increasingly familiar with this hard-working young lawyer, but saw only half the man. At both Yale and Harvard, the personable youth had met the scions of New York wealth, and through them their families. These rich folk were instantly charmed by Whitney, who seemed to have absorbed culture through his pores and to possess by instinct the grace and breeding supposedly accompanying wealth. There was never a question of William Collins Whitney being a climber; he was to the manor born.

After working long office hours, Whitney at night cut a wide swath through Gotham Society. Not only did this please the hostesses of the day, but it delighted him, for he had discovered a sybaritic streak in his nature. Having tasted luxury, he found it as necessary to his existence as breathing.

At Yale, Whitney had roomed with Oliver Payne, son of Senator Henry B. Payne of Ohio. While Whitney studied law, Payne went to the Civil War, rising in the Union army to the rank of colonel. Afterward Payne returned to Cleveland, where his counsel was heeded by John D. Rockefeller, then in the process of building the giant monopoly known as Standard Oil. With this involvement, the Payne family, already rich, began to grow wealthy.

Whitney fell in love with Flora Payne, his roommate's sister, and married her in 1869. The bride was unusually well educated for her day; she had studied under Louis Agassiz in Boston, and was said to be versed in music, sciences, languages, archaeology, sociology, and writing. It is hard to imagine such an intellect becoming a social butterfly, but without hesitation Flora joined her husband's euphoric socializing.

As a wedding gift, Senator Payne commissioned architect Russell Sturgis to build the Whitneys a fine townhouse at 74 Park Avenue. Young Colonel Payne, unmarried and intensely devoted to his sister, lavished gifts on the newlyweds. Inevitably the Whitneys became one of the most sought after young couples in Society.

The fact that his wife's father and brother spent money so prodigally may have aroused competitive envy in Whitney, causing him to think again of piling his own millions. But these ideas were put in abeyance as he accepted the responsible post of Corporation Counsel of the City of New York. As the man advising the metropolis on legal matters and fighting its battles in court, Whitney made a notable record and saved the city millions. Among other aspects of his six-year tenure, he guided the construction of the first city elevated railroads, gaining invaluable knowledge of franchises and public transit. He also displayed exceptional political adroitness and rose to be the most powerful Democrat in town.

After quitting as Corporation Counsel in 1882, Whitney seemed ideally equipped to function as a corporation lawyer. Immediately employed by the Vanderbilt interests, he found that multimillionaires paid off minimally in cash and gratitude. His hard-working efforts, he wryly noted, only made the rich richer. This was not the way he projected his life; his plan was to labor solely to enrich himself.

As Corporation Counsel, he had made canny note of the city's trolley car lines which were operating in a state of unbridled chaos. At least thirty separate trolley companies held franchises to run cars along the avenues and streets of the metropolis. Each demanded its own fare, so the person seeking to go from one end of town to the other might end by paying a dozen times.

Here, indeed, lurked a golden opportunity for a man aware of recent developments in the seamy world of transit monopoly, especially the activities of Peter A. B. Widener in Philadelphia and Charles Tyson Yerkes, who had imposed the Widener pattern on Chicago. These two men had waxed rich and famous as the transit kings of their communities, even though colossal greed caused them to cheat their stockholders as well as others.

A nation prone to admire self-made millionaires considered the traction magnates fully entitled to their ill-gotten gains. The same was true of the financial community. As with Henry Villard's watered stock, Wall Street approved such depredations, considering that financial ends justified any means. Once in a while the government tried to control the mighty monopolists, but its weapons were weak. Meanwhile, the public went on respecting the princes of finance, considering them superior human beings, entitled by their superiority to follow through on any project. This, at the time, was the American Way.

Studying Manhattan's street railways, Whitney concluded that whoever gained control of the borough's transit must own a dominant Broadway line. Oddly enough, none existed at the moment. Proud New Yorkers called Broadway their Appian Way, and rich and poor joined in efforts to keep trolleys off the stretch between the Battery and Union Square. Above the Square—an area comparatively unimportant—one Jacob Sharp ran trolleys up Broadway to Fifty-ninth Street. This operation brought Sharp millions of dollars and he was fighting vigorously to obtain a charter for lower Broadway.

Also in the fray was a group of financiers led by Thomas Fortune Ryan, a hyper-ambitious Barefoot Millionaire. Ten years younger than Whitney, Ryan too was tall, handsome, personable, and a natty dresser. He had enormous energy, great resource as a manipulator, and strong political connections.

Most of his financing and counsel in public transit came from the experienced P. A. B. Widener of Philadelphia.

At first Whitney tried to fight both Ryan and Sharp for the all-important Broadway franchise. Then he took the step that permitted his dreams to come true. Combining with Ryan, he set out to gain control of Sharp's line and the others crisscrossing the city.

In appearance and personality, Whitney and Ryan might seem the most gentlemanly of the Robber Barons, but their harsh tactics soon taught lessons to other members of the breed; historians of finance rhapsodize over the way these two meshed as a conscienceless team. Whitney performed as the master-strategist who conceived broad plans. Ryan served as the operator with a flair for the intricacies of finance, as well as the basic mechanics of stocks and bonds. Whitney thought up the ideas, Ryan followed through with the know-how; each richly complemented the other.

Yet at first these two superlative minds made the mistake of underestimating Jacob Sharp, a seventy-year-old diabetic. The wily oldster drew $500,000 out of the bank and passed it around as bribe money among eighteen of the city's twenty-two aldermen, who by accepting earned the infamous name "boodle aldermen." Overnight, Sharp won the lower-Broadway franchise.

The true amassers of wealth needed a steely ruthlessness, as well as the massive gall to reverse any previous stand. On their part, Whitney and Ryan had also tried to bribe the aldermen, promising to pay as high as $750,000. But they offered the corruptible legislators half-cash and half-stock. By giving cash only, the wily Sharp got his way.

Yet as true tycoons, Whitney and Ryan felt no sportsmanlike compunctions about suddenly donning the robes of virtue to begin exposing Sharp as an enemy of the people. Posing as public benefactors, they launched a carefully contrived campaign aimed at public opinion, the courts, and the legislature. First, they pointed out to newsmen how the boodle aldermen had suddenly begun sprouting diamond rings, expensive equipages, and hideaway mistresses.

Next, they exerted their considerable political muscle to con-
vene a committee of the legislature for an investigation of the
Sharp franchise. With this, the boodle aldermen scattered to
Paris, Montreal, Havana, and Mexico City. Enough evidence
remained, however, to prove that bribery was involved in the
franchise and Jacob Sharp was tossed into jail. Did this change
the legality of the franchise? Not one bit—Whitney and Ryan
saw to that! As Sharp's plight worsened, the shameless pair were
able to buy his precious Broadway franchise for a paltry $25,000.

At this dramatic moment, further drama intervened. Grover
Cleveland had been elected President of the United States in
1884 and Whitney had been one of his counsellors. The
President-elect asked Whitney to be his Secretary of the Navy.
With his mind full of money, Whitney hesitated, but his wife and
the ever-present Oliver Payne persuaded him to accept. He did
not sever financial ties with New York, but continued active in
the so-called Syndicate with Ryan. Colonel Oliver Payne and the
shrewd lawyer Elihu Root protected his interests and carried out
the millions-making plans he sent from Washington.

As Secretary of the Navy, Whitney garnered high praise. Since
the Civil War, this branch of the service had fallen into disre-
pute, not to say disrepair. Whitney worked heroically to restore
its former glory. "Never since the office was instituted has it been
so thorough, systematic and efficient as at present," read one
tribute to his end-efforts. Grover Cleveland rated Navy Secretary Whitney the sharpest mind in his Cabinet, with an ability to
pierce through to the center of knotty problems and a deep
reservoir of self-confidence that kept him poised under pressure.

Whitney not only made an impression on the federal government, but on social Washington as well. He and his wife remod-
eled a mansion on I Street, adding a Louis XVI ballroom so big
that, one Senator said, a two-horse wagonload of hay could turn
around in it. Here the Whitneys gave parties that transformed
the Capital's social life. Because of them alone, a social leader
believed, Washington displayed better manners, greater
refinement, and higher culture. Whitney also found time to become a sportsman, riding and raising horses on his Grasslands

Farm outside Georgetown. Here was a man who worked hard and played harder. Washington had not seen his like before.

With Cleveland's defeat in 1888, the Whitneys returned to New York. Colonel Payne was by then treasurer and a large stockholder in Standard Oil, and the scribe who used the word "magnifico" to describe Whitney chose "eminento" for Payne. He lived up to this designation by paying $600,000 for the F. W. Stevens mansion at 2 West Fifty-seventh Street, then giving it to the Whitneys. This was really a Fifth Avenue mansion, since its east side extended along the Avenue; the doorway stood opposite the family entrance to the Cornelius Vanderbilt mansion across Fifty-seventh Street. Today the Hecksher Building fills the land.

Covering four city lots, the gabled Whitney residence was of red brick with brownstone trim. Its style was combined Queen Anne and Romanesque, with the Queen winning out, for thick clinging ivy, meticulously clipped around rectangular windows on the first floor and the arched ones above, brought the look of Merrie England. The entrance was guarded by iron-grille doors and the interior has been described as rich and splendid, especially in tapestries and oriental rugs. Whitney had also found time to turn himself into an art connoisseur and collector and the new home made a suitable background for his impeccable taste.

But whatever the delights of his new abode, Whitney's thoughts were mainly beamed on money making. With Ryan as fervent partner, he set about plundering the field of metropolitan transit. As a first step the rapacious pair watered stock and disposed of it to a gullible public, acting in line with the precepts of Peter Widener who once said, "In good times, someone can always be found to buy any stock at any price."

Using their political clout—by then greater than ever—they easily forced transit rivals to sell out to the Syndicate. Bribing city officials and state legislators, they obtained trolley and elevated railroad franchises covering Manhattan Island and large sections of Brooklyn. Whitney and Ryan had an unerring instinct for the right man to bribe; they preferred the fellow at the top and the greater his power the more they paid—and expected!

Whitney's biographer, and presumably his family, have sought
to downgrade his depredations, calling him typical of the times.
But those who have studied the pirates of fortune—notably
Whitney's contemporary Burton J. Hendrick—cite the former
Navy Secretary as the most inspired of these human predators.
The smoothest member of the group, he had the sharpest mind.
According to Ferdinand Lundberg, "His crimes and those of his
associates were of such boldness and magnitude that even his
cynical class was moved to astonishment."

Whitney and Ryan electrified most of their trolley lines and
offered slightly improved service to riders. But public service
was never a major concern. The average trolley rider mattered
to them only because his daily five-cent fares kept the transit
companies alive—it was the companies that served as pawns in
the frenzied game of millions-making as played by the Syndicate.

The partners' peak inspiration arrived with the consolidation
of multifarious operations into a single unit named Metropolitan
Transit, said to be America's first holding company. The
shadowy jugglings of this concern are hard to fathom, for it has
been called one of the most complex and bewildering outfits
of all time. With it as cover, the partners leased their own trolley
cars to themselves at exorbitant prices; paid one another excessive fees for performing routine executive duties; bought new
trolley lines and renovated the cars in their own yard at fantastic
cost. After paying $250,000 for the Wall and Cortlandt Street
Trolley Line, they sold it to Metropolitan Transit for $965,000,
pocketing the $700,000 difference. And so it went, day after day,
at the expense of public and stockholder. Said Ryan to Elihu
Root, the canny lawyer who drew up the Metropolitan Transit
Charter, "You have just made us a great tin box."

For all Ryan's skills, William C. Whitney was the important
man. One Wall Streeter wrote, "He was at will the most polished
and fascinating person in the world, or the most overbearing
and intolerable bully. He had a knowledge of men, and I think a
contempt for them, beyond anyone I ever knew. His associates
seemed to fear as much as admire him; there are records of
directors' meetings absolutely terrorized by his indomitable will."

Only a few legislators, newspaper editors, reformers, and muckrakers saw anything wrong in the enormous robbery of the public and Metropolitan Transit stockholders. Muckraker Burton Hendrick paid ironic tribute to Whitney by writing that even in corruption his bigness was apparent—he was a grandee of graft never content with thousands but demanding millions from the common man. Yet any estimate of Whitney, ironic or otherwise, becomes insignificant beside the cold fact that in a little over five years he made himself $40 million from New York transit, and that partner Ryan did the same.

According to a biographer, Whitney thus achieved "his supreme end . . . the millions essential to his happiness and to the gratification of his expensive personal tastes . . . to live consistently in an atmosphere of luxury and ease."

There was more. Whitney, the wizard of finance, had kept a hand in politics, master-minding Grover Cleveland's successful bid for the Presidency in 1892. With this, Whitney was dubbed the modern Warwick, or Kingmaker. From this eminence he could pick any political plum, including Secretary of State or Ambassador to the Court of St. James's.

Along with his hard-hearted money making, Whitney remained the man of culture and social sparkle. Indeed, his socializing continued at such a rate that a friend cited love of gaiety as the basic impulse of his life.

Yet there were periods of misery. He suffered a nervous breakdown from overwork while Secretary of the Navy and endured a long period of melancholy. A far greater blow came with the death of his wife in 1892. This bereavement arrived at the moment of his fame as a modern Warwick and drained pleasure out of triumph. He deeply mourned Flora Payne Whitney and more than anything else her demise altered the course of his life. The pomp of an ambassadorship seemed unthinkable without her at his side, and he forever renounced political activity.

But whatever his sorrows, Whitney kept on making money. He joined Ryan in raiding the American Tobacco Company trust of James Buchanan Duke and in other ways flexed financial muscle. But the gears of his life had shifted to concentrate on spending rather than earning. Whitney had twelve more years of life and by one estimate spent no less than $28 million over that span. He did not present large sums to charity, as some Splendor Seekers eventually did, but spent it on his own princely pleasures. At the time of his death he had no fewer than ten city mansions and country estates, private railroad cars, uncountable paintings and other works of art, and one of the finest racing stables in the world. He had also achieved every sportsman's dream by winning the English Derby.

His family brought more satisfactions. The Whitneys had four children—Pauline, Dorothy, Harry Payne, and William Payne, the last of whom confused the public by calling himself Payne. In 1895, Pauline Whitney married Sir Almeric Paget, one of those adventurous Englishmen who made money in the American West. As parent of the bride, Whitney had charge of the affair and reputedly spent $1 million to make it one of the fanciest weddings in city history. Special cachet came from the presence of President Cleveland, who traveled from Washington to attend the ceremony.

For it, the interior of St. Thomas's Church on Fifth Avenue was transformed into a florist's dream—or nightmare—with a triple series of white chrysanthemum arches spanning the nave. In curious contrast, the chancel was shrouded by tropical foliage. Eighteen other arches of laurel studded with giant chrysanthemums lined the middle aisle. Madame Nordica and Edouard de Reszke sang "Ave Maria" as the bride and her father moved down the aisle. Six bridesmaids, carrying feathered muffs, wore prismatic poplin, trimmed with Russian sable and small velvet hats copied from a Dutch painting. A supercilious society reporter made note of President Cleveland as the only male in the assemblage without gloves.

A year later Harry Payne Whitney married Gertrude Vanderbilt, the unprepossessing but highly talented daughter (she became a noted sculptor and founded the Whitney Museum) of Cornelius Vanderbilt II. Believe it or not, this had been a childhood romance, for the Whitney mansion stood across the street from the looming Vanderbilt mass, making Harry and Gertrude practically boy-and-girl next door. These nuptials have come down in history because bandleader Nathan Franko unexpectedly struck up the "Star Spangled Banner" at the reception. He explained later, "It is so rarely that an American girl of fortune marries one of her countrymen that I thought the selection decidedly in keeping with the occasion."

Only a month after Harry Payne's wedding, Whitney himself astounded the world by marrying Mrs. Edith S. Randolph, the Baltimore-born widow of a British army officer and a lady fifteen years his junior. A quick, quiet ceremony was performed at Bar Harbor, Maine. It turned into a bittersweet event, for none of Whitney's children saw fit to be present. His former brother-in-law, Colonel Oliver Payne, infuriated that Whitney dared marry again, was attempting to influence the children against their father. For the moment he succeeded, but eventually only son Payne Whitney remained obdurate.

Whitney adored his second wife, as he had the first. Entertaining in his home had always been varied, with the politically presentable joining the fashionably wealthy and the artistically gifted. Now his parties became more catholic, with Paderewski, Madame Nordica, Fritz Kreisler, and Nellie Melba performing as friends rather than hirelings.

The new Mrs. Whitney enthusiastically joined her husband in his passion for horseflesh, on which he proceeded to spend millions. Some of the sporting gentry questioned the ex-Secretary's true dedication to the sport of kings, noting that he went about it like a monopolist gobbling up competition. He used his multimillions to build the finest stables, buy the best horses, lure top trainers, and hire jockeys like Tod Sloan, the finest of the day. It is an indication of the Whitney charisma that, with his new employment, Sloan began billing himself as James Todhunter Sloan.

Wife at his side, Whitney set about acquiring land and shortly emerged as one of the major landowners in the East. First he bought a country estate at Westbury, Long Island, its sweeping acreage dominated by a mansion described as a Venetian palace. Nonetheless, this establishment existed primarily for horse-raising and he promptly spent $2 million on stables with stalls more luxurious than the living quarters of many of his fellow human beings.

Love of horseracing also impelled him to buy property at Sheepshead Bay, near the Coney Island racetrack, where a 150-year-old mansion served as lodge. In Kentucky, he purchased Blue Grass Farm, surrounded by 3,000 acres, together with stables and private racetrack. In Aiken, South Carolina, he acquired 2,000 acres of hunting land, complete with mansion, stables, and track.

Whitney also interested himself in conservation and in Lenox, Massachusetts, bought the 11,000 acres of October Mountain, stocking the property with moose, elk, buffalo, deer, pheasant, and quail. In the Adirondacks, he acquired 33,744 acres of combined sporting facilities and game preserve. This domain included fifty-two lakes and an entire township in Hamilton County which, an observer said, Whitney purchased as carelessly as another man might buy a pair of gloves. In addition, he owned a cottage in Newport and a shooting box in England. With such vast and far-flung properties he could, if nothing else, choose his own weather.

"He may be said to lead not only a luxurious, but perhaps an ostentatious way of life," read an account of the Whitney existence. To this prodigal man, the vine-covered urban mansion at 2 West Fifty-seventh Street began to seem inadequate. Accordingly plans were initiated to give that home to son Harry Payne Whitney, while the father purchased the dwelling of the late Robert L. Stuart, sugar refiner and candy manufacturer, at 871 Fifth Avenue, on the corner of Sixty-eighth Street. This imposing French château on a Manhattan corner sat high, wide, and solid, its sternness modified by a pleasant mansard roof. Slim, vertical windows of all types were in profusion, along with bay windows, balconies, and strong rustication.

Whitney decided to leave this exterior alone and concentrate on redecorating the inside. For the job he picked Stanford White . . . naturally, no one else would do! Of White it was said, "He scoured Europe to lay at the feet of his rich and not always cultivated patrons the spoils of European palaces and auction rooms and made himself the master of artistic revels in sumptuous decoration."

This was precisely the aspect of the famous architect that Whitney desired to utilize. He carefully explained that, while a great admirer of French decoration of the various Louis periods, he felt more at ease surrounded by Italian Renaissance style. In line with this, he wished the interior of his mansion to be as close as possible to a Florentine or Roman palace of the time of Leonardo and Michelangelo.

So matters stood when, only two years after the marriage, Mrs. Whitney set out on a solitary horseback ride along the paths of the Aiken estate. Failing to lower her head passing under a bridge, she struck herself a shattering blow that sent her to the ground critically injured. For months she lay in a coma, with Whitney constantly at her side. A specially fitted railroad hospital car finally carried her north, where a private ambulance waited at the Forty-second Street ferry. A grief-stricken Whitney walked beside this ambulance, as it traveled slowly to Fifty-seventh. Several times the multimillionaire ran ahead to clear objects from the path. Mrs. Whitney lingered fifteen months before dying. Again Whitney, the man who had schemed to get everything, seemed left with nothing at all.

Still, he did have his racehorses, as well as the mansion being re-created for him by Stanford White. Though the architect was normally responsible for a mammoth job of redecoration, Whitney flung himself into the endeavor as a sort of partner. Alone or with White, he subjected southern Europe to one of its most sophisticated forays of art-pillaging. As portals for his mansion, for example, he bought (or bribed his way to) the tremendous bronze and wrought-iron gates of the Doria palace in Rome.

The remodeling of the Whitney home took four long years, its cost being estimated close to $3 million. Not only were art treasures laboriously transported from Europe at great expense, but native and overseas artisans put their unique skills into duplicating ceilings and frescoes in Italian Renaissance style. When at last he moved in, Whitney inhabited the latest and most tasteful of the "finest" mansions on Fifth Avenue.

The Whitney mansion was saluted as possessing "the rarest

and most remarkable furnishings possible—the purse of a Fortunatus has combined with rare good taste and judgment." One critic who scrutinized the mansion called it a consistent example of Italian Renaissance decor, with only the floors of modern construction. He then reminded readers that it was far more difficult and costly to design a mansion in a single period than to hit the high spots of several. "When decorations are all original, it becomes well-nigh impossible, except for the expenditure of large amounts of money and time," he concluded.

This tribute indicated that Whitney, in the manner of arrogant millionaires, had not allowed the writer inside for a view of the premises. For hardly less than others, Whitney and White had delved into the art treasures of five centuries and at least three cultures in evolving a superlative decor. It may be that the Whitney mansion had less variety of style than others and that its overall magnificence projected an aura of Leonardo. But it was still a mixture of numerous styles, backgrounds, and artists.

The furnishings in the huge ballroom of a newly constructed wing of the mansion had been laboriously brought from a French château near Bordeaux. From the château of the Sieur Franc de Conseil at Aigues-Mortes, Whitney had grabbed a cavernous Henri II fireplace of carved stone, capable of burning a small tree. From the Château of the Vicômte Sauze, he obtained other rare objects, including historic stained-glass windows. Hidden away on the first floor was a dainty, multimirrored Marie Antoinette salon, a powder room for ladies furnished at a cost of $10,000 in blue brocade and gilt furniture, with draperies to match.

The splendor that began with the Doria palace portals continued in a green onyx vestibule with three immense chandeliers of bronze. This led to an entrance hall with white marble walls, dark green columns, and a marble floor inlaid with 10,000 pieces of bronze in bold mosaic.

Here stood the tree-size fireplace from Aigues-Mortes. The ceiling was of Florentine wood, the windows stained glass from a cathedral. Additional decoration included rare cupids from a Greek palace, a looming oak table from an Italian monastery, an elaborately carved sarcophagus, and a silver hanging lamp hailed as a masterwork of old Italian craftsmanship. Portières of deep crimson contrasted with the surrounding white marble. On the walls were a religious rendering by Lorenzo Costa and a striking, full-length portrait of Charles I by Van Dyck.

In the rear of this imposing entrance hall stood a grand staircase of chiseled Istrian marble, with an elaborate balustrade carved and pieced to create an interlocking design of lacelike beauty. On the walls of this grandest of staircases hung the two famed Diana tapestries, with entwined monograms of Henri II and Diane de Poitiers.

This led up to a great hall on the second floor extending the entire length of the house, with ceilings two stories high, fittings of marble and carved wood, the furniture along the walls heavy and baronial.

Among the art treasures in the Whitney mansion were a Renaissance ceiling with 100 golden coffers from a palazzo in Florence; a noble door from the Château de la Bastie d'Urffe on the Loire; a statue of Dionysus dredged from the Tiber; stained-glass windows from churches, convents, and monasteries; and a Flemish tapestry said to be worth $100,000.

Throughout hung a breathtaking array of other tapestries by Gobelin, Boucher, and Boekel. On the floors lay rugs by Aubusson and Gobelin, as well as flowered Persian floor coverings, and smaller, silken ones from Oriental mosques. Among the countless paintings were Tintorettos, Raphaels, Angelo Donis, Gaetanos, and two more portraits by Van Dyck. One of these was of the Duke de Villiers, the other of Viscount Grandison, a young man in court dress with gold brocade doublet and plumed cavalier hat. Contrasting with these European masterpieces were panels by the American John La Farge.

The drawing room was considered an artistic triumph, with hangings of Florentine embroidery in rich, soft hues. The ceiling was an epic work in gold, green, and copper done by Bardini for a Roman prince. Covering the floor were priceless Persian prayer rugs, while overhead hung a chandelier of hammered bronze. On a fireplace of cupid design two standing lamps matched the chandelier. Furniture was carved mahogany. Facing the entrance was Hoppner's *Dancing Girl*, painted in 1791. Nearby hung Millet's original sketch for *The Sower*.

The dining, or banquet, hall featured the magnificent Brussels tapestries *Wars of Flavius Titus,* once on loan to a King of England. Other walls had tapestries by Audran representing the elements. Underfoot lay a Persian rug worth $14,000. Overhead was a ceiling painting by Bardini, delicately sliced from a Genovese palazzo. The huge medieval dining table could seat 100 or more people, each place with golden dinner plates and table service.

Leading from the entrance hall to the music room was an arcade, or corridor, lovingly lifted from a French monastery. Walls were inlaid wood panels depicting religious themes; the main one, representing the Betrayal of Christ, was signed *Francisci Orlandini Veronensis Opus* 1547. This arcade got its light through stained-glass windows and by chandeliers of wrought iron and staghorn.

The huge ballroom had been transferred at a cost of $50,000 from the Bordeaux castle of Phoebus d'Albert, Baron de Foix, a field marshal under Louis XIV. Its colors are recalled as gorgeous, dominated by tapestries of red and gold hung between panels of oak and dull gilt. The floor was inlaid oak, the ceiling a 200-year-old allegorical painting framed in smoky oak. At one end, over a carved fireplace, hung Sir Joshua Reynolds' *Portrait of a Lady*, valued at $45,000. Above and encircling part of the room was the famed Gallery of the Monkeys, inspired by the writings of Voltaire and given its name because monkeys were repeated in its wrought-iron design. Here musicians played for dancing.

In the library were bookcases carved by Renaissance craftsmen. The paneling was by Cranach the Elder, and paintings included a Reynolds, a Gaetano, and a *Madonna and Child* attributed to Filippo Lippi. Amid the greenery of a nearby conservatory stood a playing fountain and statues taken from Italian flower gardens.

As luxury-loving men, Whitney and White had installed the most modern electricity, heating, refrigeration, and plumbing in the midst of this old-world sumptuousness. Yet even here the atmosphere recalled past centuries. The master bathroom was of the finest Carrara marble, relieved by onyx and precious materials, the floor of glass and stone mosaic. The bathtub was cut from a solid block of marble, and fixtures throughout were of pure gold.

So many glowing compliments were paid to the charm and personality of the Honorable William Collins Whitney that it becomes difficult to select the most flattering.

From a High Society standpoint, however, the summit is found in the fact that the social whirl of the new century was not considered to begin until Whitney gave a housewarming ball at the mansion. This did not happen until the night of January 4, 1901, so the social history of Gotham stood in limbo until the century achieved the age of twelve months and four days. The Whitney affair appears as the First Ball of the Century.

The ball took place just as soon as the mansion was ready. In accordance with social protocol, the official justification for the occasion was the debut of Miss Helen Tracy Barney, Whitney's favorite niece. Some 700 representatives of the upper crust were invited, and a large crowd of lesser folk clustered outside to watch them arrive at 10:30 on the allotted night.

The interior of the Whitney mansion was already so lavish and colorful that little decoration was necessary for a gala. Still, banks of poinsettias lit up the cold white marble of walls and staircase in the reception room. Whitney stood at the head of the stairway receiving his guests. At his right stood his sister, Mrs. Charles Barney. Her gown of mirror velvet and brocade turned back to reveal a petticoat of silver cloth embroidered with roses of varying shades of pink; her court train was soft red velvet. Diamonds hid roguishly in her coiffure and strands of pearls festooned her neck. Debutante Helen Barney stood at her uncle's other side, somewhat less strikingly garbed in white *mousseline de soie*, delicately embroidered in gold and trimmed with flowers. Rivaling their attire was that of Mrs. Astor, now aged 70, who wore a magnificent Marie Antoinette costume of purple velvet, massive tiara, dog collar of pearls with diamond pendant attachments, diamond corsage ornament, and stomacher of twinkling diamonds.

In the ballroom, the ancient-château interior had been embellished by Southern smilax placed in windows, baskets of pink begonias dangling from the center of each. Large clusters of electric lights covered by diaphanous material were in turn veiled by asparagus vine on which lay pink and white orchids.

Whitney had decided to place his forty-five dinner tables in his state rooms, salons, and halls—everywhere, indeed, but in the ballroom. The Table of Honor, with Whitney, his sister and niece, Mrs. Astor, and top-echelon guests, had been placed in the great hall on the second floor. Tables were decorated and laid on the third floor, then carefully carried downstairs to indicated spots by an army of footmen. On each table stood pink and white orchids. Sherry's Hungarian Orchestras were stationed in strategic spots so diners everywhere could hear the music. At 12:30, supper was announced and those in the ballroom filed out to locate place cards and begin a simple supper catered by Louis Sherry—

Bouillon en Tasse
Terrapin
Canvas-back Duck
Poussins Grillés à la Diable
Pâté en Croute
Salade

| *Gâteaux* | *Glace* | *Bonbons* |
| *Champagne* | *Café* | *Apollinaris* |

After this, guests returned to the ballroom to watch the various fancy dress quadrilles performed by younger, talented members of Society, who had been practicing for weeks. In one of them, hobby horses ridden by supposed jockeys sported the Whitney racing colors of pale blue and chocolate brown. The riders handed out riding crops as presents to the guests. Other favors were numerous, among them scarves for the ladies and gay sashes for the men.

As the entertainment ended, the fifty couples who were to take part in the cotillion formed on the dance floor. Cotillion-leader Worthington Whitehouse had outdone himself in devising stunts for this First Ball of the Century. One required the fifty males to step inside balloons of tissue paper, no two colored alike. The ladies were told to avert eyes during this process. Then they turned to face the multicolored balloons and pick the color combination appealing to them. Ripping open the tissue paper, each found inside her partner for the first part of the cotillion, which was led by Whitehouse and Mrs. Barney.

Next a six-foot-high, furled fan was wheeled to the middle of the floor. As it opened wide, the ladies were instructed to gather on one side and men on the other, with the fan hiding one group from the other. A tiny, colorful fan was given each lady, who held it high enough to be seen over the rim of the bigger fan. This time the gentleman chose the color scheme that intrigued him, and so located his partner for the remainder of the cotillion.

Having scored the ultimate in social success, the Honorable Mr. Whitney once more concentrated on horseracing. Making full use of his millions and political influence, he joined other men of wealth in reconstructing the Saratoga racetrack, improving the grounds, the track itself, and the grandstands to make one of the finest courses in the world.

He then achieved the peak racing honor when his thoroughbred Volodyovski won the English Derby at Epsom. It was a muted triumph, however, for Whitney had only leased the oddly named horse when its owner died. Sadly, the Yankee Croesus was not even in England to enjoy this rarest of victories, and missed the dinner with King Edward VII that customarily followed a win. It was one of the few disappointments in his public life.

Whitney had suffered several attacks of appendicitis, an affliction that was a giant killer of the day. Spurning an operation, he continued his sybaritic life. In January 1904, three years after the First Ball of the Century, he experienced so acute an attack that an operation was necessary. Peritonitis set in, followed by blood poisoning, and he died at age sixty-two.

With his death, those who disapproved of his life again had their innings. Amidst tributes from Presidents, Kings, and Cabinet members, one obituary said, "He was a conspicuous example of those who, having the ability, use wealth to get more wealth for which they have no need."

9

Breaking into Society

THERE seemed to be no dearth of Splendor Seekers as the world closed in on the twentieth century. This remained true despite the several financial slumps in the country. Each money crisis appeared to produce a fresh gaggle of millionaires. One writer who observed the money-parade toward Fifth Avenue made note of fortunes deriving from barreled pork, mile-deep copper, grain, sugar, sewing machines, barbed wire, five-and-ten-cent stores, telegraph lines, and potency pills. "Castles of solid marble rise on understructures of chewing tobacco," he ended.

Nor was there a paucity of land on which to erect mansions. It may be hard for us to visualize an upper Avenue gap-toothed with empty lots, but such was the case. Desirable corners remained for mansions, along with mid-block space for slim, twenty-five-room townhouses. On the empty lots a few squatters' shacks actually remained.

More than ever, Millionaires' Row had become a prime tourist attraction. Few visitors to New York failed to hire an open carriage for a ride up Fifth Avenue to ogle the palaces of the rich, while a garrulous driver passed out information or misinformation. The carriage riders could guide themselves with a list of mansions with addresses and salient facts published at the beginning of each summer by the enterprising New York *Herald*.

It was only natural for these tourists to wonder what life must be like in these baronial piles. Were they comfortable or as alien to human ease as they looked? By erecting such dwellings the multimillionaires had, in effect, built a wall between themselves and the rest of humanity. Did it make them a different breed of person—a super-race, perhaps?

Those who wondered—and got no answers—might have received a few jolts of surprise had they been allowed to penetrate the world of the envied families inhabiting mansions. One would derive from the fact that most mansions failed to retain the motif of the exteriors. Whereas the outside might resemble an intricately patterned Roman palazzo, the inside often offered a contrasting decor.

This was the Victorian age, with all its horrors. In addition, the taste of the rich no less than the rest of the country had been influenced by the Philadelphia Centennial of 1876, and the Chicago World's Fair of 1893. Both had sparked a Yankee passion for the culture of exotic lands. This impelled those who could afford the price to order Spanish Music Rooms, English Oak Dining Rooms, Greek Rooms, Egyptian Rooms and Flemish Libraries, as well as Louis Quatorze Salons, Turkish Corners, and such gems as Cornelius Vanderbilt's Moorish Billiard Room.

Thus to move from room to room in a mansion often provided a series of surprises. Also, there was disappointment in the fact that the rooms, no matter how exotic, were usually dim and gloomy, since the stern etiquette of the times decreed that draperies be drawn across the outside windows that might otherwise let in glorious sunlight. Calla lilies, aspidistras, potted palms, and century plants were favored decoration, in part because their size fit the magnitude of the domiciles. Further Victorianism derived from the fact that, unless restrained by a hand like Stanford White or Louis Comfort Tiffany, the occupants happily succumbed to the contemporary love of clutter. State rooms dominated by huge, jutting medieval fireplaces from the Loire also included busts of Homer and Socrates on marble pedestals, paintings draped on easels, heavy bronze ornaments, towering vases, massive furniture, knitted fringes on damask curtains, footstools, knick-knacks, curio cabinets, blackamoors, urns with or without plants, wood nymphs peering into reflecting pools, and whatnots loaded down with Dresden china figurines, statuettes, or conch shells.

Those who wondered about the interiors of mansions might have gotten greater surprises if they had been allowed to penetrate the upper floors. The first two floors were usually for exhibition, and guests were encouraged to wander through them on gala nights. The floors above were the quarters where the family actually lived. Surviving photographs not only show these domestic rooms to be more cluttered than those below, but reveal clutter of a variety that made them look amazingly lived-in. Formality was abandoned in favor of comfort, with Victorian rocking chairs, scatter rugs, family photos, and brass beds. Unlike the marble halls, these rooms indicated the presence of people, and sometimes warm-hearted ones at that.

The upstairs atmosphere provided a good barometer of how each multimillionaire family treated its offspring. Those who retained stiffness and formality in their living quarters were usually stiff and formal with progeny, and the reminiscences of the rich offer the searing recollections of children allowed to see parents only once a day, usually for a quick goodnight as mama and papa left home in party attire. The children of Cornelius Vanderbilt III communed with their parents twice a day—at 9:00 A.M. for breakfast and at 5:00 P.M. when they were displayed to guests at tea time. On neither occasion did the youngsters speak until spoken to.

Yet others among the super-rich cared about the young. Mrs. Astor, so forbidding to the outside world, was tender with her children and grandchildren, and both generations adored her. William Kissam Vanderbilt had the instincts of a devoted father, though his formidable wife Alva would not allow their use. Consuelo Yznaga, a beauty with Cuban father and New England mother, married the Duke of Manchester but managed to spend time on Fifth Avenue. Once a friend visited Consuelo in her bedroom, where her young son also amused himself. The child seemed enchanted by his mother's chamber pot, cradling it in his arms and putting it over his head. The friend remonstrated, but ever-loving Consuelo murmured, "Let him do it, nothing else seems to amuse him."

The Aristocratic Rich—as opposed to those Suddenly Rich —living in New York at this moment in history considered themselves the most fortunate folk alive. They were probably right, for the country had turned into a land of plenty far exceeding previous dreams. Yankee independence, enterprise, and ingenuity had created comfort and commodities no other nation possessed and naturally the rich had access to more than anyone else. Why, in just a few years the rich would be the first to own motor cars!

Those aristocrats who chose to inhabit Millionaires' Row might radiate greater splendor than the rest of the Four Hundred but they remained part of it, with every assurance deriving from membership in a close-knit, self-approving group. The Suddenly Rich might grow lonely in their ornate homes, but never the Social Rich. Mrs. Winthrop Chanler has recalled how, as a bride fresh from Rome, she was obliged to launch two motherless sisters-in-law in Gotham Society. Brought up on a Hudson River estate, the girls had few friends in the city. Worse, they were "not tuned to ballroom pitch, and lacked a certain lightheartedness." Mrs. Chanler felt qualms, but needlessly. The girls had Astor blood on their mother's side and on the night of their debut gratifying numbers of aristocrats showed up. From then on, they were socially occupied every night. Truly, the Four Hundred took care of its own!

Inside the mansions, servants of the rich rose before dawn to do their unobtrusive cleaning before 9:00 A.M. Milady usually breakfasted in bed and did not show herself until noon. The master of the house might or might not go to work. If he belonged to a family rich for generations he had no need to hustle to an office. After taking his time to dress and breakfast, he probably went to the gymnasium of the mansion for a workout or a massage by a male masseur who was a full-time member of the household staff.

Then he might repair to the office of his family estate, or to his club, there to peruse stock reports and racing forms. If truly sporty, he went to the track or placed bets at his club. After lunching with congenial members, he could pass the hours snoozing in his favorite upholstered chair at the club window. Asked how he passed his days, one fellow of entrenched wealth deigned to explain, "I go to the club every forenoon, read the headlines in the newspapers, then go home after lunch and explain them to my wife."

One reason for this good life was an abundance of servants. The mansions of the rich were staffed first of all by an all-important butler or butlers, a valet for the master, and ladies' maids for the mistress and her daughters. Then came ten or twelve footmen, who worked under the butler, a housekeeper, chef, assistant chef, and a profusion of parlor, upstairs, and scullery maids. The butler, often more snobbish than his employer, was responsible for the smooth running of the visible part of the household; the housekeeper ran the rest. Many old-roots families had inherited faithful butlers. Others employed butlers who claimed to have worked for the English nobility, and may have done so. Supplementary footmen, grooms, maids, and others could easily be hired from the swollen ranks of immigrants from overseas, preferably England or Ireland. Incidentally, the quarters under the roofs of mansions where the lower servants lived have been described as "unspeakable."

Members of wealthy families knew how to treat servants, having been surrounded by them from childhood. There was a line across which no servant dared step, and within this area the hireling did a job well or got fired on the spot, without back pay or references. Mrs. Cornelius Vanderbilt was not the only great lady of Society to don a single immaculate white glove and run an index figure over tables, chairs, and knick-knacks. If the whiteness of the glove was marred by one smudge of dirt, the housemaid lost her job.

One day a growing Vanderbilt watched a maid shaking a rug from a window. "Mother," he asked, "what's that lady doing?"

His mother nearly swooned, but finally found herself able to say, "That's no lady, that's a *woman*." Then she proceeded to lecture the child, stressing the point that never under any conditions did a lady perform a menial task or anything resembling one.

Our grande dame of Society might seem to live in a vacuum in the center of enormous riches, but this existence was sufficiently populated to please the lady herself. Once dressed, she communed on social matters with a social secretary, and on domestic ones with butler, housekeeper, and chef. Her rooms and the rest of the house would be already filled with fresh flowers, for Fifth Avenue families not only had carriage houses on side streets nearby but private greenhouses as well. Milady might approve the flower arrangements done by a parlor maid, or take the time to tell her butler or social secretary how to do it better.

As a viable social figure, she was required to entertain on, say, alternate Thursday afternoons; this meant being at home to a select number of social equals and an inferior or two. Social secretary and butler joined her in making out this list. Once the names were selected, the secretary would write on cards in a shaded Spencerian hand, "I hope you will come to my next Thursday at home." A groom in a carriage would then leave them at the proper residences.

The first visitors of a lady's day were likely to be the milliner or dressmaker from the New York shop of Madame Osborne, sole local rival of Worth and Paquin in Paris. Mrs. Cornelius Vanderbilt made the proud boast that from the day of her marriage she never entered a store, and other ladies of Society believed in having merchandise brought to them. Still, a few restless spirits did prefer personal shopping expeditions to Lord & Taylor or Arnold Constable.

After a lunch shared by her social secretary, the social lady might be visited by close female friends, with the addition of a male hanger-on or two. Ward McAllister smoothed the existence of Mrs. Astor, while Harry Lehr brightened the long hours for Mrs. Stuyvesant Fish. Lesser Wards and Harrys livened the intimate circles of others. These males might be indigent noblemen from abroad, home-grown homosexuals, or suave fortune hunters. In a few cases, this hanger-on might also function as a lover, in which case there came the ever-present danger of blackmail.

At three o'clock a lady's victoria, polished body by Brewster, usually pulled up before the portals, with two grooms and two spanking horses. This might take her briskly around Central Park for a dose of fresh air. More likely it deposited her at another mansion or townhouse where the occupant was holding an Afternoon. Or she might attend a gathering of females of high social stratum in a so-called cultural group improving minds by a discussion of recent operas or the novels of Mrs. Humphrey Ward or Mr. Howells, with a daring deviation into the best-seller *Trilby*.

The social rich enjoyed special privilege—or so they believed—in the matter of paying bills. The rest of the world was expected to pay up on time, or else. But the aristocrats whose lives were paved with gold believed themselves possessed of a divine right to be dilatory. Three years was considered a suitable period to let a bill run, and butchers, specialty shops, or florists went out of business because the filthy rich considered tradespeople lucky merely to serve them.

Male offspring of the rich were brought up by English nannies and then tutored at home until old enough to enter exclusive prep schools like St. Paul's or Groton. During these years of home schooling, daughters might sit in on the lessons and could receive a good educational grounding as a result.

But once a girl entered her teens, with skirts dropping to hide her legs forever, she was no longer obliged to think of anything but marriage, motherhood, and the challenge of social life. The presence of young male tutors in households sometimes produced interesting results. In her later years, novelist Edith Wharton reached the surprising conclusion that she must be illegitimate, since it did not seem possible that anyone with talent could emerge from the loins of her smugly patrician parents. Mrs. Wharton decided that her true father was an older brother's tutor.

Day inevitably led to night and our lady of Society, along with milord, usually had a dinner or a ball, perhaps fancy dress, to anticipate. Around five o'clock the female mind turned to the all-important matter of dressing for this occasion—which dress, how many jewels, what coiffure? If·she had young children or grandchildren, they might be allowed to visit with her as the process of adornment began. In rare households, the husband might appear for a warm family hour.

Chances are, however, that the husband greeted eventide by drinking cocktails or whiskey at his club. Only the best wines would be served at the night's dinner with no cocktails beforehand, so the male who liked his beverages potent consumed them early. If the gentleman worked downtown, he directed his coachman to stop at the Waldorf Men's Bar or some other stimulating oasis on the way home. There he drank pleasantly with the men he would meet that night at dinner.

Or maybe the gentlemen spent these precious hours with a *petite amie* in a hideaway love nest. Pretty girls were easily available at a time when the Personal columns of newspapers carried blatant advertisements of girls of tender years in quest of older protectors. If it still proved difficult for a man to find a tempting girl, the Wall Street area offered fresh young maidens who went from office to office supposedly vending flowers and candy, but in reality offering themselves for long- or short-term use. It was simple for a man of means to set up a girl in a boarding house around Twenty-third Street, an area suitably distant from upper Fifth. The scandal sheet *Town Topics* had operatives sleuthing this district, detecting the illicit romances of the rich.

When the husband reached home, sated with alcohol or sex, he too dressed for dinner; in an era before the tuxedo was accepted, white tie, stiff shirt, and tails were in order. Possibly he drank more whiskey while dolling up.

With his richly adorned wife and her personal maid, he was then driven by carriage to an 8:30 dinner at another palatial mansion that seemed to lose its incongruity on Fifth Avenue as smart carriages laden with the fashionable Four Hundred deposited the guests at the *porte cochère*. Inside, the handsomely dressed throng made the tapestries and suits of armor seem right; the grand staircase took on greater majesty as guests moved upward past the two lines of liveried young footmen.

If this was a formal dinner, vast amounts of elaborate food had been provided for the delectation of those invited; hundreds of pounds of fresh lobster and such in similar abundance had been lovingly prepared. After greeting hosts and locating designated dinner partners, the diners trooped into a richly decorated dining room to enjoy this monumental meal. Behind each chair stood a footman who would, in reality, serve two full meals. For after the oysters, soup, fish, and heavy entrées there came a sorbet, or digestive, providing a pause that refreshed. Then followed more entrées, salads, and finally dessert, with each course of the dinner accompanied by the best wines a butler could buy. Ladies in whalebone corsets may have found eating capacity limited, but not so the males. One socialite believed, "Each of the men toyed with enough food to sustain a clerk for forty-eight hours and sipped enough wine to send a day-laborer into night court."

Social critic Ralph Pulitzer had charted the progress of these mighty dinners—"culinary vaudevilles," he dubbed them. One he mentions was a dinner for eighty-eight, at a table 58 feet long and 14 across, with no less than 3000 white roses adorning it. Toward the close of this dinner the huge centerpiece was removed in order that host and hostess, at opposite ends of the table, might signal to one another when time came to rise.

The first fifteen minutes of such repasts were by far the best, Pulitzer tells us, for then guests were hungry. Also, such dinners acted as the climax of a day and all were prepared to make the most of them. "Frank pleasure permeates the Gothic dining room," Pulitzer wrote of one dinner-beginning. But as the pangs of appetite were assuaged a certain fastidiousness took over—"unreasoning appreciation gives way to analysis." As diners ate less and tasted more, they evaluated each dish and formed conclusions about milady's chef. On her part, the hostess at the head of the table cocked an ear to see if the talk seemed spontaneous or forced. If the former, she relaxed—her dinner party was a success.

Another expert warns us not to imagine Society dinners as quiet, decorous affairs. Society folk had excellent manners, but over the years—most guests were middle-aged or over—many of these privileged persons had become rampant individualists, accustomed to speaking in loud tones and crassly pressing individual views on others. So conversation at a high-life dinner party might consist of males speaking loudly in the general direction of dinner partners, while others nearby did the same. "One was rarely amused by one's neighbor," wrote Mrs. Chanler coolly.

If a dinner made a mansion spring to life, a ball—costume or otherwise—did an even better job.

For an elaborate ball of 500 people or more, it might be expected that the lady of the mansion would turn commander-in-chief, supervising not only her own servants, but caterers (a function this size being too big for her own staff), interior decorators, orchestras, and a private eye or two. Yet such was the training of domestic staff that once again milady needed to dwell only on her own image. Her most responsible chore was to winnow the guest list, updating for marriages, divorces, and deaths. Then she endured the fittings for her gown, the selection of jewels, supervision of her coiffure, and finally a manicure and massage.

While she did this, her staff coped expertly with the million and one details of an affair supposedly beginning at 10:30 at night, but actually getting underway an hour later when guests began arriving from the opera. Those lacking opera invitations for the night passed the early evening hours at home, for it was considered gauche to attend the theater in décolleté.

After mounting the stairway to the melody of their own names, guests found themselves ushered into a ballroom freshly and lavishly decorated with flowers, colorful lights, and bright draperies. Though the decor might offer a delightful surprise, there were few among the assembled guests—"Here you all are, older faces and newer clothes," shrieked maniacal Mrs. Stuyvesant Fish at one of her galas.

Two orchestras provided uninterrupted music, but because of the age of most guests little dancing seemed to take place at first. "In the more seasoned breasts, the sight of the unfilled dance

floor aroused feelings of despondency," a socialite observed.
True, young men and women were in evidence, but the girls at
first stuck close to families, since the young males at balls were
often of a type eager to advance social position. "Dancing men,"
they were called and their charm was initially beamed at matrons
who might provide invitations to upcoming dinners, balls, or
nights at the opera.

Slowly the guests began spilling out on the ballroom floor,
making dancing almost impossible. People greeted one another,
exchanged small talk, observed others and were themselves observed. In the center of the floor a few intrepid souls might try to
waltz, but these early moments of the ball usually involved meeting and mingling. This aspect especially delighted some. "Music
and laughter flooded the place, as sunshine floods the fields,"
exulted Frederick Townsend Martin, describing the prelim-
inaries to one ball.

Finally the hostess signaled the musicians to cease and guests
began making their way through the mansion to the dining room
or the gymnasium (or both) for a buffet supper of nearly as
many courses as a formal dinner. Diners sat at tables of four, six,
or eight, with footmen attending each guest. The libation was
wine, though at a ball the host might set up a hard-liquor bar in
an alcove. But it is sad to report that a few ladies who had arrived
alone with high hopes of pleasure had seen fit to vanish. If no
gentlemen asked the pleasure of their company at supper, they
rushed home in tears, since no table was provided for single
women. Males, on the other hand, were free to sit at a noisy
bachelors' table, without partners.

After supper the well-fed throng trooped back to the ballroom
for the cotillion. This dance may sound like the pleasant, graceful exercise we have often seen in technicolor movies. As practiced by High Society, however, it had turned into a complicated
contest.

First, the hostess or her daughters passed out wrapped, expensive favors to the young dancing men, who then dashed
across the room to bestow them on the females desired as partners. Again, the honors went to older ladies of social eminence,
rather than young pretty girls. One commentator believed this

selection of partners was "not for the delectation the ladies arouse, but for the invitations they command; the young men waltz for weekends and two-step for yachting parties."

After a circuit of the ballroom, the cotillion stopped again and the ladies resumed their seats. Once more favors were passed out to the men who presented them to new partners. Still, young ladies were neglected in favor of dowagers, most of whom, it was noted, smugly accepted the favors as their due. Finally, the cotillion wound to an end, and the orchestra began to play for dancing.

It had grown late, and older folk were saying goodnight. Host and hostess stayed until 4:00 A.M., then went upstairs to bed. But the dancing went on, so that at last the young were free to dance until dawn. In a stuffy room downstairs the maids of the young ladies fought to stay awake, for it would be unthinkable for any of the girls dancing so gaily upstairs to be escorted home by her young man.

Close by the mansions of the Aristocratic Rich stood those of the Suddenly Rich. Often the dwellings of the *nouveaux riches* were considerably more ostentatious than those of the Social Rich, a circumstance Edith Wharton described in these words—

> That Granier house, now—a typical rung in the social ladder! The man who built it came from a milieu where all the dishes are put on the table at once. His facade is a complete architectural meal; had he omitted a style his friends might have thought the money had given out. Not a bad purchase, though; it attracts attention and awes the Western sightseer. Bye and bye he'll get out of that phase and want something that the crowd will pass and the few pause before.

Interiors were less stately, the atmosphere less calm and assured. Decoration might appear to be the same but it often lacked authority, as if architects and decorators knew the owners were not as well informed or as fussy as the Aristocratic Rich.

One fact which contributed to laxness of atmosphere was that the Suddenly Rich did not know how to handle servants. Families who had never beheld a butler stood in awe of their own, especially if this most dignified of men claimed to have worked for the English upper classes. After insisting that their footmen dress in livery, the Suddenly Rich felt uneasy in their presence. Parlor maids might be careless or flip of tongue, while the chef downstairs often refused to follow orders.

If the Suddenly Rich were anxious to break into Society— and they would hardly have been on Fifth Avenue otherwise— their households included a functionary not to be found among aristocratic neighbors. For want of a better name, this person might be called the Social Guide, since he or she had undertaken, for a large fee or annual salary, to do everything possible toward launching the family into Society.

Sometimes this Guide was a female poor-relation of a Knickerbocracy family, or perhaps a brash young man with good connections who failed to enjoy working on Wall Street. Or it might be a maiden gentleman on the order of Ward McAllister or Harry Lehr. If a hard enough bargain had been driven with the ambitious family, the Guide might live in a suite in the mansion, tended by maid or valet, with carriage or limousine for personal use.

This Guide was expected to propel his charges into what the New York *World* called "the gay world of Society, Fifth Avenue, terrapin, Newport, dry champagne, servants in livery, men who don't work, women with no serious thoughts, and all the other charms of fashionable existence." To this end, the wife and daughter of the Splendor Seeker might be ordered to take diction lessons, as well as instruction in French. Etiquette had to be mastered in all its complexity and clothes and other finery assembled. Dancing teachers, riding instructors, hairdressers, and others, all collecting good pay, were involved.

Often the head of the house entered into this. He was not likely to take diction lessons, but he might agree to brush up on his table manners, as well as patronize a better tailor. To highly competitive males who had slickly put together monopolies in starch or barbed wire, the matter of social climbing was just another challenge, much like the ruthless take-over of a competitor. Mrs. Wharton pictures such a man—

With slow unalterable persistency . . . he was making his way through the dense mass of social antagonisms. Already his wealth, and the masterly use he made of it, were giving him an enviable prominence in the world of affairs, and placing Wall Street under obligations which only Fifth Avenue could repay. In response to these claims, his name began to figure on municipal committees and charitable boards; he appeared at banquets to distinguished strangers, and his candidacy at one of the most fashionable clubs was discussed with diminishing opposition.

Certain things could be done by the Splendor Seeker who was pulling—or being pulled by—his family into Society; by far the best was Commodore Vanderbilt's old gambit of accumulating Wall Street obligations that only Fifth Avenue could repay. This meant, of course, that in the world of finance the plutocrat did a favor for an aristocrat and demanded repayment. He might be lucky enough to save an aristocrat from dire bankruptcy.

Charity was another *modus*. Mrs. Astor's idea of a charitable act might have been to send turkey dinners to patients at Bellevue Hospital on holidays, but other upper-crust ladies showed interest in the Foundling Home or the ASPCA. Instructed by the family Social Guide, the plutocrat's wife might write a substantial check to one of these, with the subtle understanding (unmistakably conveyed by the Guide) that an invitation to a dinner party or an Afternoon would be appreciated.

Others took pains to travel to Europe in first-class cabins on the same ship with families desirable to cultivate. Social barriers fell on shipboard and, if nothing else, the children of the families might become friendly. Society always contained a few traitors who for diverse reasons reached out to help an outsider. Often these turncoats were the young, who found their parents' existence restricted and dull.

The closer a family group cooperated on this, the more hopeful the result. Before the glistening eyes of the *nouveau riche* shone the success of the Richard Thornton Wilson family, which by the 1890s had gained respectful designation as "the marrying Wilsons." Wilson himself was a handsome, courtly Southerner who had contrived to make millions from the Civil War. Facing an existence cushioned by profiteering wealth, husband and wife discovered a mutual desire to crash Society in a big way. As their children grew up, the parents were gratified to find them alight with the same fire.

Even so, the process took time; despite the senior Wilson's distinguished appearance and business acumen, twelve long years passed without mentionable success. By then the children had reached marrying age and Wilson *père* concentrated on them. He sent his daughters to Paris to be superbly gowned by Worth, then took expensive quarters in a social summer and winter resorts where the girls and gowns would be seen and talked about. His calculated maneuvers began paying off when May Wilson met and married Ogden Goelet.

"The strength of the Wilsons lay in the fact that they always stuck together," says one admiring account. In 1884, young Orme Wilson attracted the winsome interest of Carrie Astor, that favorite daughter of the one-and-only Mrs. Astor. The leader of the Four Hundred branded this puppy love, but reputedly found herself won over by the adoring looks the youngsters exchanged. During this interlude May Wilson Goelet joined her parents in working tirelessly to advance the match. In due time, a wedding took place.

Belle Wilson next captured the Hon. Michael Herbert, who became Sir Michael and eventually British Ambassador to the United States. But the greatest Wilson coup was scored by beautiful Grace, youngest of the brood, who married Cornelius Vanderbilt III despite the ferocious opposition of his family. Cornelius' father cut off his oldest son's primogeniture inheritance of $40 million, leaving him with a mere $5 million with which to muddle through life. The reason for the Vanderbilt objection to Grace remains the foremost untold story of Gotham Society, reputedly so sensational that no one has dared reveal it. As for the marrying Wilsons, their powerful ambition carried unto the third generation, when grandchild May Goelet shopped diligently among English titles before becoming the Duchess of Roxburghe.

With the example of the Wilsons before them, other families kept marching, sometimes to the drumbeat of success. Ralph Pulitzer has recorded the emotions as a Suddenly Rich family received the invitation that put a toe in the door of Society—

> Fingers tremble as they tear open the envelope and, having
> found their hopes realized, (they) gloat over the little piece of
> pasteboard as though it were a love-letter. . . . After their years of
> Sisyphus-labor, pushing their precious stones up the heights of
> social prominence, they have reached their successful end at last
> and feel that here is their letter-patent of nobility. Thus can this
> little card unloose that mighty passion . . . called snobbishness.

Working in favor of the Suddenly Rich was a certain whimsi-
cality on the part of aristocrats, who without apparent reason
sometimes picked out a family of climbers and hefted it up the
social ladder. Newport, reflecting New York Society in micro-
cosm, proved a good place to observe this. There a few of the
nouveaux riches built expensive cottages in the hope of attracting
Society's notice. In this, they went against the advice of Harry
Lehr, who said, "Avoid Newport like the plague unless sure you
will be accepted there." Yet Newport Society occasionally bestowed its whimsical smile.

How else to explain the acceptance allowed E. J. Berwind, the
coal baron, whose efforts to crash Newport seemed no different
from others in his exalted income bracket? On a first trip abroad
after striking it rich, Berwind and his wife were vastly impressed
by Buckingham Palace. Determined to assail the Four Hundred
by the backdoor of Newport, they bought property and erected a
cottage reminiscent of the British royal palace. It turned out to
be the only Newport cottage with three massive doors that could
open simultaneously to admit guests to dinners and dances.
Perhaps for this reason Society unexpectedly embraced the coal
baron and his spouse.

The case of the William B. Leeds is easier to fathom. One of
several tin-plate kings, Leeds was an unusually handsome man
and the husband of a beautiful young wife. One summer Mrs.
John Drexel leased her cottage, Fairholme, to the Leeds, an act
that did not sit well with Society. "It's not fair to the rest of us," a
dowager raged at Mrs. Drexel. "How can you possibly lease to
those vulgar, horrible people?" Mrs. Drexel kept calm under
fire. "We're going to have the house redecorated anyway," she

responded. "We may as well have it done when they're in it."

This tempest in a summer resort caught the roving attention of Mrs. Oliver H. P. Belmont, the one-time Alva Vanderbilt and the first personage of social magnitude to insist on a divorce. Having only recently become Mrs. Belmont, Alva needed to prove that she retained her social clout. Noting the superior attractiveness of the Leeds, she whimsically decided to give a dinner dance in their honor. Society gasped, then offered prayers for courage to stay at home. But to refuse an invitation from Alva was unthinkable. The dinner took place and the handsome Leeds achieved social eminence overnight.

On Fifth Avenue, inspiration and luck counted. Mrs. Pembroke Jones, wife of a southern cereal king, also seethed with a yen for social heights. Consulting Society's court-jester, Harry Lehr, she implored him to instruct her in making an impression on the upper crust. Lehr studied her and saw a woman who obviously loved food. "Feed Society well and it will eat out of your hand," he answered merrily.

Mrs. Pembroke Jones took him at his word and began giving Southern-style dinners, a type of cuisine intriguing to the elite. If nothing else, she introduced the Mint Julep to New York and Newport. In the dead of winter she transported rice, birds, and Indian corn from her North Carolina estate. With them arrived a Negro cook who specialized in cornbread, corn fritters, yams, Southern fried chicken, and sugar-cured ham. Word of her finger-licking meals got around and Mrs. Pembroke Jones won social acceptance, though her husband was the boisterous type Society usually shunned.

Presumably Harry Lehr beamed with pride at the triumph of Mrs. Pembroke Jones. But it did not prevent him from playing his favorite trick at her dinner parties. While others masticated their rich food, Lehr delighted in ordering his footman to bring him a hard-boiled egg and glass of milk. "I always love to do it at a party of this sort," he giggled. "Champagne may flow like water, but you will see the whole staff won't be able to produce one glass of milk."

Prodded by Social Guides, the *nouveaux riches* gave increasingly elaborate dinners. "You don't give parties to enjoy yourself, but to advance yourself," one declared. Dining rooms and ballrooms were wholly redecorated for galas, turned into simulated rose gardens with caged nightingales twittering in bowers of roses, drugged swans sitting in pools, and hot-house grapes laced to arbors. Fortunes in flowers festooned the walls, while chandeliers blossomed with twined roses, lilies of the valley, and jasmine. *Espergnes* of flowers and fruit dotted long dining tables.

Hostesses vied with one another over the expensive favors slipped under the napkins of dinner guests. After sending out 100 invitations, a Suddenly Rich hostess felt pleased when twenty people showed up. If her favors, decoration, and food turned out exciting enough, more might attend next time. One hostess put a black pearl in every oyster served to her guests, at a cost of $30,000. Another gave the gentlemen cigarettes made of tobacco wrapped in $100 bills. Others handed out gold matchboxes and cigar cutters to the men, jeweled pins, charms, and rings to the ladies. It was customary to buy such bijoux at Tiffany's, where they could easily be exchanged.

Another hostess invited fifty people to a dinner party, but only twenty appeared. Under the napkins, the fortunate few discovered staggeringly expensive gifts—gold cigarette cases, plus gold mesh purses actually studded with diamonds and other costly baubles. Astounded by such extravagance, they nonetheless pocketed the gifts with pleasure.

Next morning Social Register circles buzzed over the atrocious taste of a hostess who gave such dazzling presents. One soft-hearted lady of Society undertook to contact the woman in question, hinting that her display of crass wealth added up to social error. Suitably chastened, the hostess planned a second dinner. This time she sent out sixty invitations and received seventy acceptances.

On the night of the dinner, guests sat down and probed feverishly under napkins to find only tasteful, moderately priced favors. A sigh of disappointment swept the table. Following a doleful meal, the hostess concluded her second solecism had been worse than the first.

Meantime, Society enjoyed many jokes at the expense of rough-edged newcomers. The greatest was always the self-made extrovert who heartily shook hands with the butler on leaving his first (and last) social function.

"Do you want a *porte cochère?*" an architect inquired of a Croesus who had commissioned a mansion. "You bet I do," the man answered. "Put in at least five on each floor and make sure they don't make too damn much noise when they flush." "Do you like *petit pois?*" a *nouveau riche* lady asked a group of visitors, and led them to her *petit point*.

A few climbing ladies became lah-de-da under the tutelege of Social Guides. One informed friends that her household included a Groom of the Chambers. "But what does he do?" demanded a lady who didn't have one. Said the first, "He arranges the note paper in the guest rooms and makes sure the flowers are changed daily."

Another lady who had stood by her husband's side during the tough battle to the top professed to be unfamiliar with trolley cars. "But what does one do after one gets aboard?" she wondered. Amazingly, a blue-blood did know and sought to puncture pretense by saying, "You put a $5 bill in the box by the conductor." Before she could check herself the first lady burst out, "Oh, no, it's only a nickel."

Mrs. Stuyvesant Fish, known to intimates as Mame, was a female of impeccable social background who prided herself on speaking her mind. Once at home Mame had a coughing fit and her husband asked, "Can I get you anything, dear?" "Yes," she said, "you can get me that diamond and pearl necklace I saw today at Tiffany's."

Mame Fish's restless intelligence made her enjoy meeting people, even if they were climbers. Stories of her encounters with the Suddenly Rich became legion.

Mrs. Fish inhabited a thirty-five-room Stanford White doge's palace at 25 East Seventy-eighth Street, which for a brief time was the finest in the city. As others outdistanced her, Mame found herself the object of condescension by the New Rich. One dared inquire about the size of the Fish mansion. "I can't tell you how big it is because it swells at night," Mame answered. Another ill-mannered lady sought to compliment her by saying, "Yours is the largest small house *I've* ever seen." Answered Mame, "And yours is the smallest large house *I've* ever seen." Showing off her mansion, another said to Mrs. Fish, "This is my Louis Quatorze Room." "That's what you think," barked Mame.

Time continued to favor the Suddenly Rich. Mrs. Astor was growing older, inviting too many rather than too few to her prestigious annual balls. Ward McAllister had died; Harry Lehr contemplated life in Paris. The public now thought of the money-grasping multimillionaires as barons rather than buccaneers.

Led by the indomitable Mrs. Fish, Society had begun cutting its formal dinners from three hours to fifty minutes, with wine served with the courses instead of between. When her stream-lined dinners were over, Mrs. Fish brought in opera stars, musical comedy choruses, ballet dancers, and darktown strutters to entertain; prior to that time, Society had amused itself.

"The Four Hundred would have fled in a body from a poet, painter, a musician, or a clever Frenchman," wrote Mrs. Winthrop Chanler. Now the Suddenly Rich manifested interest in bizarre types like explorers, sculptors, and authors of books.

The humor magazine *Life* quipped that the Four Hundred had become the Fifteen Hundred because the Robber Barons had got control and watered the stock. Aided by the Suddenly Rich, the Four Hundred had transmogrified into High Society. It might be a Society but, like the circus, it looked bigger and better than ever.

10

"I Know Charley Yerkes Loves Me"

THE matter of the sex lives of the plutocrats is probably of more interest to us today than to their contemporaries. For in the late Victorian era, it was not considered "nice" to ponder such topics.

Nor did much background for sexual speculation exist. Sad to say, the trial of the Pittsburgh coke scion Harry K. Thaw for the murder of Stanford White first really set on the American record the fact that prominent men lusted after young girls. And that girls who aspired to the gay life of the Great White Way might find themselves in the hands of men—like Thaw—who followed the pleasure precepts of the Marquis de Sade.

From the White House, President Theodore Roosevelt branded testimony at the Thaw trial "filth," and expressed the opinion that newspapers should refrain from publishing it. But the papers went ahead and the sexual higher-education of America had commenced.

We do know these Robber Barons to have been males of the species, harboring varying sex urges. They were also a group possessed of an exceptionally strong competitive drive, amounting in most cases to the predatory. So it is reasonable to assume that a drive to trample fellow humans extended to the frequent conquest of the female. Inevitably the women who succumbed came from a wide variety of backgrounds, for each plutocrat had different roots and patterns. The women involved might be friends of wives, daughters of friends, friends of daughters, girls of stage or street, or occupants of the many plush brothels on New York side streets catering to the fathers, sons, and uncles of the ultra-rich. A superior place for contacting willing flesh existed in the corridor known as Peacock Alley in the Waldorf-Astoria. There lovely, well-dressed girls invitingly dropped their lace handkerchiefs at the appearance of prosperous looking males.

It is impossible to imagine John D. Rockefeller or Andrew Carnegie being unfaithful to a lawful wedded spouse. On the other hand, J. P. Morgan flaunted his mistresses. The most celebrated of them was Maxine Elliott, a statuesque actress for whom he built a theater. Maxine was an international beauty, but with his other mistresses this Croesus was not so selective. Someone said he collected "old manuscripts and older mistresses."

In the days after his divorce, William Kissam Vanderbilt could be seen paying courtly attention to various French music hall stars. Not for a Vanderbilt were girls who dropped handkerchief along Peacock Alley; even the women the males of this effulgent family slept with had to be winners. Frederick Gebhard, a dashing fellow of Society and friend of Stanford White, gained fame as the lover of Lily Langtry, who came to him with references from King Edward VII. When affection between these two cooled, he married a young member of the Florodora Sextette.

By tradition, males of Society were supposed to sow wild oats before marriage, then live ever afterward in uxorious bliss. Social matches were frequently arranged by ambitious parents, usually the bride's. This led to the sad love affairs of Society wherein husbands and wives found others of the Four Hundred to be more compatible than their mates.

As some aristocrats and plutocrats grew into self-satisfied old age they often came to imagine themselves irresistible to the opposite sex. Women who sat beside these amorous types at dinner parties called them members of the Paw-Knee or Feel-a-Thigh Clubs.

The scandal sheet *Town Topics* claimed to find instances of adultery, incest, transvestism, lesbianism, homosexuality, cuckoldry, masochism, sadism, and satyriasis in the hallowed ranks of the Four Hundred. A few scandals of High Society were indeed red-hot, proving that fact easily surpasses fiction. One dealt with a young man who fell in love with the beautiful daughter of a climbing family. Unfortunately, the girl was having an affair with his father, a fact known to both the youth and his mother. With her future in mind, the young lady opted for the son and married him, at which the enraged father disinherited both.

Embellishing the social record is the chilling story of a dowager of impeccable position who wished above everything to see her worthless son married. Accordingly, she chose a young girl of excellent family and invited her to the country estate for a weekend. There the dowager dismissed servants and tacitly collaborated while her drunken offspring raped the girl guest. By the rigid mores of the time, the girl then had to marry her deflowerer.

Beginning in 1899, there actually existed as an adornment of Fifth Avenue a millionaire whose life—for those who took the trouble to look—was an open book the lurid pages of which included a stretch behind bars and the sex life of a dedicated satyr. This unabashed fellow was Charles Tyson Yerkes—pronounced Yerk-*eez*—who might be called Chicago's gift to New York. For Yerkes had won fame in the nation as the Traction King of the Windy City, gaining tight control of surface transportation—trolleys, elevated railroads—as had Whitney and Ryan in New York. It is hard to say which of these three transit monopolists was the more brilliant and ruthless. Yerkes in Chicago seemed to have devised every possible scheme for mulcting the public, while Whitney and Ryan came along to perfect his inspirations.

Yet it was always difficult to imagine those two polished New Yorkers in connection with anything as lowly as public transportation; the mind cannot encompass the thought of Whitney or Ryan in a trolley car. Yerkes, on the other hand, was an earthy, pungent type who marked his rise in the world of finance by coining suitable maxims. One of the first was "Buy up old junk, fix it up a little, then unload it with a profit on the other guys." Another of his cherished mottos was "Buy, buy, buy!"

Yet his definition of *buy* did not fit the dictionary. Rather, he meant "Bribe, bribe, bribe!" For Yerkes was a man who believed every human being had his price, and little in his lifetime of frenzied activity refuted him. Yerkes did not believe in bribing underlings but, like Whitney and Ryan, went straight to the top, offering handsome, under-the-table sums to mayors and aldermen—since Chicago, no less than New York, had its boodle aldermen. He also bribed the officers of rival companies and anyone else who obstructed his road to riches.

Yerkes soaring dream was to accumulate $100 million and for twenty years his efforts in Chicago were aimed at that goal. "It's the straphanger who pays," was another of his favorite sayings and to riders he gave minimal service for maximum profit. His surface railways ran slow, broke down, lacked heat, screamed for repair, and kept no visible schedules. Yet Yerkes was allowed to gobble up one territory franchise after another, with no protective strings attached. He was lord of the city's transportation system, so well entrenched that he could laugh aloud when citizens' groups appeared in his office to demand improved service. When they handed him petitions signed by an outraged citizenry, he grandiloquently ripped the papers in half.

A description of Yerkes in his prime says, "He was handsome, physically strong, and stridently masculine, with hypnotic shallow-set eyes that were deceptively frank and a face that was an intriguing mask of sensuality." Another observer speaks of his dead-white skin, bristling mustache, and imperturbable, almost mesmerizing, manner. In photographs, he looks straight at the camera as if sincerely interested in it.

Yerkes was born in 1837 to a well-off Philadelphia Quaker family. As a youngster he showed extreme precocity in arithmetic and mathematics. Eschewing the games fellows play, he began

at age eight to work after school. At seventeen he quit his studies
altogether, to devote full time to making money.

Over the next ten years he impressed Philadelphia as a potential financier-promoter on a genius level. By age twenty-five, he
had his own brokerage house and four years later expanded it to
include banking operations. Yerkes early recognized the importance of friends in high places. He cultivated the companionship
of the City Treasurer of Philadelphia and the two began gam-
bling on the stock market with municipal funds. Even then,
Yerkes felt a kinship with the raw city of Chicago and he and his
friend invested heavily in enterprises there. When Mrs.
O'Leary's cow kicked over the lantern that set the town afire, the
investments went up in the flames. The two were exposed as
embezzlers and sent to jail for three years. Yerkes got out in
seven months, largely through the tireless efforts of a doting
wife.

Yerkes cogitated hard in jail, setting his mind to locate a field
of endeavor where the service would be indispensable to the
public and the opportunities for bribery great. He had noted the
success of the former butcher Peter A. B. Widener in public
transportation, then largely a matter of horse-drawn trolleys.
Widener was not yet Philadelphia's grand traction monopolist,
and Yerkes elected to get control of a trolley company of his
own. He did so on release from jail, and by judicious bribery
extended its franchise. Then he improved service slightly, and
watered the value of its stock from $15 to $100 a share. Next he
sold the company for $1 million, thus for the first time living up
to his maxim, "Buy up old junk, fix it up a little, and unload it on
the other guys."

Still, he found the Widener traction interests so well entrenched that a move to attractive Chicago seemed advisable.
Yerkes was a noisy blusterer, but so was the Chicago of the late
1870s. Arriving there, he noted with pleasure that the city's trolley lines were in dilapidated shape. The mind of a true
financier-speculator-promoter contains a precious sixth-sense,
alerting him to coming events. Yerkes sensed that the next few
years would see a revolution in transit that would multiply
profits a thousandfold. He was proven right by the advent of
electricity, which enabled trolleys to run by overhead cable. In-

deed, the success of nearly every plutocrat of the era was due in some way to one new invention or another.

Not the least of Yerkes' distinctions was that Theodore Dreiser wrote three novels about him—*The Financier, The Titan,* and *The Stoic.* In this trilogy Yerkes is named Frank Algernon Cowperwood and at one point the novelist tries to capture Yerkes-Cowperwood's emotions about street cars—

> One might have said of him quite truly that the tinkle of car bells and the plop of plodding horses' feet was in his blood. He surveyed these extending lines, with their jingling cars, as he went about the city, with an almost hungry eye. Chicago was growing fast, and these little horse cars in certain streets were crowded night and morning—fairly bulging with people at the rush hours. If he could only secure an octopus grip on one or all of them; if he could combine and control them all! What a fortune! That, if nothing else, might salve some of his woes—a tremendous fortune—nothing less. He forever busied himself with various aspects of the scene quite as a poet might have concerned himself with rocks and rills. To own these street railways! To own these street railways! So ran the song of his mind.

Yerkes used his Philadelphia million to buy Chicago trolley lines and slowly his transit empire came to cover the city like a spider-web. On the credit side, the Traction King replaced horse lines with cable cars, widened service, built elevated railroads, and initiated the ingenious downtown Loop. But he was always the plunderer laboring less for the public good than for his own aggrandizement. The service rendered by his trolleys and elevated lines remained slow and uncomfortable, with profits lining his pockets rather than utilized for repairs and improvements.

Chicagoans came to consider Charley Yerkes a burden that had to be borne. Self-made tycoons in other fields tried to topple him from his eminence, but he thwarted them by concocting schemes wonderful in their slippery boldness. Downtrodden Chicagoans were forced to feel a sneaking admiration for this wily, arrogant fellow, who cared nothing for city or people.

Yerkes' primary support came from the politicians who granted him street franchises free of obligation to the public.

More than ever he became a past master in the seamy art of civic bribery and legislative manipulation. Even the mayor stood in awe of him. He kept on hand a perpetual fund of $1 million from which he offered bribes so big few could resist.

His main conspirators were always Chicago's boodle aldermen of whom the muckraker Burton J. Hendrick wrote, "They attained a depravity which made them notorious all over the world—they openly sold Yerkes the use of the city streets for cash."

Yerkes did not stop there. Cleverly, he turned his operations into a tangle only he could understand. He owned engineering companies, repair companies, holding companies. He watered stocks, heaped bond atop bond, reorganization on reorganization. Selling his properties from one Yerkes company to another, he pocketed the profits involved. He created interlocking firms, dummy corporations, dummy directors. No one but Yerkes comprehended this maze and he gloried in manipulating it, sneering at press and public alike.

Propelling him forward was that burning determination to make the sum of $100 million and, to his manic mind, the process was taking far too long. Needed was a gargantuan coup, and he dreamed up the idea of obtaining 100-year franchises for his surface lines. Or, if not 100, at least 50. With these long-term leases in hand he could command untold millions.

As word of Yerkes' plans leaked out, press and public gave them the name Eternal Monopolies. Only Yerkes favored them, and he stood impregnable in his power. The Traction King began to wave larger bribes than ever under the noses of his boodle aldermen and put aside the sum of $500,000 to be offered to Mayor Altgeld.

Such were the contours of the financial career of Charles Tyson Yerkes, Traction King of Chicago. Citizens of a city perpetually fascinated by him also knew of other aspects of his colorful life. One was his love of art and the other his love (if this word can be applied) of women.

Back in the year 1876, Yerkes had been one more rough fellow whose life had been amazingly enriched by the Philadelphia Centennial Exposition. Like Henry O. Havemeyer, Yerkes first viewed the art of foreign lands at the Centennial and never again was he the same person. Wrote a biographer, "He discovered the enchantments of bygone times and foreign cultures."

While prospering in Philadelphia, he sought to express himself by building a $60,000 Gothic mansion and filling it with chromos of famous paintings, Victorian bric-a-brac, and heavy maple furniture. His conservatory, with potted palms, rubber plants, and singing birds in cages, won the admiration of friends.

Yerkes' ideas of art and beauty changed drastically during a first trip to Europe, early in his career as a Chicago man of millions. At first he was a humble purchaser of art and statuary, lending an ear to dealers who touted Meissonier, Gérôme, Detaille, and Alma-Tadema. One of his proud purchases, painted to his order by Adolphe William Bouguereau, bore the title *Invading Cupid's Realm*; a critic said it belonged in a brothel.

Then his own sound instincts took over and he began buying artists like Rembrandt, Breughel, Steen, and Hals. He paid $35,000 for the Franz Hals *Portrait of a Woman*, now in the Frick Collection, $40,000 for Troyon's *Going to Market,* and $32,500 for Falconet's *Bacchante*. Like other acquisitions, these were carefully crated and sent back to the handsome Yerkes residence at 3201 Michigan Avenue.

Yerkes also developed a passion for—of all things—rugs. He was the second American collector in history to become fascinated by them and the first with the wherewithal to purchase the finest available to the western world. Yerkes brought home a forty-foot Persian state carpet which, it was said, gave off a glow of royal magnificence. He obtained three carpets from a historic mosque and shelled out over $1 million for thirty rugs considered the rarest on the market. Some of those he bought weighed half a ton.

Yerkes possessed astoundingly good taste in art matters and eventually became one of the first great American collectors to venture into French Impressionism. Yet it is possible to believe that a good part of his pleasure in acquiring paintings and statuary lay in the fact that they could so readily be *bought*.

This man's total belief in the buying power of money also extended, as Chicago knew, to a raunchy sex life. Charles Tyson Yerkes can easily be labeled a satyr, or sufferer from satyriasis. This may account for Theodore Dreiser's great interest in him, since the novelist nursed the same compulsive drive to possess women.

Yerkes not only maintained a shifting seraglio of mistresses in Chicago but managed to have willing females awaiting him in the other cities he visited on business. In Chicago and New York, the satyr was especially known for his nonaltruistic interest in girls who aspired to acting, singing, or painting careers. In the area of business, he awarded himself *droit du seigneur* privileges over the wives and daughters of employes and other males beholden to him. Sometimes, he went so far as to support entire families in order to get his paws on the daughter of the house. Yerkes liked his girls young, dewy-eyed, and compliant. When introducing them to fellow financiers, he called them "wards" or "nieces."

At the same time he insisted on having a Mrs. Yerkes. The wife he married in Philadelphia bore him six children and worked with energy to get him sprung from prison. Her reward was a divorce that left Yerkes free to wed a beautiful youngster named Mary Adelaide Moore. After renaming her Mara, he took her to Chicago for the important years of his life.

Yerkes' pursuit of youthful sex partners developed into a major Chicago scandal, but he never divorced his Mara. Eventually she learned of his multifarious infidelities and added to their notoriety by confronting him and his inamoratas in public. Her hysterical scenes on such occasions had no effect, for Yerkes never changed his wicked ways. Asked if he preferred blonds, brunettes, or redheads, the lecherous fellow rubbed hands gleefully together and chortled, "God bless 'em all!" It is small wonder that Mara Yerkes began to reach for the gin bottle. In her cups, she assured people, "I know Charley Yerkes loves me."

Every summer Yerkes and Mara went abroad for a grand tour. In each city visited, Yerkes managed to have a mistress or two stashed away. He also bought art in large and ever-improving quantities. Once, to please his wife, the Splendor Seeker bought no less than 300 landscapes by a mediocrity named Jan van Beers, who had the foresight to paint a highly flattering portrait of Mara, a woman growing plump but still good-looking. Simultaneously Yerkes acquired Rodin's sculptures *Cupid and Psyche* and *Orpheus and Eurydice,* both today in the Metropolitan Museum of Art.

The city of Chicago had ambivalent feelings about Yerkes, the demon collector. Was he demonstrating a commendable interest in art, or wasting the money gouged from a long-suffering citizenry? Yerkes never gave a damn about his image, but Mara did and she began urging him to make some gesture to win public approval. He put out feelers and discovered that the astronomy department of the University of Chicago needed a telescope. "Get them the best money can buy," he ordered offhandedly. It was Yerkes first and last effort to woo the public.

Now, in the midst of his efforts to win the Eternal Monopolies, word leaked out that the Traction King of Chicago had commissioned a mansion on the sidewalks of New York. The revelation could not have come at a worse time, for it caused Chicago's love-hate feelings toward the Yerkes to become sheer hate. It had seemed that his adopted city would take almost anything from the man, but at last he had gone too far. Said a newspaper editorial, "Chicago has no use for a man who treats the city as a milch cow, and who takes the butter and cream to New York to be consumed there; who grabs franchises in Chicago and puts their excessive profits to erecting a palace in New York."

Folk who had feared to critize the Eternal Monopolies began rising to protest vocally. "Revolutions are caused by just such rapacity," a Chicago paper declared. Civic groups organized indignation meetings where the disenchanted reviled Yerkes with cries of "Lynch him!" and "Throw the rascal out." The impassive fellow merely increased his bribes to aldermen and waved his $500,000 before the eyes of Mayor Altgeld.

The Mayor spurned the money, and Yerkes retained enough power to have him defeated in the next election. But it was the Traction King's last victory in the Windy City, for under the glare of publicity the Eternal Monopolies became such a shameless grab that even the boodle aldermen feared to vote them in.

All at once Yerkes' exciting Chicago career had fizzled; he could no longer function in his adopted city. Reluctantly, he disposed of his manifold transit holdings to another Syndicate headed by the outlanders Whitney, Ryan, and Widener for $20 million, three-quarters of the sum in cash and negotiable securities. Then he turned his thoughts eastward.

The mighty Transit King of Chicago had fallen!

Yerkes' downward plunge had consumed several years from start to finish, and during that period his Fifth Avenue mansion at the corner of Sixty-eighth Street had been erected. The *New York Times* called it "The palace on Fifth Avenue that awaits the coming of the master." As such, it enjoyed a hidden distinction. As imposing as any mansion along the Avenue, with an overall cost of $5 million, it had as owner a man who failed to qualify for membership in the ultra-exclusive $50 Million Club. Even with the $20 million payment for his Chicago utilities, together with his own personal millions, Charley Yerkes still had a fortune far below the sum supposedly necessary to keep up with the Vanderbilts and dwell in peace along Millionaires' Row.

The continuing incompatability of Yerkes and his Mara was apparent in the manner of their approach to Fifth Avenue. Mara, ever credulous and forgiving, had allowed herself to nurse the dream that life in a mansion would change her errant husband into a faithful stay-at-home. She also aspired to success among the Four Hundred, or its contemporary counterpart. In brief, Mara Yerkes could hardly wait to get to New York and arrived there alone before the mansion was finished.

Had anyone bothered to warn Mara of the necessity of hiring a Social Guide to chart her path into Society? If so, the plump, attractive, forty-year-old paid no heed. Rather, she determined to rely solely on her own charms, good nature, and multimillions. In line with this independence, she took an elaborately decorated suite in the Waldorf-Astoria Hotel on Thirty-fourth Street. There she found herself inhabiting a social half-world with uncertain boundaries.

The most celebrated resident of the Waldorf was John W.

"Bet-a-Million" Gates, who had made his money as a barbed-wire monopolist. Gates would bet on anything and earned his nickname for a million-dollar wager that one rain drop would reach the bottom of a window pane ahead of another. Before his nightly poker game, Bet-a-Million would dine in one of the hotel dining rooms with his wife, who wore her justly celebrated diamond choker. Gates was known to eat peas with his knife, jam everything on his plate into his mouth at once, masticate greedily, then belch in supreme contentment. At the end of the meal, he would yank out a gold toothpick, plying it with skill and pleasure. In time, Bet-a-Million Gates achieved fame as the first to bring American bad manners to Europe.

In such surroundings, Mara Yerkes easily let her fondness for drink and conviviality push her toward a Broadway theatrical and sporting crowd rather than Fifth Avenue Society. The millionairess from Chicago surrounded herself with an entourage of hangers-on, who flattered her and drank her drinks. Mara gave elaborate dinner parties with champagne only, and ordered that all corks must pop at the table. Amidst so much giddy fun, she did not bother to note the difference between Fifth Avenue and Broadway.

As for Yerkes, nothing in his Chicago years became this man so much as his departure from the metropolis he plundered. It resembled a scene in an epic novel, but strangely enough Theodore Dreiser, who researched his fiction like fact, made nothing of it.

The ex-traction magnate hired a complete railway train and ordered the Pullman and other seats removed, leaving a flat surface in each car. On these floors, he tenderly laid his paintings, face up. Other art treasures, statuary, and rugs occupied the freight cars attached. The departing Splendor Seeker was the sole passenger as this long train rattled east. In Manhattan, a caravan of vans waited to haul the art treasures to the Yerkes abode.

Already Yerkes had brightened life in the metropolis by providing an anecdote for its citizens. This had roots in the fact that the rich men of the time, seemingly so invincible, lived in quaking terror of a popular uprising that might strip them of lordly wealth. They especially feared anarchists of Russian extraction who might attempt to assassinate them. The fact that in 1892 an anarchist did shoot Henry Clay Frick of Pittsburgh gave credence to these fears.

Yerkes was not above such terrors, particularly because of his unpopularity in Chicago. He was also exceedingly proud of the handsome bronze doors of his Fifth Avenue mansion, which had been stripped from a Venetian palace. These two emotions met head on when a friend warned him that the conspicuous doors might incite the public to revolution. Yerkes was shaken. Soon the friend noted the doors looked dull and lackluster. "What did you coat them with?" he asked Yerkes. "Platinum," the Chicago Croesus answered.

The Yerkes mansion, designed by architect Robert Henderson, turned out to be an Italianate palazzo, sprawling rather than high and mighty. Over the years it sprawled further, as Yerkes bought adjacent brownstones to the rear and tore them down for additional art galleries and pleasure domes.

Here was another domicile that cheated the public, for the Yerkes residence, like that of Collis P. Huntington, offered an exterior of gloomy stone, giving small hint of a lightsome interior. Yet those who penetrated the palazzo, passing through its platinum-coated bronze doors, found one of the most picturesque interiors ever to decorate Millionaires' Row.

"Seemingly endless were the changing moods confronting the wanderer in this labyrinthine château," writes Wesley Towner, in his book *The Elegant Auctioneers*. He goes on to list countless rooms, halls, vestibules, art galleries, and salons, each exquisite in its fashion. Among them were a Louis XV Room, an East Indian Room, a Japanese Room, and an Empire Room transported *in toto* from France. Another room was lined with wood from Robin Hood's Sherwood Forest. Still another was a museum featuring such curiosities as Oliver Cromwell's sword.

The Yerkes mansion had halls of mirrors, halls of marble, halls of story-telling panels, halls of honor. Also great vaulted ceilings, huge Norman fireplaces, and columns of green marble topped by armored figures supporting crowned friezes. For $80,000 Yerkes had acquired the bed of a former King of the

Belgians. Another bed, once the property of Mad King Ludwig of Bavaria, cost less but looked grander. Not counting the green velvet steps leading to its dais, that bed stood twelve feet high. At its head, large male torsos of bronze finished to look like gold stood guard over a sleeping Goddess of Light in enamel. At the foot, violet ebony cupids held green draperies surrounding a nymph couchant personifying Morning. The whole was topped by a dome of ebony and ormolu, plus green silk damask with gold lace trimming.

The place was full of marvels. A mighty conservatory, or Winter Garden, sprawled L-shaped through the center of the edifice, forming a vast inner courtyard covered by opaque skylights and surrounded by a balcony supported by thirty-two white marble columns. The walls were of bark, the floors of black and white marble. Plants were profuse, with cockatoos and toucans flying happily among them. Fountains in the Winter Garden were simulated springs trickling water from varying heights over moss-covered rocks to form rivulets and woodland pools. Immense plate-glass windows separated the Winter Garden from a Great Hall of Siena marble. In the unlikely event that the Yerkeses gave a ball for Manhattan's *bon ton,* the windows could be lowered to the basement, creating a vast expanse of ballroom.

Off the imposing balcony lay a second conservatory called either the Italian Palm Room or the Vatican Garden. Its glass floor formed the skylight of one of the picture galleries below. Exotic fruits grew on wires and trellises, and doves cooed among busts of Roman emperors. Hundreds of singing birds flitted over the branches of palm trees and splashed in marble fountains.

One observer saw the Yerkes mansion as a congeries of splendors. It contained no less than three different art galleries for the masterpieces, near-masterpieces, and non-masterpieces the Traction King had assembled over the years. The largest gallery, with its own entrance on Fifth Avenue, boasted a marble staircase costing $250,000, lifted from a doge's palace. Here too were sculptured figures by Rodin and Houdon, as well as the finest Oriental rugs.

People allowed to wander through the art galleries came across ladies of the English aristocracy painted by Reynolds, Gainsborough, and Blakeslee; Dutch burghers by Rembrandt and Hals; nudes by Rubens and Bouguereau; Alma-Tadema Roman ladies, Watteau garden parties, and the finest Gobelin tapestries. Connoisseurs said his finest paintings were Corot's *The Fisherman*, Troyon's *Going to Market*, Diaz' *Gathering Fagots*, Rousseau's *Paysage du Berry*, and Millet's *The Pig Killers*.

Art lovers who feasted eyes on the wonders of 864 Fifth Avenue usually staggered from the confines in an ecstatic daze. The young artist Walter Tittle rushed home to write in his diary—

> It is the most splendid place I have ever seen. Millions have been spent adorning it. Some of the furnishings were formerly in the Louvre. One rug in the hall cost $150,000. The stairway is worth a quarter of a million. The library paneling was brought from Holland; the dining room is a copy of that in Warwick Castle. I saw the great picture galleries, their collections being among the finest in America. Their Dutch and Italian masters are immense. Four Rembrandts, a Raphael, a Botticelli, four superb Hals, a fine Rubens, an excellent Van Dyck, two Ruysdaels, two Potters, and innumerable other Old Masters. For modern masters some Corots and Millets, together with specimens of Diaz, Porot (enchanting), Tousseau, Daubigny, De Beers, Benj Constant, Boldini, Troyon, and lots of others.

Having created this magnificent urban palace, Yerkes proceeded to spend little time in it. Indeed, the splendid mansion practically became the exclusive province of Mara Yerkes. More than ever the belle of a high-stepping Broadway crowd, she turned the mansion into an after-the-theater supper club, where her fine feathered friends guzzled liquor and cavorted among priceless possessions.

The reasons for Yerkes' long absences from his personal Taj Mahal were, as usual, business and sex. This man of self-made millions not only found inactivity impossible to bear, but still dreamed of raking in $100 million before his death. The traction picture in New York was hopeless for him, since Ryan and Whitney gripped the city as tight as he had once controlled Chicago.

On a trip abroad, Yerkes had noted the sorry state of the London underground, where soft-coal-burning locomotives slowly pulled cars through foul-smelling tunnels. Though an expert in surface traction, Yerkes began to dream in terms of subways. He proposed the building of tubes, or miles of tunnel, below the surface. Aired by new-style vents and accessible by elevator, the rails in the tubes would be electrified to carry modern trains. After much jockeying, his plan was approved by Parliament and the former Traction King of Chicago set about becoming the Subway King of London. If nothing else, this mighty endeavor kept him away from Fifth Avenue.

The other reason for his continued absence from an opulent hearthside was a girl named Emilie Grigsby. Or should it be *Miss* Emilie Grigsby? For seldom has the young mistress of an old man appeared so far above reproach. Officially, Miss Emilie was Yerkes' "ward," but few who knew the old fellow's credentials as an amorist were fooled by the Victorian euphemism.

Yerkes' acquisition of Miss Emilie reads like a naughty Victorian novel. On a trip to Cincinnati, the plutocrat had been taken to a plush whorehouse operated by Emilie's mother. Theodore Dreiser, who reveled in such situations, characterized Mrs. Grigsby as "not good, but entertaining." Her effervescent personality delighted Yerkes during his night of joy on her premises. Returning for more, he got to know Mrs. Grigsby better and was eventually shown a picture of her daughter Emilie, then being educated in a convent.

What bargain was struck between these two—or three—the world will never know. But when innocent Emilie departed the convent at age eighteen, she slipped effortlessly under the protection of Charley Yerkes, a sexagenarian still hearty and handsome. At about the same time her brother, Braxton Grigsby, became Yerkes' private secretary.

Miss Emilie Grigsby glowed with china-doll loveliness and a description pictures her "in the full bloom of adolescence, bedewed with modesty and religious ecstacy." Another observer raved, "Her chief possession is marvelous red-gold hair, obviously natural and as luxuriant as her complexion is alabaster."

Dreiser, naturally, was fascinated by the lucent girl and in *The Titan* calls her—

a Circe, tall and delicately sinuous . . . a creature of an exotic mind and opalescent heart . . . a born actress, lissome, subtly wise, indifferent, superior, taking the world as she found it and expecting it to obey—to sit up like a pet dog and obey . . . You would not call her sensuous—though she was—because she was self-controlled. Her eyes lied to you. They lied to all the world. They looked you through and through with a calm *savoir faire*, a mocking defiance, which said with a faint curl of the lip . . . *You cannot read me, you cannot read me!*

Emilie Grigsby, so lovely, devout, and virginal in appearance, is hard to visualize as a rich man's toy. Yet she was one, though her status as a kept woman remains unique. In New York and London, she gave sedate dinner parties to which her proud benefactor brought financial and engineering associates. Yet for the most part Yerkes was content to remain in the shadows, allowing Miss Emilie to emerge as a personality in her own right. Her stance before an admiring world was that of a girl with unlimited funds and a craving for the better things in life, which she accumulated as fast as possible.

Claiming to be an heiress from Kentucky, she traveled in top style, mingling with Society folk at luxury hotels and in the first-class salons of ocean liners. In London, she was called The Kentucky Beauty and moved in the exalted set dominated by Edward VII. Men of title and wealth proposed marriage but Miss Emilie, apparently satisfied with her life, explained that eventually she planned to enter a nunnery and could not consider wedded bliss.

Miss Emilie had been Yerkes' ward for a year when she moved into a graystone gabled and turreted townhouse just completed at 660 Park Avenue, two blocks behind the Yerkes palazzo. This quickly became one of the most lavish back-street residences in history. Over all lay an ambiance of religious devotion, for Miss Emilie remained pious, no matter what her way of life. Doors to the establishment were cathedral-like and the library lighted by lamps of silvered bronze from the palace of Cardinal Serafine Vanatelli.

Still, a few non-religious items were visible among the profusion of *objets d'art* in the five-story residence. Miss Emilie's opulent Regency drawing room featured a gold harp; the dining room was decorated in a voluptuous crushed-grape color, set off by maroon draperies and purple carpeting. At one end of her purple-brocade bedroom stood the slightly naughty sculpture *Temptation of the Vestal by Cupid.* At the opposite end was a bust of the worldly-wise Madame Du Barry. Miss Emilie slumbered on a large bed once the property of an Indian rajah. In her closets hung so many gowns that it was necessary to keep inventory in notebooks.

With the art work that embellished her numerous rooms —nine servants took care of the place—Miss Emilie did something no other Splendor Seeker had thought of. She had her own face painted into frescoes and panels so that her loveliness gazed down on her, no matter where she went.

"Ecstacy is perhaps the best word for the grand salon," a writer has said of another of Miss Emilie's rooms. Gilded throne chairs stood at one end, while the golden pipes of a full-size organ brought stateliness to the other. This organ likewise introduced a note of mystery to the ménage. For behind it a secret door and staircase led through the bowels of the house to a tiny, whitewashed cubicle containing a narrow iron cot, a prie-dieux, and the figure of a saint. Beside the cot stood a full-length cheval glass.

What was the meaning of this barren cell? Did Miss Emilie atone for her sins by nights in these chaste and cheerless quarters? Or was it, as she once explained, a bedroom for the nuns from Ohio who sometimes came to visit? Or did she and the jaded Yerkes indulge in bizarre sexual practices there? The presence of the large mirror might indicate this.

These questions are only compounded by a concealed elevator running from this cubicle to the basement, opening into another secret apartment as richly furnished as the other was bare. "A vast room containing every appeal to the senses," it has been called. What transpired in this sumptuous room?

Yerkes was now in his mid-sixties, and it is amazing to report that his life included two other "wards" in addition to Miss Emilie. For the most part, these girls remained in London, living in fashionable hotels close to Yerkes' expensive townhouse. One of them was reported to be even younger and lovelier than Miss Emilie, while the third was reputedly younger and lovelier than both. To bring matters close to the incredible, this last girl was a blood-relative of the plutocrat. Ethel Link Yerkes by name, she was a grandniece, the granddaughter of his half-brother.

Yerkes was living all his life on the same improbable scale. Construction of the London subway was proceeding too slowly to be profitable and his millions were gradually shrinking. No one would guess this from his behavior, however. He lived as extravagantly as ever, in one way or another spending at least $2,000 a day on the upkeep of his Fifth Avenue mansion, Miss Emilie's opulent love nest on Park Avenue, and the hotel suites of his London loves.

In his London office hung J. M. W. Turner's painting *Rockets and Blue Lights*, for which he paid a record $75,000 in 1901. His purchases of other paintings were on so great a scale that he kept up a running feud with the United States Customs over the size of duties paid. To a reporter who interviewed him on an arrival in New York, Yerkes confided that he did not regret a single action of his life. The reporter wrote that he had "heaped millions on millions and always sighed for more."

Charley Yerkes got away with it in life, but at his death the edifice began to crumble.

In midsummer 1905, his Harley Street physician imparted the news that Yerkes had cancer of the kidneys and could live only a few more months. Returning to the United States, the stricken man did not go to his Fifth Avenue mansion, where a new art-gallery wing was under construction, nor to Miss Emilie's elegant quarters on Park Avenue, also his own possession. Rather, he took a suite at the Waldorf-Astoria and prepared to meet his Maker.

Relations between Yerkes and Mara had reached the breaking point and she made few, if any, visits to his sickbed. Miss Emilie, however, was devoted in her attentions and one memorable afternoon he pressed a check for $200,000 into her hot little hand along with 47,000 shares of gilt-edged London Underground stock. Still a damsel in her mid-twenties, Miss Emilie Grigsby would thus be able to live in accustomed luxury for the rest of her life.

Next, Ethel Link Yerkes arrived from London. Ship news reporters were bowled over by her sublime looks. "Blithely exuberant, like a girl fresh from college," one enthused. To the press, this girl burbled, "Oh, Uncle is just the finest, grandest-hearted man in the world!"

On his deathbed, Yerkes apparently faced up to the fact that his millions were gone. In his private safe reposed a grandiose will dictated and signed years before. This bequeathed the Yerkes mansion and art collection to the people of New York, and provided funds for the construction of a hospital to serve the sick and needy. His millions were to be Mara's until her death, at which time money and mansion reverted to the city; the hospital bearing his name was to be started at once. No mention was made of Miss Emilie or any of his other illicit silken-sheet partners. Ethel Link Yerkes received $100,000, but after all she was a relative and her mention in his will quite proper.

Late in December 1905, Yerkes summoned a lawyer to dictate another will, presumably more realistic. Then he lapsed into a coma. Next day doctors refused to rouse him from the coma in order to sign the will. So the old document remained in effect.

Half an hour before his death on December 29, Mara was summoned to the hospital, so newspapers could report his widow had been at his bedside. But on New Year's Eve, as Yerkes' body lay in a coffin in a candle-lit wing of the mansion, Mara kicked up her heels in a Broadway cabaret. Crowds lined the street as the Splendor Seeker's body was lifted into a hearse and transported to Greenwood Cemetery, where a bronze-doored mausoleum with sarcophagus awaited his remains.

Mara and the people of New York rejoiced as the signed will became public. But joy was short-lived, as lawyers and creditors intervened to declare Yerkes as poor as a multimillionaire could

get. A trickle of money allowed Mara to dwell in the mansion for
the next five years. As it grew shabbier, she kept on drinking,
entertaining, and muttering, "Charley Yerkes loved me." In
1910, her fortune finally gone, she moved to allow a public auction of the mansion and art treasures. The tearful woman took
up residence in the Hotel Plaza, carrying with her a few precious
paintings and sixty trunks of personal possessions.

The three-day Yerkes art auction turned out to be a fantastic
affair, with international dealers like Sir Joseph Duveen vying
with socialites like the Harry Payne Whitneys and Splendor
Seekers like Thomas Fortune Ryan and Henry Clay Frick for the
cream of the Yerkes collection. Sums paid for the better items
reached all-time highs. "No sale like this ever took place in
America," said one account. "Records fell like glasses from a
table, the dollars seeming to be rolling along the floor." Turner's
Rockets and Blue Lights fetched $129,000 and Franz Hals' *Portrait
of a Woman* went to Frick for $137,000; the Hals, of course, had
cost Yerkes $35,000 in 1893.

In all, the Traction King's paintings, statuary, tapestries, rugs,
and bibelots brought $2,207,866.10. However, the sale of the
mansion itself was not so fortuitous. This was the first residence
along Millionaires' Row to fall under the auctioneer's hammer.
The asking price for the massive mansion, annexes, arches, and
amazing architure was $1.4 million, but the knock-down price
only $1,239,000. The Yerkes mansion was bought for specula-
tion that never eventuated and for years it stood empty and
neglected.

Mara Yerkes, who had only a year before she died at age
forty-nine of heartbreak and alcoholism, received little of the
$3.5 million earned by the sale of the art and mansion. Again
lawyers and creditors grabbed it. Mara always felt that her late
husband's attorneys had cheated her on a vast scale, but never
could prove it.

A year later, Miss Emilie Grigsby auctioned off the effulgent
contents of her Park Avenue townhouse, with a 427-page
catalogue listing such items as the friezes with her loveliness
painted into them. Far from impoverished, the girl nonetheless

welcomed the $200,000-plus the public sale netted her. After it, the convent-bred daughter of a Kentucky whorehouse madam embarked to make her home in London. "One is treated so much better there," she explained prettily.

11

Clark's Folly

IT is difficult to imagine anything as magnificent as the William Collins Whitney mansion being used as a ploy in the devious game of social climbing. Yet this is what happened following the death of its owner.

Nor was the Fifth Avenue dwelling on which Whitney and Stanford White labored with such artistic fervor bought by an established aristocrat, whose name was a household word. Rather it was purchased and used as a pawn in the social game by a self-effacing bachelor named James Henry Smith.

He was known to friends as "Silent" Smith because he seldom spoke of his own accord and never answered a question without carefully mulling the answer. Sometimes he did not answer at all. Short and broad of body, Smith was a stockbroker by profession, rated by Wall Street colleagues as "having few intimates, not given to making a display of himself, and in business noted for the characteristics that give him his nickname." Another source saw him as "torpescent . . . with a wilting black mustache and a rimless *pince-nez*."

Silent Smith was neither prominent nor successful as a stockbroker. He lived alone, read books and magazines, and passed hours in a fantasy world where social prominence miraculously came his way. In these aspirations, if not in personality, he resembled blustering Sim Rosedale in Edith Wharton's *Age of Innocence.*

The daydreams of Silent Smith were not altogether lacking in foundation, since his only living relative was an elderly uncle who had amassed $60 million in his lifetime and had conserved it by living on $200 a month. Silent Smith lived in expectation of inheriting this fortune and, oddly enough, he did. Possessed of millions overnight, he tossed off his mantle of torpor to reach out and buy the Whitney mansion for $2 million. Behind this grand gesture lay the knowledge that the tongues of Gotham Society would wag as a result.

The thought of James Henry "Silent" Smith inhabiting the Whitney mansion staggers the mind. Whitney had been a noted figure and a gregarious soul, with the world beating a path to his door, but Silent Smith was unknown and friendless. Yet after moving in he was not awed by his surroundings. Boldly he bought and hung Gainsborough's *The Woodsman's Return*, a painting Whitney probably would not have liked. He also placed a Japanese fountain in the Renaissance reception room, while scattering Imperial Chinese rugs and other bits of Oriental art throughout the premises. On the floor of the imposing great hall he placed a polar bear rug measuring seven feet, tip to toe.

Then he bought Rubens' *The Holy Family with St. Francis* and presented it to the Metropolitan Museum of Art, knowing the splendid gift would win him added notice from Society's top ranks.

Changes in Gotham's upper crust operated in favor of this curiously ambitious man who, in the words of Elizabeth Drexel Lehr, "was still dazed at the sudden change in his fortunes, uncertain where to look for entree; he wanted to get into Society, he did not know how to do it." Society's old order was changing, with some reigning dowagers bored, restless, and hungry for bizarre diversion. Paramount among them was Mrs. Stuyvesant Fish who, with Mrs. George Gould, one day decided to divert herself through a social season by sponsoring the dreams of Silent Smith. Approaching him like tiara-topped fairy godmothers, the ladies promised, "We are going to promote you in the right set. You must give a ball! We will organize it for you!"

Overjoyed, Silent Smith allowed them *carte blanche* to spend his money for invitations, decoration, and gold cotillion favors. He did not hold his function at the Whitney mansion, but rather in the ballroom of the Waldorf-Astoria, where it proved the success of the season. "He became the fashion," writes Mrs. Lehr, "the quarry of the matchmaking mothers of New York." Once he began scampering up the social ladder, Silent Smith discovered in himself the ability to spend money prodigally. He gave parties in the Whitney mansion at which Caruso and others sang, built a country home in Tuxedo Park, and rented a yacht owned by the Anthony J. Drexels.

With all this, he remained something of a ridiculous figure. *Town Topics* made fun of his pretensions, referring to him as The Silent One. Yet the ambitious man must have possessed a certain charisma. "How I envy that man!" the usually bitchy Harry Lehr wrote in his secret diary. "It takes a lot of personality to bring a newcomer to Society to the front like that!" To this, Lehr's wife makes the addendum that Smith had money, not personality.

Still, Silent Smith demonstrated the magic powers noted by Harry Lehr by becoming an intimate of the high-toned William Rhinelander Stewarts. In 1906 Mrs. Stewart astoundingly divorced her spouse to become the bride of Silent Smith. Society all but collapsed. After the wedding the newlyweds boarded the Drexel yacht to sail for the Orient, accompanied by the Duke and Duchess of Manchester and other deluxe guests. The cruise got as far as Kyoto, Japan, where Fate suddenly quit smiling at Silent Smith. He died there, and in chronicling his meteoric social rise an obituary labeled him "an interesting eccentric."

As for the Whitney mansion, it was put up for sale by the Smith estate and an auction of its treasure trove announced. At the last moment, Harry Payne Whitney stepped in to buy back his father's residence. He lived there with wife Gertrude Vanderbilt Whitney until his death.

The short, happy social whirl of Silent Smith had its tender, even amusing, aspects. As such, it is notable as one of the few

sagas of Society to evoke mellow feelings. For Society was a serious matter to those involved, much like a giant wheel of fortune
on which members of the Gotham elite and Climbers fought to
remain erect. Those in the calm at the center of Fortune's wheel
might have had little trouble remaining upright, but those
farther from the center frequently stumbled, fell, or vanished.

As the ranks of the Four Hundred grew to an unruly Fifteen
Hundred even the ladies of established Society grabbed at the
morning *Herald* to see who had dined with whom the night before. To be omitted from a certain dinner list might be a slight,
rebuff, or insult milady had to endure with grace. For the
climber, omission from a dinner party might spell social oblivion.

But for all the earnestness of Society, occasional levity cropped
up. Mrs. Stuyvesant Fish, of course, was famed for her reckless,
acidulous wit. One day she found herself faced by an angry
woman friend who gritted, "I heard what you said about me last
night, Mame—you said I looked like a frog!" Calmly looking the
lady up and down, Mrs. Fish replied, "No, my dear, a toad, a
toad!"

A gentler type of wit came from two young females who married into Millionaires' Row. One wed a scion and was taken on a
tour of the Fifth Avenue mansion. Later she confided to a
friend, "They seem to have everything in that place except the
Mad Hatter."

Another who joined the Suddenly Rich by Wedlock got from
her father-in-law an imposing four-poster-with-canopies seized
from a château in the Perigord. Viewing it for the first time, she
said, "I'll have eight children if I ever get into that bed!"

Society's cherished male wit was William R. Travers, who left
behind enough witticisms to fill a joke book. A slight stammer
added to the humor of his spontaneous remarks. One day he
walked past the Union Club with a friend who asked if the men
in the comfortable armchairs at the windows were habitués of
the club. "No," Travers answered, "s-s-some are s-s-sons of
habitués." Once he addressed the bald-domed banker Henry
Clews, "I s-s-say, Clews, since you are a self-made man, w-w-why
the devil didn't you put more hair on your head?" At Newport,
Travers watched the passing procession of yachts owned by the

great stockbroking families and asked, "But where are the c-c-customers' yachts?" On viewing the Siamese Twins for the first time, he stammered, "B-b-brothers, I presume?"

For the most part, though, the laughs of Society fall into the category known as black humor. What, for instance, could be more darkly ludicrous than the members of the Fifty Million Club—those mighty gents who seemed to have conquered the universe—quaking in terror at the thought of blackmail by Colonel William D'Alton Mann, publisher of the scandal sheet *Town Topics*? Colonel Mann was a diabolical oldster who pretended to look admiringly on Society folk as "the show figures of the social *musée*." In his paper, the words Four Hundred were printed in boldface numerals—the **400**. But actually his rheumy eyes saw in High Society a collection of dingbats.

Among the multimillionaires who at one time or another paid blackmail to *Town Topics* were William K. Vanderbilt, J. P. Morgan, Charles Tyson Yerkes, William C. Whitney, and Thomas Fortune Ryan. The sums, which could rise as high as $25,000, were not necessarily to cover up sexual peccadillos, though some did. More often they were paid out of fear of what *Town Topics* might print about family, relatives, or friends.

For Colonel Mann was capable of printing an item that said, "Miss Van Alen suffers from some kind of throat trouble—she cannot go for more than half an hour without a drink." Or, "Seldom does a brunette make a pretty bride, and Miss Marie Arnot was no exception." Or, "Mrs. Frederic Nielsen has aged a great deal lately; her complexion has become almost blue, and the crow's feet around her eyes are visible at a distance."

Colonel Mann was insatiable. Not only did he extract bribe money over *Town Topics*, but he also published at $1,500 a copy a weighty volume titled *Fads and Fancies of Representative Americans*. Any rich man who failed to order it could be sure of ridicule in *Town Topics*. Presumably this was true of Herman Oelrichs, whose remarks before a distinguished gathering were called "a speech compounded in equal parts of drivel, bathos, and attempted humor."

The $25,000 shelled out by William K. Vanderbilt to Colonel Mann did not win long immunity for him. After Vanderbilt's second marriage to Mrs. Lewis Rutherfurd, *Town Topics* wrote, "Mrs. Vanderbilt's gown actually glared with shining spangles the size of a dime. The background of the gown was black net, but all one could see was a gleaming, flashing mass of changing lights. Diamonds were worn about her throat and in the hair. Mrs. Vanderbilt looked remarkably well and her new husband appeared exceedingly proud of her, but that did not hinder her from looking like a circus rider."

Colonel Mann used the same snapper technique when the newly opened Waldorf Hotel refused to advertise in his scandal sheet. Paying a reportorial visit to the hostelry, he wrote a laudatory description of its furnishings and decor. He then described in detail the noble repast served him in one of the hotel dining rooms, ending "but the oysters were hot and the soup was cold."

Occasionally the Colonel wrote not so much with malice as with common sense. Describing one newly completed mansion he said, "The dining room is decorated in Henry II style—and, by the way, these Henry II dining rooms are getting to be as great a bore as Du Barry boudoirs and Louis XIV salons."

For another sardonic chuckle at Society's expense, look at the mansion built by Stanford White for Joseph Pulitzer, editor of the New York *World*. Over the years Pulitzer had slowly gone blind and with this worsening of sight his hearing became more acute. Able to hear a pin drop and sensitive to the tiniest noise, he began spending his time on an ocean-going yacht. Nonetheless, he decided to build a château-like home at 7–11 East Seventy-third Street, a few steps off Fifth Avenue.

Before going blind, Pulitzer had seen enough ornate mansions to know he did not desire one. Instead he ordered his to be built around a fine courtyard, but with no excess ornamentation. Stanford White provided a plaster model of the outside over which the publisher ran sensitive fingers. For the interior, Pulitzer instructed, "No ballroom, no music room, or picture gallery under any disguise . . . no French rooms, designed or decorated to require French furniture. . . . I want an American

home for comfort and use and not for show or entertainment."
Either White could not be controlled or the Pulitzer family
stepped in, for the completed job had a ballroom, music room,
and swimming pool.

Naturally, this man so allergic to noise had impressed on
White the importance of sound-proofing his personal quarters,
especially the bedroom. White stuffed walls with insulation,
triple-plated windows, and put floors on ball bearings to prevent
vibration. The architect shut himself inside the room while men
outside shouted and pounded; no sound penetrated. Yet on his
first night in the mansion, Pulitzer claimed to hear a hollow,
ghostly knocking from the depths of the building.

It is interesting to visualize the confrontation between the im-
perious Pulitzer and Stanford White, a man so justly proud of
his skills. In the course of it, the publisher accused the architect
of trying to drive him mad. A shaken White took to questioning
his different contractors. One broke down to admit that a bubbling spring had been uncovered during the excavation. On his
own authority, the fellow had diverted this spring by feeding it
into a sump pit. The pump for this had been placed under
Pulitzer's bedroom, in the belief that the extraordinary
soundproofing would kill the sound. But the drum of a nearby
heating system acted as sounding board, sending an eerie
thumping upward.

The pump was moved outside the château and buried under
the sidewalk. Even so, Pulitzer refused to sleep in his bedroom
and branded the entire mansion a wretched failure. Finally, an
annex was built in consultation with a Harvard authority on
acoustics. Again walls were packed with mineral wool, windows
double-plated. Fresh air came in by the fireplace chimney only,
and after one night Pulitzer angrily declared that through it he
could hear street noises and early morning factory whistles.
White solved the problem by stretching thousands of silk threads
back and forth across the chimney opening.

"Now at last," sighed a Pulitzer associate, "he has found
zero—the room is so still as to be uncanny."

Of all the centimillionaires, the public derived the most fun, or thought it did, from William Andrews Clark, the Copper King of Montana, a man widely believed to garner $1 million a month from multiple holdings.

Among other things, the popular attitude of the public toward Senator Clark—he served a term in Congress—exposed a drastic change in the nation's thinking. No longer was the widespread attitude toward members of the Fifty Million Club one of mute reverence. With extreme slowness, the people had come to realize that the much admired plutocrats had got to the top by exploiting their fellow man. Theodore Roosevelt, President of the United States, was shaking his big stick at the large trusts, branding their operators malefactors of great wealth. Never had Teddy Roosevelt been an admirer of the predatory breed. "I am simply unable to make myself take the attitude of respect toward the very wealthy men which such an enormous multitude of people evidently really feel," he wrote once. At long last, the public was catching up with him.

The nation was also becoming bored by the denizens of Millionaires' Row. For suddenly the Great White Way of Broadway seemed more exciting as it provided characters like Diamond Jim Brady and Lillian Russell, who seemed to live surrounded by glamor, sex, and sin. The American theater had likewise leaped to life, sending across the country strong-jawed matinée idols like Richard Mansfield and Kyrle Bellew, who caused female hearts to flutter and excited males to envy and emulation. The newspaper world simultaneously produced Richard Harding Davis, the most romantic male figure of his generation, immortalized by artist Charles Dana Gibson as the Gibson Man.

Beside these glorious creatures, the skinflint Croesus, shadowy in his Fifth Avenue mansion, began to seem drab, despicable, and old-fashioned.

So the moment had arrived when a multimillionaire like Senator William A. Clark could provoke mirth. People chuckled at the thought of this Montana Midas, a slight, dandified fellow with a neatly pointed beard, standing (as he did) on the corner of Fifth Avenue and Seventy-seventh Street to intone, "I will build here the finest mansion on the Avenue, one that will make ex-Secretary Whitney's look poor by comparison."

The mansion that slowly arose as a result took eight years to build and cost nearly $7 million. Finally completed, it provided not only Mrs. Wharton's full architectural meal, but an indigestible repast as well, for it displayed nearly every classical style of architecture on its cluttered facades. By then, people had become discriminating judges of mansions and, in *Collier's*, Will Irwin poked fun at this one—

Senator Copper of Tonopah Ditch
Made a clean billion in minin' and sich,
Hiked for Noo York, where his money he blew
Buildin' a palace on Fift' Avenoo.
"How," sez the Senator, "Can I look proudest?
Build me a house that'll holler the loudest—"

Forty-eight architects came to consult,
Drawin' up plans for a splendid result;
If the old Senator wanted to pay,
They'd give him Art with a capital A.

Pillars Ionic
Eaves Babylonic,
Doors cut in scallops, resemblin' a shell;
Roof wuz Egyptian,
Gables caniptian,
Whole grand effect, when completed, wuz—Hell!

Yet in ridiculing Senator Clark, or dismissing him as a vulgarian, the world made a mistake. Though never in a cultural class with William Collins Whitney, Clark was still a fastidious man well aware of what went on. With the arrogance of the truly self-made, he did not give a damn for the praise or ridicule of the public. Senator Clark knew he was not the fellow the world thought him. The last laugh, he felt, would one day be his.

Each saga of a Robber Baron has its individuality and dapper William Andrews Clark carved out his own colorful segment. Born in Pennsylvania of a second-generation Irish family, he was taken to Iowa while still in his teens. Behind him, he left a pretty childhood sweetheart who promised to await his return.

In the rough Midwest, Clark grew up light of body, but phenomenally quick of mind—"a driving, grasping, ambitious youth of truly astonishing energy." He attended Iowa Wesleyan with the intention of studying law, but lack of funds turned him into an eighteen-year-old schoolteacher. Throughout a long life, Clark reveled in titles and was overjoyed when his fellow Iowans saw fit to address him as "Professor."

Outstandingly ambitious, he avidly read newspaper accounts of gold and silver discoveries in parts of the West. Abandoning teaching—though retaining the title Professor—he traveled at age twenty-three to Central City, Colorado, to labor with pick and shovel in the mines. In 1863, he moved to the Montana Territory and, after many hardships, staked out a claim at Jeff Davis Gulch, near Horse Prairie Creek. Months of panning gold netted him $1,500, a fair return but hardly a marvelous one. Like other millionaires-in-the-making, he saw greater profits in providing supplies for prospectors. Turning trader, he ordered provisions from the East and sold them at his rough-hewn general store.

In the accepted manner of the paleface conqueror, Clark found solace during this period of struggle in the arms of various Indian maids. As was the custom, he abandoned each of these young redskin girls once she bloated with pregnancy. Later on, his legitimate progeny feared that an Indian by-blow might rise to claim a share of the Clark fortune, but none did.

Eager, or greedy, for any endeavor that would bring precious pelf, he contracted to deliver the U.S. Mail between Missoula, in Montana Territory, and Walla Walla, Washington, a hostile Indian territory. He usually hired pony express riders for this hazardous duty, but occasionally the vibrant little man did the riding himself. He also led militia forays against the Indians and from them earned the title Major, which seemed preferable to Professor.

As Major Clark he established a department store and a bank bearing his name. He also optioned four abandoned gold mines around Butte. At this vital moment in life, Clark took the step that raised him above fellow Montana miners and prospectors. Leaving his affairs in the hands of a brother, he traveled to New York to study geology and minerology for a year at the Columbia School of Mines. On the way home he detoured to claim the hand of the sweet Pennsylvania girl who had waited thirteen years for him.

Back in Montana, he knew far more about mines and minerals than his rivals. Among much else, he had learned that the blackish substance impatiently tossed aside by gold miners was in reality silver ore. Accordingly, he bought other abandoned gold mines. And, after silver, a beneficent earth yielded him copper.

By working sixteen to eighteen hours a day, Clark made his first million by age thirty-four, emerging as the Territory's leading mine owner, banker, merchant, and owner of water-power resources, timber lands, and herds of cattle. In private life, he had become the proud parent of two sons and two daughters. Montanans considered him vain and unscrupulous, but there was no denying his energy and financial genius. "He accumulated capital by grasping every opportunity and making the best of it," says an account of his life. Withal, he remained one of two men in the Territory who always wore white shirts. An admiring Montana selected him as Official Orator at the Philadelphia Exposition of 1876.

Clark's fortunes soared as Butte became the copper capital of the world—or, as natives put it, "the richest hill on earth." He started his own newspaper, acquired the local traction monopoly, reached into Arizona for the hugely profitable United Verde Mine, and invested in Mexican tobacco. His only rival was Marcus Daly, discoverer of the Anaconda Mine. The two hated one another and battled for control of the Territory.

Clark led the fight for Montana's statehood, which finally came in 1889, when he was fifty-four. With his lust for titles, he aspired to be the first United States Senator from the third largest state in the nation. "He was eaten to the core by a desire for public office," a friend recalled. Daly opposed him, putting up his own man. According to one account, "Clark and Daly rolled up their sleeves, spat on their hands, and prepared to throw dirt aplenty at one another. The whole struggle was one of the most wretched in the history of Montana. Sordid were the details. . . ."

To the Robber Baron, bribery was the best means of attaining any end, and Clark and Daly employed it to the utmost. "How much are they paying for votes today?" became a joke that was no joke. In those days senators were elected by state legislatures, so a candidate for the office first had to bribe voters to elect men susceptible to his bribes. For Clark and Daly an off-shoot of this lay in the fact that, with enough amenable men in power, taxes on their properties and operations could be reduced.

In his efforts to win a Senate seat for himself Clark bribed everyone possible. His candidacy was ably encouraged by the Butte City Cornet Band and the W. A. Clark Marching Club, both attired in white uniforms with gold leaf. Handing over hundreds of thousands of dollars to his campaign managers, Clark virtuously claimed to be untainted by bribery because he did not know precisely where the money went.

So great was Clark's expectation of winning his first campaign that he wrote an acceptance speech. But he lost and remained a loser until 1898 brought him victory. Then, on the day of taking his seat in Washington, his enemies handed the Senate Committee on Elections proof that Clark had paid forty-five state legislators $430,000 for votes. He had no alternative but to resign, which he did in a ringing speech that ended, "I have never in my life been charged with a dishonorable act, and I prefer to leave to my children a legacy worth more than gold—an unblemished name!"

His words tore the hearts of senators who had similarly bribed themselves into office. But sympathy proved needless, for back home in Montana the lieutenant-governor maneuvered the governor out of the state and appointed Clark to fill his own vacant Senate seat. By this and other stratagems the Copper King managed to serve out a full six-year term.

By that time William Andrews Clark had entered his sixties, an astounding little man with a neat mustache and dandified beard. He aspired to be Ambassador to France and patterned his trim appearance on a Parisian *boulevardier*; indeed, he resembled a Whistler painting of one. Ever a powerhouse of energy, he mocked Senate colleagues by his feats of vitality. Where others had large staffs, he cut his to a bare minimum and answered his own mail in longhand. Twenty-six millionaires occupied seats in the Senate but Clark, as head of fourteen thriving corporations, was by far the richest. Senator Robert M. La Follette of Wisconsin rose one day to castigate him as one of "the hundred men who own America."

There was always speculation about Clark's total worth, usually listed in newspapers as $50–80 million. But those figures did not take into consideration his potential wealth. The Senator owned gold mines, copper mines, ore deposits, smelters, railroads, trolley cars, wireworks, and other enterprises, as well as banks, newspapers, and giant herds of cattle. Possibly his actual riches were twice any newspaper estimate.

In addition, the Montana Midas made a fetish of owning his properties outright, with no partners or stockholders. Said a tribute, "Of all the great undertakings with which he was connected, not one share of stock nor bond issue by any of them was either listed or quoted or could be bought on any stock exchange in the United States or elsewhere."

The world was fascinated by this Croesus with wealth impossible to estimate, and Clark obliged his admirers by becoming something of a cosmopolite. By sending his four children to the best Eastern schools he became familiar with the parents of their classmates. After buying a handsome townhouse in New York he achieved inclusion in the Social Register. One day his trim figure stepped into the auction rooms of the American Art Association, forerunner of Sotheby Park Bernet. There he took his first step as an art collector by paying $3,150 for the painting *Weary Wayfarers*, by Jean Charles Cazin.

But he did not achieve fame as a collector of paintings until the acquisition for $42,000 of Mariano Fortuny's striking, naughty *The Choice of a Model,* wherein a group of male connoisseurs of womanflesh gather in a richly decorated studio "to criticize a nude female who is posing before them in an attitude of studied grace." This put his name in newspapers and with ownership of other works by the same artist, the Montana family became known as "the Fortuny Clarks."

To the multitudes who considered Senator Clark a ridiculous figure the idea of him as an art collector always seemed the most absurd. Yet he set about collecting art with the same determination applied to his study of mining at Columbia. "I mean to have the finest collection of paintings in the United States," he told associates. With that, he sailed for Paris, to take cram courses in art history and the French language. In the process he became an ardent Francophile who for the remainder of a long life tried to spend three months of each year in Paris. On his first trip he dabbled enjoyably in the fleshpots of the city; back in the United States his proper wife heard of it and all but left him.

Almost as rapidly as he had turned into an art collector, Clark became a full-fledged citizen of New York. A short time before entering the Senate, he had bought the property at Fifth Avenue and Seventy-seventh and issued the order, "Build me the finest mansion in New York."

The architect to whom these Aladdin-like words were spoken was J. M. Hewlett, of Lord, Hewlett, and Hull. Clark approved the plans drawn by the firm, then irritably disapproved on grounds of insufficient scope and grandeur. Carrying them abroad on his next trip to Paris, he consulted M. H. Deglane, designer of the Grand Palais on the Champs Elysées.

Deglane reworked the plans in extravagant fashion and Clark instructed Hewlett to follow them. Somewhere along the line architect K. M. Murchison also became involved. While Clark served in the Senate his mansion slowly rose. The centimillionaire slowed the job considerably by making structural changes himself. Further delays stemmed from his stubborn insistence on gaining possession of every company that furnished him major materials. In the end, he became the only potentate along Millionaires' Row to inhabit a mansion built of his own marble and granite, with bronze entrance doors cast in his own foundries and woodwork and decorative plaster from his own shops.

Clark's resentful wife had died in 1893, and within a year the elegant Copper King had acquired a "ward." Two stories exist regarding how Anna LaChapelle, a French-Canadian girl of fifteen or sixteen, entered his life. One says Clark saw the luscious child posing as the Goddess of Liberty in a Fourth of July parade in Butte. By the other, Anna boldly walked into his office, to declare herself the possessor of musical talent and aspi-

rations far beyond the rough life of Montana. Then she mean-
ingfully suggested that Clark subsidize her education.

Whichever, the Copper King quickly became her official
guardian and dispatched the girl to Boston for musical studies,
with his own sister as chaperone. Then Anna journeyed to Paris,
remaining eight years.

The world did not know about Anna LaChapelle, but in other
ways the name of Senator Clark appeared in newspapers as
much as any American millionaire. Periodic reports were
printed about the progress of his mansion and from the West
came word of fresh mining endeavors. The Copper King bravely
undertook to combat the railroad barons by building the San
Pedro, Los Angeles & Salt Lake Railroad, capitalized at $25 mil-
lion, which opened up the iron fields of Utah to the West Coast.
He was sued for breach of promise by a lady journalist and an
anarchist picturesquely named Joe Peg threatened to shoot him
on the elementary grounds that he had too much money.

Newspapers eagerly recounted his continuing art purchases as
he shelled out $180,000 for Rembrandt's *Portrait of a Young Man*;
$150,000 for Raeburn's *Portrait of the Artist's Daughter*; and
$100,000 for Corot's *Dance Under the Trees*. The art world buzzed
as he went on to buy twenty-one Corots, twenty Monticellis, eighteen Cazins, and works by Titian, Hogarth, Rubens, Reynolds,
Van Dyck, Gainsborough, Blakelock, Daubigny, Whistler,
Troyon, and Jules Breton. Especially admired by him and the
contemporary world were six panels by Boutet de Monvel depicting the life of Joan of Arc.

As a collector, Clark preferred to buy at auctions, eliminating
the profit usually extracted by an art dealer. He attained stature
in art circles by purchasing the Sir George Donaldson collection
for the low price of $350,000. Sir George knew he could get
more by bargaining, but haughtily refused. "To do so would
have brought me to the level of an American money-grubber,"
he pontificated. Clark was promptly sued in London for a five
percent commission by the dealer who had introduced him to Sir
George. An unsympathetic court ordered him to pay up.

Beyond these news stories lay real drama. In Paris, Anna

LaChapelle had borne him two girls. Anna's existence was still a dark secret to the world and no one (not even his grown children) knew the United States Senator had a young mistress and family of toddlers in France. Clark seemed reluctant to marry Anna, perhaps considering her a cut below him culturally. He was especially opposed to having her inherit his vast millions.

Yet his love for their children brought a dilemma. In 1904, he settled a few million dollars on her, getting in return a document renouncing her claim to his fortune. Next, he married her and used his wealth to falsify French records to make it appear the wedding took place before the birth of the first child. He was then prepared to break the news to his unsuspecting sons and daughters, as well as reveal to a credulous world that he had been secretly married for over five years.

Mrs. Anna LaChapelle Clark, forty years her husband's junior, walked at his side on the day the Senator took possession of his mighty metropolitan mansion. Presumably the owner was pleased with the finished product, but New Yorkers, by then sophisticated on the subject, labeled it "Clark's Folly" and sarcastically dismissed its architectural style as "Mid-McKinley Renaissance." The word "monstrosity" was freely tossed about and one wit made reference to "A Gold Brick for the Copper King."

About this massive conglomeration of architectural samplings one writer sniffed, "The house would be the ideal dwelling for the late Mr. Barnum; it is as flamboyant as he could wish—an airy fantasy in granite block." Added another, "If, as Schelling said, architecture is frozen music, this edifice is frozen ragtime discord."

Senator Clark's hearth and home rose an overpowering four stories with a steep mansard roof giving two additional floors. Nobility and grace were conspicuously lacking in an exterior that seemed to combine every classic architectural design, stuck together clumsily, as if by giant hands wielding putty. "There is not one bit of detail upon which a human being can look with pleasure," an observer declared.

The mansion had a seventy-foot front on Fifth Avenue and extended back two hundred feet on Seventy-seventh Street. A slight amount of beauty may have been visible on the Fifth Avenue facade, with its classical columns, abutments, high windows, balustraded balconies, and urns and bunches of flowers carved in high relief. Yet one detractor compared this central mass to an umbrella poked in the public eye.

The decoration of the whole was characterized as a relentless pattern of lines, with the deep rustication between heavy blocks of granite a particular affront to the human eye. (One critic said this deep rustication indicated that the real derivation of the mansion was the log cabin.) Dominating the edifice was a commanding cupola on the Seventy-seventh Street side. As if that were not enough, the cupola served as base for a clumsy steeple or spire. Also prominent on the steep, cluttered roof was a high Renaissance chimney with utilitarian flues.

If the public reacted to the Clark mansion with amusement, the architectural profession registered outrage. *The Architectural Forum* called it an "aberration" and an "erection." *The American Architect* objected to "our biggest, boldest, and brassiest example of domestic architecture." The steeple atop the cupola provoked special vilification, with an architect professing to be unable to define it—"Is this steeple, belvedere, crowning lantern, belfry, or what?" Another declared, "A more meaningless or fatuous feature than this steeple would be impossible to find in the wildest vagaries of art."

Newspapers were equally harsh on the mansion. One said, "Nobody could possibly infer from style, size, shape, or treatment that this is a dwelling." Nor was Senator Clark himself exempt: "The only way this mansion can be deemed good art is that it correctly represents the personality and taste of the Copper King who inhabits it."

The Senator met the hurricane of scorn by ignoring it and by that shrewd tactic slowly won a victory in the battle of public opinion. A later critic has looked back on the Clark mansion and seen it as "French baroque eclecticism of the exuberant Ecole des Beaux Arts variety." As the public grew accustomed to the mansion it seemed to be less Clark's Folly and more exuberant Beaux Arts. By sheer bulk and arrogance of design it began to impress a fickle populace, advancing in the public eye from monstrosity to curiosity to landmark cherished for size, boldness, and atrocious taste.

From printed sources the people learned that inside Clark's Folly lay 130 rooms and twenty-one vaulted marble bathrooms. A writer found these bathrooms the most successful feature of the house—"the coldness, the stoniness, the marbleness of the halls and staircases grope timidly toward what the bathrooms alone achieve." Each of the main floors included a large dining room and hotel-size kitchen, so master and mistress could dine anywhere at whim. The first, or state floor, included a Reception Room, Grand Salon, Petit Salon, Morning Room, Music Room, Staircase Hall, Sculpture Hall, Banquet Hall, and no less than four sizable Picture Galleries. The Grand Salon was furnished in the style of Louis XVI with ceiling by Fragonard, while the Petit Salon reflected a room in the Hotel Soubise at the time of Louis XV.

The Banquet Hall boasted three striking balconies, walls of spotless Greek marble, and a ceiling from a 2,000-year-old tree taken from Sherwood Forest, carved with shields, wreaths, and cherubim. For dining, there were available one $120,000 gold service and another silver service of Renaissance design. Also on hand was a $7,000 tablecloth with fourteen paintings from the Louvre reproduced in *point de Venise* lace.

The Morning Room was of oak overlaid with gold leaf; the Breakfast Room had 200 walnut panels, no two alike; the Library offered small mullioned windows and furniture of Empire mahogany; the Reception Room was of Circassian walnut; Billiard and Smoking Rooms were English oak; the Music Room featured marble, bronze, and satinwood, with a $100,000 pipe organ and picturesque organ loft.

Walls of the state rooms were hung with priceless tapestries from France and Spain; so were labyrinthine halls and corridors. Oriental rugs covered marble floors and French porcelains adorned shelves. Fireplaces from French châteaux jutted into state rooms. Exotic birds twittered from nine-foot ivory cages. The walls and floors of Mrs. Clark's bedroom were of sandalwood, giving off a delicate scent.

Clark's main staircase was of ivory-tinted marble, from his own quarries in Maryland. Some ceilings were of hard-to-install stone. The Gothic Poolroom, with Caen stone fireplace and mantel, was authentic to the legs of green-topped tables. Also embellishing the premises were a fully equipped theater, complete with dressing rooms; a Conservatory for orchids only; and a varicolored Faience Marble Room. In the midst of such magnificence were incongruities like electric floor lamps.

The ground floor contained a full-scale suite of offices for the Splendor Seeker to use on the rare days he did not go to his Wall Street office. In the basement lay a Turkish bath called "unrivaled" by a newspaper; it had rubbing rooms, steam room, massage table, and twenty-eight-foot colonnaded pool. The depths of the building also held a Limousine Room, or garage, with space for a dozen cars. Limousines entered the premises by way of a large, open Main Court at the rear of the mansion, then dipped underground through a marble-walled driveway to the garage, emerging by way of the Rotunda. There were secret doors and stairways throughout the mansion, plus a solarium, large wine cellar, cold storage plant, and furnace that devoured fourteen tons of coal a day.

Naturally, Clark doted on the four art galleries on his main floor. They could be thrown together, with the Music Room, to run along the entire north end of the mansion; for a social family this would have provided the most superb of ballrooms. The Copper King liked to guide groups of art lovers through the galleries, delivering little lectures on his paintings and sculptures.

"I have never bought a picture I did not like at first sight," he informed awed listeners. The collection was valued at $1.5 million and he liked to say, "Paintings and sculptures are selling at enormous prices as compared to five or ten years ago. My collection as a whole is worth vastly more than I spent on it. But of course it will never be sold."

The Senator yielded to none in love of country and was wont to state, "Art, like everything else, is best and sanest in America." His collection failed to bear this out. He owned Inness' *Sunset at Montclair*, Blakelock's *Moonlight*, and Wyant's *Morning at*

Neversink, but the remainder of paintings were European. His Monticellis were considered superior to those in the Louvre and his many Degas won him envy.

Clark was sixty-five years old when he finally settled in his $7 million home. In the past it had been said he built the ornate dwelling to crash a Four Hundred rapidly becoming the Fifteen Hundred, but any social ambition seemed to have drained from him. One daughter by his first wife had made an excellent marriage (the Croesus settled $1 million on the bridegroom) into High Society, and the second daughter made a good one. One son raised homosexuality to new heights on the American continent.

Had he wished, Senator Clark could had given successful dinner parties for the social elite, but he restricted social activities to nights in his box at the Metropolitan Opera. For him and other Splendor Seekers, the challenge of social climbing had gone. Amusement rather than exclusivity had become the motto of High Society and if invited, members of the jaded upper crust would flock to a dinner or ball at Clark's Folly. It was all too easy to be worth the trouble.

Clark never ceased working. With a garage for a dozen limousines, he confounded the world by daily riding to and from Wall Street by subway. Ever courtly, he probably rose to give ladies his seat, and so became a Millionaire Straphanger. He was a tough old cock who in the last twenty years of life survived an operation for the removal of an abscess at the base of his brain, and serious auto accidents in Colorado and France.

Energetically laboring through his seventies and into his eighties, the octogenarian looked back with pardonable pride over a career encompassing farm boy, country schoolteacher, miner, merchant, banker, financier, politician, lawmaker, capitalist, and patron of the arts. World War I and the spread of electricity in the United States increased his wealth to an estimated $200 million.

Always cherishing his art collection, the little Senator swelled with rooster-like pride when flatterers assured him it was better than the Louvre. Eventually, he made a will leaving his works of art to the Metropolitan Museum of Art, just a few blocks up the avenue from his home. By his strict stipulation, the collection had to be housed in a special gallery bearing his name.

This bequest, plus the extreme solidity of his mansion, seemed to guarantee Senator Clark immortality. In the meantime he lived contentedly in the mansion until his death in 1925 at age eighty-six. Edith Wharton may have predicted that the taste of the Suddenly Rich would slowly outgrow their flamboyant mansions, but William Andrews Clark never tired of Clark's Folly.

12

Twentieth-Century Kubla Khans

MILLIONAIRES' ROW reached full flower during the first ten years of the twentieth century. The stretch of Fifth Avenue once dismissed as Squatters' Sovereignty had grown into a magnificent boulevard with Central Park, the Arsenal, and the Metropolitan Museum of Art on one side and the other lined with habitations of the rich in such profusion that newspaper feature writers had difficulty conjuring up properly descriptive phrases.

One called the dwellings "palaces of paladins of princely privilege." Others dreamed up "purple purlieus," "the bullion-ated boulevard," "citadels of vested wealth and social privilege," "Society's Klondike," and "the paradise of American millionaires."

The English visitor Frederic Harrison marveled, "Each millionaire seemed to have commissioned his architect to build him a mansion of any style from ancient Byzantine to the latest French empire, provided only it be in contrast to the style of his neighbors."

It was true. French châteaux and Italian palazzi might be favored by the mightiest of these Fifth Avenue Midases, but others in the Fifty Million Club flew off on individual tangents to erect Kubla Khan pleasure domes reflecting the Medieval, Byzantine, Empire, Baroque, Rococo, Medici, Georgian Tudor, or Gothic. George Gould, oldest son of Jay Gould, favored the Oriental, with a prayer-balconied mansion almost as wide as it was high, topped by nothing less than minarets; in her bedroom, Mrs. Gould dreamed between black silk sheets. Judge Elbert Gary, a brilliant legal mind important to J. P. Morgan interests, burst forth with a dwelling of Byzantine splendor, inside and out. Henry Phipps, wallowing in profits from Carnegie Steel, erected a baroque palace big enough to resemble an apartment house. Augustus Van Horne Stuyvesant, bachelor and ninth in line from redoubtable Peter, lived with two spinster sisters in a medieval pile at the corner of Seventy-ninth Street, across from the neo-Renaissance Brokaw mansion.

Inside these mansions, wonders increased. After his mother's death in 1908, John Jacob Astor summoned the firm of Carrère and Hastings to render the family double-dwelling into a single one and conspicuously increase its lavishness in the process; divorced at last from Ava Willing, this Astor had little time to enjoy the renovation, for he went down on the *Titanic*. The walls of the home created for Payne Whitney by Stanford White hid what was called the most beautiful staircase in America; years later it served as inspiration for the one used in the film *Gone With the Wind*.

However, it is incorrect to assume that every dwelling along Millionaires' Row was an overpowering mansion. Usually the mansions occupied corners, with a frontage of fifty to seventy feet on Fifth, extending eastward 200 or more feet. The manorial entrance was on the side street. Then, sandwiched between mansions on the corners were handsome, slender townhouses equally individual in style.

Thus the block beginning with the William Collins Whitney mansion also included to the north the residences of Joseph Stickney, Daniel Reed (another Tin Plate King), and Mrs. Ogden Mills. The Astor mansion shared its block with Grant Barney Schley. Nearby stood the rounded Henry O. Havemeyer mansion, along with the townhouses of Colonel Oliver Payne and

Mrs. Benjamin Thaw. So it continued to Ninety-third Street, site of the huge habitation of beer baron Jacob Ruppert.

Altogether sixty mansions—plus the Metropolitan Club, exotic Temple Beth-El, and a block-size McKim, Mead, and White apartment house—lined Millionaires' Row, with a dozen more due to appear before the end of World War I.

Ever-popular as a tourist attraction, the residences of the vastly rich also existed as architectural curiosities. As European-style mansions on the American continent they were, of course, a hothouse growth, almost as perishable as the orchids so frequently on display within their walls. In sad truth, the palaces of princely potentates were destined for a short life.

Already active in 1900 was a lively lady whose efforts hastened the doom of Renaissance living. Elsie de Wolfe by name, she was seen as "a lanky, black-haired, black-eyed little creature." Elsie's sense of personal style was the despair of fellow females; on her "a simple cotton frock becomes a poem, a shawl thrown across her shoulders an inspiration." As a mover and shaker of American culture, Elsie de Wolfe functioned to banish Victorian clutter, render massive mansions obsolete, and bring color, air, and light into interior decoration. "Suitability, simplicity, proportion" were the oft-repeated words of her credo. At other times, she said, "The cardinal virtue of all beauty is restraint." Or "Color should be treated kindly, and never allowed to get the best of a house or room."

Elsie grew up on the periphery of Gotham Society, living in a pleasant home where Macy's stands today. As a debutante, she had traveled overseas for presentation at the court of Queen Victoria. The girl's quick eye caught everything—"My senses have always been visual," she confessed. She was likewise obsessed by "a quest for beauty that has been my dearest adventure." When her parents redecorated their drawing room, the child Elsie erupted in a tantrum. "It's ugly, *ugly*," she shrieked at her elders.

Yet it took a number of years before Elsie became America's first modern interior decorator. At first she proved so good at amateur theatricals that producer Charles Frohman put her in important Broadway plays; in one, Ethel Barrymore served as her understudy. For ten years, Elsie de Wolfe played in the sophisticated works of Sardou and others, a remarkable career for a young lady of smug society. She also formed a close friendship with Elisabeth Marbury, another well-born girl who became America's first literary and play agent. Poison-pen *Town Topics* hinted at a lesbian duo.

As a Broadway actress, svelte Elsie received invitations to the best Fifth Avenue mansions. In them, her sharp senses recoiled at "windows unkindly in their attitude toward the light; walls and ceilings without respect for one another's dimensions; colors unfriendly to themselves and to the eye; ungainly furniture whose angles denied comfort."

Elsie's sense of color was ever paramount and her head burst with ideas for using chintz and other lively materials. Elisabeth Marbury sighed, "Never can she spend fifteen minutes amid new surroundings without longing to move the furniture, rearrange ornaments and paintings." She and Bessie Marbury bought a small house on Irving Place and used old objects like Louis XVI chairs, Nattier portraits, Houdon busts, and Savonnerie rugs to redecorate in fresh, spirited fashion.

Simultaneously, in the popular pages of the *Ladies Home Journal,* the decoration-conscious editor Edward Bok printed contrasting photos labeled "Good Taste—Bad Taste." All at once, the words "good taste" were in vogue, and to the social elite Elsie de Wolfe and her Irving Place home represented it. Even Mrs. Astor came to tea in order to view the "modern" decor.

Elsie felt especially sorry for multimillionaire friends like William C. Whitney, who resided in museum-like Fifth Avenue mansions, with suits of armor conspicuous in corners. "I am often amazed at the lack of taste in the houses of those who had an otherwise high degree of culture," she observed. "Many of them, dissatisfied with their surroundings, had no conception of what was wrong."

Elsie believed a drawing room should colorfully and comfortably reflect those who gathered in it; in other words, that room and people should belong together. She advocated dainty, vivid things like lampshades, wall mirrors, mantel ornaments, and lamps made from jars and vases. A painting, she thought, ought to be beautiful in itself, not for the scene portrayed. She utilized chintz and cretonne, wallpaper, pastel rugs, and thought up the tray-table and the popular ruffled, triple-mirrored vanity table. "Where do you get all these inspirations?" her baffled mother asked. Elsie could only reply, "I don't know, they must just come to me, I guess from my heart."

Deciding to go into business, she sent out cute cards announcing herself as an interior decorator; it was probably the first time the two words had ever been used in conjunction. Her telephone began ringing at once and never ceased until her death as Lady Mendl, at over ninety years of age.

Oddly enough, Elsie de Wolfe's first important job came from Stanford White. Commissioned to design the female-membership Colony Club on lower Madison Avenue, the architect insisted on Elsie for the decoration. She produced rooms of artful simplicity with sophisticated twists. Lattice-work in the dining room brought a garden-like relaxation and flowered chintz ran rampant throughout.

Yet her first commissions from the super-rich were not from Fifth Avenue, but from Mrs. Ogden Armour of Chicago, the Weyerhausers of Minneapolis, and Mrs. William Crocker of San Francisco, who with rare inspiration named her grand new estate "New Place." However, Elsie's headquarters remained in New York, with her career shooting ahead like an idea whose time has come. Continuing to lend support on a popular level was Edward Bok, who dismissed the mansions of Millionaires' Row as "repellently ornate."

The good-taste dictates of Elsie de Wolfe may have penetrated the consciousness of wives and daughters of Splendor Seekers, and possibly a few sons. But they failed utterly to influence the minds of the multimillionaires themsleves. This came as no surprise to the common people of the era, for the magic had begun rubbing off the image of the financial titans, allowing a monumental arrogance and callousness to shine through.

These millionaire moguls did indeed live in a world of their own, cushioned by wealth, hemmed in by subservience, with the other intoxicating ingredients adding up to Power. In each other's company, they might display doubts, fears, and insecurities, stemming chiefly from fear of being outsmarted by rivals and losing a few precious hundred-thousands. Sir Joseph Duveen, by this time embarked on his remarkable career of selling works of art to selected centimillionaires, found the breed "slow-speaking, slow-thinking, cautious, secretive—[having] trained themselves to talk slowly, pausing lengthily before each verb in order to keep themselves from sliding over into the abyss of commitment."

Before the rest of the world, however, these Yankee plutocrats behaved like lords of creation, seeming far different than the rest of the herd. Having gained their millions—and smugly believing anyone else could do the same by application—they considered themselves god-like personages.

Jay Gould, one of the first and boldest among them, said before a congressional committee, "*We* made this country rich, *we* have developed the country." Similar arrogance can be found in William Henry Vanderbilt's "The public be damned," as well as J. P. Morgan's "I owe the public nothing." Told the public ought to have a hand in running the railroads, the same Morgan exploded, "*Your* railroads! *Your* railroads belong to my clients!"

With one or two exceptions, the plutocrats considered it a duty no less than a pleasure to hoard millions of dollars. Colossal conceit told them that money was best off in their grasping hands. Dismissing the government as weak and Congress as venal, they viewed themselves as the best possible custodians of the nation's wealth. These power brokers actually justified refusals to raise workingmen's wages on the grounds that the money involved was best off with them. Robber Barons paid the lowest possible wages for the longest hours. Viciously fighting unionization, they resisted attempts to better working conditions, and considered themselves performing a service to the national economy. The financiers and bankers who operated solely on Wall Street gave wholehearted backing to this philosophy.

In justifying themselves, the plutocrats leaned heavily on religion, and tried to stand before the world as deeply devout. "God gave me my money," John D. Rockefeller declared. George F. Baer, president of the Philadelphia & Reading Coal & Iron Company, said, "The rights and interests of the laboring man will be protected and cared for by the Christian men to whom God has given control of the property rights of the country." Baer's reward came to him on earth; when J. P. Morgan needed a Pennsylvania hatchetman, Baer got the job.

Most plutocrats had abandoned the simple faiths of their fathers for more elaborate religions. Purse strings shut for other causes opened wide for churchly charities and edifices. Some went further—John D. Rockefeller and Cornelius Vanderbilt II taught Sunday school, and J. P. Morgan sank to his knees in church to sing hymns along with the noonday organ recital.

To most of them, the ability to accrue money represented a gift from Above. "I believe the power to make money is a gift of God," said Rockefeller, "and having been endowed with the gift I possess I believe it is my duty to make more and still more money." Others acknowledged divine aid with equally fervent words. Clergymen, eager for financial largesse, seconded this notion. "In the long run it is only to the man of morality that wealth comes," intoned a bishop. "Godliness is in league with riches."

In view of such convictions, there was small chance of a Splendor Seeker dramatically changing his mind in the course of a lifetime. To him, a Fifth Avenue mansion had always seemed the best way to impress the world, and the dawn of a new century made no difference to this entrenched belief. So mansions continued rising along Millionaires' Row, even though the rest of the world might be ready for a cultural change.

The first magnate to reaffirm faith in mansions after 1900 was Andrew Carnegie, the Pittsburgh Steel King. Described as "a mite of a man but all of it dynamo," Carnegie was an energetic but diminutive five-foot-four, a man who weighed in at 130 and proudly wore a size five shoe. But not everything about Carnegie was small. "His head is round and big and hard and Scotch and full of brains," a friend wrote. His career had been a glowing evocation of the rags-to-riches precepts of G. A. Henty and Horatio Alger. Born in 1837 of poor parents in Scotland, he was brought to Allegheny City, Pennsylvania. By age twelve, he was working as a bobbin-boy in a factory at his father's side. Two years later the father died and Andy became the sole support of mother and brother.

As a messenger boy in a telegraph office, he mastered telegraphy and allowed his grasping mind and inherent optimism to shove him up the ladder of success. He was hired as secretary to the superintendent of the Pittsburgh division of the Pennsylvania Railroad, then got the job himself and made history by forcing acceptance of the Pullman Sleeping Car. Next, he branched out on his own in iron works, bridge building, and oil holdings.

"Whatever I engage in, I must push inordinately," he wrote in his diary. Thus the secret of his success might seem to be learning every aspect of a job before him. In part this was true, but the tiny man actually excelled as an inspired salesman in an era when the salesman, traveling or otherwise, was a vital cog in the economy. Carnegie was also a tireless flatterer, conniver, and greedy bargainer in top-echelon financial deals.

He also said, "Pioneering don't pay," and capitalized on the trailblazing efforts of others. Observing a Bessemer converter at work in an English factory, the iron-oriented man raced back to Pittsburgh to proclaim, "The day of iron has ended—steel is king!" The smartest business move he made was to drop his many activities and concentrate on steel. The sharp little man improved his factories during depressions and stood ready to gain when good times returned. As a steel magnate, he lifted America from fifth to first among world producers. In 1899, his Carnegie Steel Corporation showed profits of $40 million.

Oddly enough, this man so closely associated with Pittsburgh was more of a New Yorker, having moved there with his beloved mother in 1867. He made frequent trips to Pittsburgh, but considered Manhattan a superior field for his inspired salesmanship and skill at putting together big deals. Carnegie was able to operate that way because of his uncanny ability to pick the right associates and his willingness—rare among his breed—to delegate authority. Once he suggested as his epitaph, "Here lies a man who knew how to get around him men cleverer than himself." He held on to the right men by giving limited partnerships and paying such high salaries that another job became unthinkable. Over the years he depended heavily on the abilities of Captain Bill Jones, Henry and Lawrence Phipps, Henry Clay Frick, and Charles M. Schwab.

But this is not to say that Carnegie Steel was a big, happy family. The little man kept his partners at each others' throats by playing on their fears, jealousies, and inherent competitiveness. It was his belief that by so doing he increased production and efficiency.

Nor was tiny Andy a benevolent employer. "The most cruel taskmaster American industry has ever known," he was branded. As greedy, or greedier, than other Robber Barons, he too schemed to pay minimum wages for maximum labor. His public statements were replete with admiring references to "honest poverty," a condition in which he hoped to keep workers. Plant managers and shop foremen paid heed to his constant cry, "Lower costs, more production! More! More! More!"

Fiercely opposed to unions, he did not hesitate to close down his works to break a strike. In a weak moment, he allowed Captain Bill Jones to persuade him that men worked better on eight-hour shifts. It gnawed at him and soon he shut down operations, ostensibly to install new equipment. He reopened on twelve-hour shifts, asserting that the equipment made the work easier.

Carnegie also sailed off to his native Scotland in 1892 after imposing a wage cut at his Homestead plant, ten miles up the Monongahela from Pittsburgh. Behind him, he left general manager Henry Clay Frick, who had abdicated as Pennsylvania's Coke Baron to become the hard-nosed head of Carnegie operations. When the steel workers struck over the wage cut, Frick recruited 300 burly strikebreakers through the Pinkerton Detective Agency. In armed barges, they crossed the Monongahela River, but the steel workers fought back so furiously that the Pinkertons surrendered. Frick had to appeal to the Governor to send in 8,000 militia.

The battle of Homestead remains the bloodiest blot on American labor history. During it, Carnegie calmly fished for salmon in Scotland. Said an associate, "Andy was like the piano player in a whorehouse who tries to pretend he doesn't know what's going on around him."

As opposed to other millions-makers, Carnegie liked to relax and enjoy life. In 1878, he took a trip around the world and wrote a readable book about it. A year later he toured the British Isles and produced another volume. He had inherited a love of literature from his father, and his mind was an unexpected storehouse of quotations ranging from folksy homilies to Bobby Burns and the exalted words of Byron and Shakespeare. With this, though, he was indifferent to political and worldly matters. "His general ignorance was colossal," a friend said.

Carnegie's mother died in 1886, when he was fifty-one. Five months later he married a twenty-eight-year-old girl known to him since her babyhood. He had vowed never to marry while his mother lived, but began seriously to court his bride-to-be when she turned twenty-one. He had many anxious moments, for the pretty girl had other male admirers. Still, she held out for Andy.

After the marriage, the couple moved into the onetime Collis Huntington brownstone on West Fifty-first Street, a pleasant but not social area favored by such diverse personalities as John D. Rockefeller and Mrs. Pembroke Jones. Ten years after the wedding, Mrs. Carnegie gave birth to a daughter. To celebrate, Andy bought a steam yacht and built Skibo, a castle in Scotland surrounded by 40,000 acres, with towns and human beings under the sway of the laird of the manor. At Skibo, Carnegie was called "the Star-Spangled Scotsman."

As 1900 approached, this proud possessor of wife, child, and massive millions began to ponder retirement. Almost alone among America's millionaires, he believed that a fortune earned from the public should be returned to the people by way of philanthropy. In explanation of this he often quoted Shakespeare, "So disposition should undo success / And each man have enough." On other occasions he said, "He who dies rich, dies disgraced."

Over the past twenty years the books he had written—*Empire of Business, Problems of Today,* and *Gospels of Wealth*—touched on philanthropy. His idea was to give away every dollar of his wealth, except ten percent retained for wife and daughter. Thus the wellsprings of his benevolence lay far deeper than those of John D. Rockefeller, who began to give away money only when warned by men like Bet-a-Million Gates who said to him, "Your fortune is rolling up—like an avalanche. You must keep up with it! You must distribute it faster than it grows! If you do not, it will crush you, and your children, and your children's children."

Perhaps Carnegie, at age sixty-four, also realized his particular era had ended. In his day, small companies had been merged into large monopolies. Now, pursuant to the vision of J. P. Morgan, large monopolies were in turn being merged into huge ones. "Billion dollar trusts," they were called by Bet-A-Million Gates, a man involved in the process.

In 1901, Carnegie dramatically sold out to Morgan, figuring in his precise Scottish way that the price for the steel corporation should be $487,556,160, of which he kept $300 million himself. The rest was divided among his limited partners, with a not-too-generous $4.5 million fund set aside for the welfare of his 45,000 steel company workers. "This makes you the richest man in the world," Morgan supposedly remarked at the end of the transaction. It was not exactly true, for that eminence always remained with Rockefeller. But it was correct in the matter of fluid fortune and remains a graceful tribute from one moneybags to another. Morgan, incidentally, would have been appalled had he known Carnegie really intended to give away his fortune.

But he did. Over succeeding years, until his death in 1919, little Andy performed the herculean task of giving away his millions. During six months of the year, when not resident at his Skibo demesne in Scotland, he performed this rite from a granite-and-brick Georgian mansion designed for him by the firm of Babb, Cook, and Willard. Fifty rooms in all, it occupied the block front on Fifth Avenue between Ninetieth and

Ninety-first Streets, the official address being 2 East Ninety-first Street. Carnegie had paid $850,000 for the land and another $1 million for the mansion and its decoration; altogether he owned 201 feet on Fifth Avenue and 276 extending backward. The press named the mansion "Highlands," in part because of Carnegie's Scottish ancestry, but also because it occupied what passed for a hill on the Avenue.

Protected on all sides by a high iron fence, this elbow-room mansion was encompassed by a green expanse of well-kept lawn, gardens, and large trees, with the house itself picturesquely vine-covered. Altogether, its country-life appearance provided a welcome change from the unrelieved masonry of Millionaires' Row. Sometimes Carnegie could be seen through the fence, reading under a tree, surveying his gardens, or strolling. Once in a while, he walked over to converse with those peering in. For despite his strained, almost simian appearance in photographs, the Master of the Highlands could be a friendly fellow, with a puckish sense of humor. Mark Twain, a close friend, thought him "rollicking."

The interior of the Carnegie mansion was sumptuous but never ostentatious. None of its rooms had been transported from overseas, but the decorators provided enough satin-walled ballrooms and red-brocade drawing rooms for the owner to rank as a Splendor Seeker. Despite Carnegie's lack of stature, the rooms were unusually large and high ceilinged. One Louis Quinze salon was topped by a gilt encrusted ceiling, with paneled walls, framed tapestries, and marble fireplaces with matching mirrors on either side. It was filled—too filled, perhaps—with curved-leg chairs decorated in marquetry, marble-topped tables, delicate sofas with outsize American pillows, and footstools. Amidst this French delicacy stood a sizeable potted palm—or was it an areca tree?

Greeting the eye on entering this residence was a painting that showed what one millionaire could do for another. Before erecting Skibo, the Carnegies had leased a Scottish castle that included Hoppner's portrait of the Duke of Dorset among its treasures. Carnegie admired it greatly. As the Fifth Avenue mansion neared completion, Carnegie's colleague Henry Phipps moved heaven and earth to buy the Hoppner, finally making an offer so good the owners could not refuse. When Carnegie finally set foot in his new abode, the delighted Croesus saw the Hoppner before him.

In every room of the mansion hung homilies like "God Bless Our Home" or "Sleep Sweetly in This Quiet Room." Most were printed in gold letters on watered silk. Carnegie's own bedroom was ascetic, decorated mainly by a chromo portrait of Captain Bill Jones, who had died in a steel mill explosion. The mansion included a mighty organ that reverberated everywhere, for Carnegie was a man who believed a taste for good music was as necessary as a taste for good reading. Each morning, by his order, he was awakened by the swelling sound of the organ; at Skibo Castle, bagpipes outside his window did the trick.

Across the fireplace in the library ran Carnegie's favorite motto, "The Hearth Our Altar, Its Flame Our Sacred Fire." There the architect learned a lesson about centimillionaires. J. P. Morgan, when told the carpets for his original yacht *Corsair* were no longer being made, ordered that the design be created again and mounted on fresh looms. Carnegie's architect informed him that his pet motto had too many letters to fit over the fireplace. "Then tear down the house and build it with a larger library and bigger fireplace," the little Scotsman ordered, and apparently meant it. The architect contrived to make the motto fit.

The great and near-great beat a path to Carnegie, for among the Splendor Seekers he was the most accessible and stimulating. He told stories so well that Sir Henry Irving swore he should have been an actor. In addition, Carnegie served a Scotch known as Queen's Vat, supposedly distilled for the lips of Queen Victoria. He kept friends supplied with cases of this smoothest of libations and also sent an annual supply to the White House, no matter who the President.

Carnegie liked to spar mentally with men like Theodore Roosevelt and naturalist John Burroughs. His close friend, Richard Watson Gilder saluted him as "a tremendous personality—dramatic, wilful, generous, whimsical, at times almost cruel in pressing his own convictions upon others, and then again tender, affectionate, emotional, always imaginative, unusual, and wide visioned in his views."

In one of the fifty rooms hung the surprising aphorism "The Chief Glory of a Nation Is Its Authors." Believing it implicitly, Carnegie set aside a fund of $50,000 for needy writers and provided rooms for an Authors' Club in Carnegie Hall. Once a year he hosted a convivial Authors' Dinner in his mansion, inviting the likes of Mark Twain, Henry James, Brander Matthews, and Thomas Bailey Aldrich. Each guest signed the tablecloth and his signature was then embroidered into it. The following year an author sat by his name, while new guests added their own.

When not serving as host, Carnegie played God by brooding long hours over the endless requests for money that came his way. Every mail brought loads of begging letters from all over the world. Carnegie had them investigated and, if honest, paid off. He gave pensions to numerous people out of his past, including a grizzled Scotsman who claimed to have rocked him in the cradle. He once told the graduating class of a girls' school to write him when they married. To each, as a wedding gift, he sent $500.

Yet his real interest lay in giant benefactions. "Can you tell me how I can spend $5 million to $10 million to the best public advantage?" he inquired of a select list of prominent men. His first library was given to his birthplace in Scotland, with his mother laying the cornerstone. His initial gift as a full-time philanthropist was $5.25 million for sixty-eight Manhattan public libraries, followed by funds for twenty more in Brooklyn. Public libraries became his most publicized benefaction and he erected them in many parts of the English-speaking world, with only one-third bearing his name. In all, he gave 2,811 libraries, 1,946 in the United States, the others in England, Scotland, or Canada. Their price was $60,364,808.

But it must be remembered that Carnegie gave only library buildings. Books to fill the shelves were the responsibility of each community. He referred to his libraries as "bribes" and said, "I do not wish to be remembered for what I have given, but for what I have persuaded others to give."

Even before his retirement, he had built Carnegie Hall for

New York City and was properly respectful when Peter Ilyitch Tchaikovsky came from Russia for the gala opening. He gave away as many pipe organs as libraries, and also established a $5 million Heroes' Fund, to reward acts of heroism as well as provide pensions for relatives of those who died heroically; this was probably his favorite charity. He built the Peace Palace at The Hague at a cost of $1.5 million and supported antiwar causes. But all of his famed philanthropies faded in comparison with the millions given the Carnegie Institute to provide research facilities for increasing man's knowledge and a Carnegie Fund to perpetuate the benefactions.

In eighteen years, he gave away the stupendous sum of $350,695,653. Doing so, Carnegie presented the picture of a Croesus living a happy life. Early in the game a secretary warned him that he had exhausted the huge annual interest on his fortune and was going into principal. "Delighted to hear it, my boy," Carnegie chirped. "Let's keep it up."

The fact that within the imposing Carnegie mansion sat a man dispensing money in million-dollar chunks brought a special aura to the surroundings. People stood on Fifth Avenue gazing longingly through the iron bars of the fence, hoping to see Carnegie and engage his help. It was not difficult to find him at times, for as years passed the tiny man began a regime of fast two-mile hikes around the Central Park Reservoir, after which he rested quietly on a bench.

However, he was no help to those in quest of small loans. Long before turning philanthropist, he grew famous as one of the multimillionaires who walked around without money in his jeans; Senator Clark was another. In the last years of his life, Carnegie was usually accompanied on outside trips by a male secretary or bodyguard who paid any bills. Still, the agile little Scotsman liked to escape and run off on his own. Newspaper stories told of him boarding buses or streetcars and being unable to pay the fare. Sometimes he was recognized and given a free ride, but occasionally an irate conductor threw him off.

While Andrew Carnegie dispensed his millions at the top end of Millionaires' Row, a Midas-into-Maecenas lower down the Av-

enue hewed closer to the traditional pattern. Thomas Fortune
Ryan, fifty-four years of age in 1905, had become the latest to
enter the gilded ranks of mansion dwellers. He had established
himself at 858 Fifth Avenue, at Sixty-seventh Street, next door to
the Yerkes domicile, where Mara then lived in dwindling splendor.

Tall, commanding, determined, and broadfaced, with a wide
cleft chin decorating an iron jaw, Ryan on occasion made use of
courtly Virginia manners inherited as the offspring of an Irish-
Scotch family ruined by the Civil War. An orphan at fourteen,
the gangling, penniless youth had made his way to Baltimore.
Late one afternoon he wandered into the large dry goods emporium of John S. Barry, who hired him at $3 a week as boy of
all work. "Report tomorrow morning," Barry instructed. The
youth grabbed a broom and energetically began sweeping the
floor. "If you please, sir, I'd rather begin right away," he said.

If his respectful biographers are to be believed, Ryan even
then aspired to become the richest man in the world—not just
rich, the *richest*! The luck of the Irish aided him, for he fell in
love with Ida Barry, his boss's daughter, and she with him. John
S. Barry had connections on Wall Street, the locality Ryan had
picked as springboard to fortune. As a result of his employer's
influence he began in 1872 to work for a New York brokerage
house as runner. He quickly won promotion for, in the words of
a biography, "No firm could afford to overlook the worth of a
youth who did nothing but study and strive to get ahead in the
business." As fast as possible, he made Ida Barry his bride.

The luck of the Irish again arose as Ryan and William C.
Whitney merged formidable talents in the transit monopoly undertaken with the backing of Widener millions from Philadelphia. While Whitney, as the conspicuous front man, piled up his
first $40 million, Ryan as treasurer and backstage manipulator of
stocks, bonds, interlocking corporations, and directorships perfected his skills and acquired millions of his own. At one point
Whitney paid tribute to Ryan as "the most adroit, suave, and
noiseless man American finance has ever known."

Assuming charge of the fabulously profitable Syndicate after
Whitney's semi-retirement, Ryan proved his mettle by grabbing

stock of the badly managed American Tobacco Company for a little more than $50,000. Making use of watered stock, he promoted an initial capitalization of $10 million and by other devious means over-capitalized at $180 million with practically no cost to himself.

This might have been enough for any man, but for Ryan it meant only a beginning. Next, he won control of the Equitable Life Assurance Company, with assets of $500 million; the Morton Trust Company, soon to merge with Guaranty Trust, which among other things controlled the underlying railroad securities of Manhattan and the Bronx; the National Bank of Commerce, second largest in the nation; and other less prestigious holdings.

As his victories multiplied, an admirer said the financial world had become Ryan's plaything. His net worth had reached at least $75 million, of which he kept a balance of $10 million perpetually in his bank account. Unlike Carnegie and Senator Clark, he never left home with less than $10,000 on his person.

In matters beyond business, Ryan inclined to follow the star of William C. Whitney. At times, he tried race horses, but lacked the true passion. Strangely, he made no attempt to rescue the Whitney mansion as it slipped into the possession of Silent Smith. But in 1905, having contentedly raised a large family at 60 Fifth Avenue, he began to dream of a mansion on Millionaires' Row. Like Whitney, he decided not to build from the ground up. Instead, he purchased 858 Fifth Avenue and set an army of workmen to gutting the interior for the latest Manhattan wonderland.

Mrs. Ida Barry Ryan emerges as one of the few Splendor Seeker wives to have visible effect on a Fifth Avenue palace. In her lifetime, this devout lady presented $20 million of her husband's money to the Catholic Church and as reward earned the title of papal countess. Of her it was said, "The only elegance Ida esteemed was that found in church interiors." Her husband considered this predilection depressing and solved a potential domestic schism by purchasing the mansion to the south of him—the Yerkes mansion stood to the north. By throwing the two houses together, Ryan made a background for both his own and his wife's taste.

Ryan's half of the premises came to be called an American Louvre, which raises the question of this man's extraordinary artistic sensitivity. William C. Whitney's superlative taste was cerebral. Ryan's, on the other hand, was visceral or intuitive; he instinctively "felt" what was good. Many people have pondered the mystery of Ryan's taste. Writes Andrew Tully, "He bought only what he liked; and liked and understood what he bought." But this does not explain how a notably secretive and mercenary man had enough good taste to amass an art assortment thought by some to be "more solid" than the Whitney, Morgan, and (eventually) Frick collections. Finally one man sighed and said, "He must have acquired his taste for art behind the underwear counter back in Baltimore." It seemed as good an answer as any.

The Ryan mansion, completed in 1908, was furnished for the most part in heavy Florentine style, with a sprinkling of touches in French and English. Ryan's private chapel, with four-ton altar and choir stalls, had been wrested from an Italian palazzo. This Maecenas did not favor large paintings, either Old Masters or Barbizons, though he did own a few. For the most part he expressed himself by means of tapestries, triptyches, and porcelains. His state rooms abounded in sixteenth-century Florentine furniture, Gothic and Renaissance paintings and sculpture, Belgian tapestries, Oriental and 32-foot Persian rugs, Etruscan bronzes, Limoges enamels, Italian majolica, and Chinese cloissonné. His collection of Limoges enamels was called the world's finest; his most cherished Italian works of art came from the Davanzati and Montevecchio palazzi, whose furnishings set the standard for Renaissance art. A cassone, or chest, bore the coat of arms of the Barbarini family, another the Salvati crest.

Ryan had torn out the ballroom of the original Fifth Avenue mansion and replaced it with his art gallery, the ceiling after Ricci, the Venetian disciple of Tiepolo. Sixteenth-century stained-glass windows from the Flavigny Abbey in Lorraine cast light over the collection. Ryan owned the magnificent triptych *Crucifixion and Admiration of the Infant Jesus,* from the Monvaerni *atelier,* and *Entry into Jerusalem* by Nardon Penicaud, the latter exceptional for its "wealth of incandescent blues, purples, and greens." He also owned twelve plaques once the property of a

King of Portugal; a wondrous woven Pieta; and peerless Isfahan carpets. Some of these items may have shown the influence of his religious wife, but Ryan's own taste burst forth in robust Rodin sculptures, among them a muscular nude figure of John the Baptist, plus a brooding *Napoleon Wrapped in His Dreams*. At the same time, many of his favorite paintings were by the living Spanish artist Sorolla y Bastida, one of Ryan's friends.

Ryan had a deep fondness for his Renaissance Room, and sat there for hours soaking up the classic vibrations. Once in a while he curled up on a couch and passed the night surrounded by treasures like a duo of angels by Pavia, a Rossellino Madonna and Child, a Gothic marble Pietà, a massive Florentine fireplace, and a gorgeous tapestry of woven silver and gold. Among his sculptures was the near-priceless head-and-shoulders of Beatrice of Aragon, done in 1475 by Francesco Laurana.

Ryan passed other nights in a bedroom as notable for cost as for antiquity. He had paid $200,000 for a carved ivory bedstead, inlaid with gold; $65,000 for walls of enamel and gold; $20,000 for a ceiling of elaborate carvings; $2,000 apiece for ten pairs of filmy window curtains; $125,000 for a medieval wardrobe; $65,000 for a dressing table; $8,000 for chimney piece and overhanging mantel; and $50 a yard for bed hangings.

From time to time after 1908, the iron-jawed Robber Baron informed the world that he planned to quit his corporations and thirty-two directorships to retire and enjoy life. Ostensibly for this purpose, he had also bought a 4,000-acre farm at Lovingston, Virginia, his birthplace.

It never happened. In fact, Thomas Fortune Ryan's outstanding moments came after the completion of his mansion when he bought into railroads, public utilities, and became influential in Democratic politics. King Leopold II of the Belgians appointed Ryan head of a syndicate to exploit the resources of the Congo. The Congolese diamonds, gold, and copper shot his fortune into the hundred millions. In 1913, he humored his devout wife by building the $1 million Church of St. Jean Baptiste at the corner of Lexington Avenue and Seventy-sixth Street.

Yet for our purposes, Ryan becomes celebrated for the most prodigal gesture ever made by a Splendor Seeker along Millionaires' Row. This incredible man loved flowers as much as art. Already his property displayed a stunning, well-tended expanse of roses, lilies, birch trees, jungle vines, and Italian statues and fountains. Deeming this insufficient, Ryan shelled out $1,239,000 for the now-vacant Yerkes mansion next door and had it razed solely to make way for a bigger Ryan garden, with teahouse and wrought-iron pavillion. Of the Yerkes mansion, he saved only the famed doge's palace staircase and thirty-two marble columns. He retained these to allow his roses and vines to twine around them.

Thus the Croesus had a private cloister covering nearly half a block of fabulously expensive real estate. Like Carnegie, Ryan could sometimes be seen in the glory of his garden. But where Carnegie was always primly dressed Ryan favored a picturesque Chinese robe, floppy straw hat, and carpet slippers. Thus attired, he liked to breakfast in the teahouse or pavillion. At other times, he sat reading in his garden. His partisans declared his favorite books were Plutarch and Gibbon; enemies claimed he read nothing but corporate reports and stock quotations.

But what of the super-capitalist who erected his mansion on Riverside Drive, rather than Fifth? How can such an aberration be explained?

He was Charles M. Schwab, president of United States Steel, the monopolistic giant created by J. P. Morgan with the purchase of Carnegie interests. Schwab had also been president of Carnegie Steel, with Carnegie himself chairman of the board. Lively, personable, irrepressibly young, Charley Schwab seemed an odd man to find among the Robber Barons. Yet no one ever appeared more at home in their company.

Schwab's life had all the ingredients of an operetta with a background of the American scene in its colorful industrial and financial aspects. This would be especially appropriate because Schwab was a music-minded fellow, with a fine singing voice and an ability to play musical instruments, including the organ.

Schwab, with his pleasantly Germanic looks, emerges as the golden boy of American industry. Outgoing and friendly, he was

popular with his fellow moguls and the sweaty workers before
blast furnaces, who respected his rapid progress from bottom to
top in the steel business. "He was a man of many sides and
enjoyed them all," says one tribute. An upright young man from
the small town of Loretto, Pennsylvania, he journeyed at age
sixteen to nearby Braddock to labor in steel mills owned by Carnegie. Behind him lay two years in a college run by Franciscan
brothers who gave him a grounding in Latin and Greek, music
and mathematics. He was cocky and assured, but never annoy-
ingly so.

Charley Schwab's first job in steel was driving stakes at $1 a
day. Two miraculous years later he was chief engineer of the
works. Schwab was a student of any job he held, studying it in
depth until its mastery made him superior to colleagues and
competitors. In his first days inside the plant, he became aware
of the importance of chemistry in the steel process. Making
friends with the company chemist, he learned that aspect of the
job. He also married the chemist's daughter. At first, money was
so tight for the newlyweds that Charley gave music lessons at
fifty cents an hour.

Carnegie's rare ability to pick the right men was never demonstrated better than with Schwab, who not only became a master
steelmaker but specialized in such elementary psychological
tricks as provoking day and night shifts into competition. Like
Carnegie, he was also a superb salesman. His personal
philosophy of success was, "I expect every man to do a little more
than he's paid for—*I do*!" Early on, he learned how to amuse
Carnegie and keep him laughing. After the shameful Homestead battle, Schwab was appointed general manager of Homestead and Braddock. He too was anti-union, capable of capitalis-
tic statements like, "I will not permit myself to be put in a position where labor can dictate to management." Yet he was such a
capable, democratic guy that workers found him impossible to
hate.

When Carnegie and Henry Clay Frick fought between themselves, Schwab became president of Carnegie Steel at age
thirty-five. Carnegie paid him $1 million a year, and six percent
of profits. With this stimulus, he lifted annual production from a

million annual tons to twelve million with profits rising from $7 million to $40 million a year. This brought his annual salary close to $3 million.

With this amount of lucre rolling in, Schwab's aspirations naturally turned to thoughts of a Manhattan Island palace. But why Riverside Drive? We can only guess that he was unable to find a suitable corner along Millionaires' Row; that he wished to demonstrate his own individuality; or that he was alert enough to realize that lacking suitable lawns and gardens the majority of mansions on Fifth Avenue looked a trifle ridiculous. By choosing a block on Riverside Drive and West End Avenue, between Seventy-third and Seventy-fourth Streets, Schwab not only found a great river at his door, but also had elbow-room grounds for baronial gardens, walks, and proper statuary.

It was strange that other moguls had not built on Riverside Drive, for the view from floors above street level gave the uncanny impression of hanging over the river. Mrs. Graham Fair Vanderbilt lived on Riverside Drive, as did Bishop Potter and William Randolph Hearst. But for the most part High Society and the Big Money had passed it by, leaving the Drive to be filled with small, attractive Beaux Arts residences. With his full block there, Schwab had grabbed one of the finest sites in the city.

In 1900, the extroverted Schwab acted as catalyst in the Morgan monopoly of steel. At a dinner in his honor, the golden-tongued man rose before 100 top financiers and industrialists to wax so eloquent over the potential of steel that J. P. Morgan was smitten with the idea of a monster trust. Schwab easily persuaded Andy Carnegie to sell out, and as a result became the first president of Morgan's United States Steel, with a salary of $2 million a year and share of the profits. Yet he was not altogether comfortable as head of this billion-dollar trust. "Too many bosses," he complained about Morgan and his grim-visaged partners. "Those fellows think running a steel company is the same as floating a bond issue."

Nevertheless, he dared to emulate Carnegie by placing experienced men in the major posts of the corporation, while making New York his home and reserving himself for summit duties. Said he, "I am making more than two million a year, but it's hard work; the luxuries and pleasures I enjoy in New York will keep me in better shape to do that work."

Schwab kept a firm hand on U. S. Steel, and even bought the moribund Bethlehem Steel Company as kind of hobby. His Riverside Drive mansion was underway and already people labeled it as the most impressive in town. The land had cost him $800,000, the construction amounted to $2 million and the elaborate interior decoration raised the total to the vicinity of $5 million. "Have you seen that place of Charley's?" Andrew Carnegie asked. "It makes mine look like a cottage."

During the construction period, Schwab hired the ever-available Drexel yacht for $25,000 a month and took wife, mother, and father on a Mediterranean cruise. For several nights he appeared at the Monte Carlo gaming tables, and an American newspaper erroneously reported him breaking the bank. The American public was tickled, but the barons of U. S. Steel took on a grimmer look; strangely, their disapproval was supported by Carnegie who may, after all, have been jealous of the spectacular rise of his personable protégé. Morgan and his associates failed to realize that, at a time of growing antitrust feeling among the populace, good-time Charley Schwab shone as a walking advertisement for capitalism. On Schwab's return to this country tense confrontations took place, and he quit U. S. Steel.

His mansion, named by Schwab "On the Hudson," was still a-building, with the plump and wholesome Mrs. Schwab in almost daily attendance to supervise. "On the Hudson" rose four stories of gabled and turreted magnificence, with state rooms on the first floor, living rooms and bedrooms on the second, guest rooms for seventy people on the third, and servants on the fourth, together with basement and sub-basement. The building was of cream granite and reddish stone, surmounted by slate roofs. As designed by architect Maurice Ebert, its strong facade and courtyard on the Drive derived from the cherished château of Chenonceaux, with the great wings showing intimations of the châteaux at Blois and Azay-le-Rideau. Inside were seventy-five rooms and forty bathrooms.

Out of his job at U. S. Steel, Schwab applied his brilliant energies to reviving the weakling Bethlehem Steel, improving it to
the point of competition with the colossal steel trust. Still in his
early forties, he was a whirlwind of industry and inspiration,
operating in a field that never bored him. "He was always talking
about steel," said a friend, "and I never saw him in the doldrums
where it was concerned." His was admittedly the sharpest mind
in the business, and he set about evolving profitable new techniques. Sensing the imminence of war in the world, he quietly
bought shipyards.

This required him to be away from New York, but he still
found time to spend in the Riverside Drive mansion that became
his delight. The Schwabs moved in over Christmas 1905, though
scaffolds and ladders still filled the premises. When completed,
the mansion stood as probably the purest example of Renaissance style in the United States. Schwab may have hired the
services of decorator Arthur Brunet, but the steel master himself
reputedly designed the first and second floors. Decoration
reflected the period between 1450–1500, generally considered
the flowering of French architecture. The first floor stood twenty
feet above Riverside Drive, with the imposing Francis I main hall
rising another two and a half stories to a vaulted ceiling. Statues
stood in niches and light from John La Farge windows threw
mellow light.

Around this hall at second-story level ran an elaborate gallery,
or balcony, leading to the principal chambers on the floor, one a
music room containing the inevitable organ which Schwab could
personally play. A steep staircase of white marble with bronze
balustrade mounted to the gallery. The house also boasted three
elevators with heavy bronze doors and velvet-topped banquettes.
Until now no mansion in New York possessed more than a single
elevator.

Schwab's library was patterned after Fontainbleau and his
state drawing room copied Le Petit Trianon, with the addition of
Boucher tapestries. The arched dining room was Louis
Quatorze decorated by Gobelin tapestries representing the four
seasons, matching those hanging in Versailles. A large conser-

vatory could be combined with the dining room to make a banquet hall for 1,500 diners.

The art gallery, occupying the entire Seventy-fourth Street wing, displayed paintings by Rembrandt, Hals, Velásquez, Diaz, Corot, and Inness; the owner's favorite was Titian's *Portrait of Cardinal Pietro Bombo.* Schwab also owned Turner's *Rockets and Blue Lights*, once the Yerkes' pride. A smoking room was Flemish; a breakfast room Louis XIII; a billiard room Henry II, with an African mahogany wine closet on one wall. There were also a colonnaded swimming pool, bowling alley, and steam rooms. The tall Renaissance towers at the Riverside Drive corners rose 116 feet, giving an incomparable view of the Hudson and the Palisades. Schwab slumbered on a wide, canopied bed.

Three chefs labored in the electrified kitchen, where the refrigerator could (and did) hold twenty tons of meat—a radical publication figured this would feed a family of five for eight years. Those who stayed at the Schwab mansion often felt like guests in a hotel, a comparison not exactly unsuitable. The residence had its own flashing telephone switchboard, together with heating and lighting plants, and other facilities suitable for a 2,000 room hostelry. Altogether the cost of annual upkeep came to $500,000.

In these opulent confines Charley Schwab, always a devout Catholic, had mass said for him every morning in a private chapel with a ten-ton altar that had cost $35,000; a priest from a nearby chapel officiated. The master of the mansion also played his organ every day but Sunday, when the professional Archer Gibson gave a recital for selected guests. Top musical and theatrical names flocked to Schwab's dinners and parties, with Caruso, Kreisler, Sembrich, Schumann-Heink, and Zimbalist prominent. When Schwab dined and wined his capitalist friends, Caruso sang for a fee of $10,000.

"Charley Schwab enjoyed ostentation," thinks Lucius Beebe. Another author says he aspired to graceful rather than grand living, though his surroundings can only be called grand. Motherly Mrs. Schwab, who did not seem to mind her increasing girth, supervised the care of lawns and gardens, a not inconsiderable task in view of the grandiose landscaping around the Schwab château.

Friends said Mrs. Schwab would have been much happier back in Loretto, Pennsylvania, where the couple also maintained a home; Schwab had named his elegant private railroad car *Loretto*. But if Charley Schwab was happy amidst his surpassing decor, his ever-loving spouse was prepared to go along cheerfully.

The public repeated stories of the democratic Schwab shooting craps with his help and introducing a manservant to the King of Sweden with the words, "King, this is my valet—he's a Swede, too!" New Yorkers looked at the Schwab mansion, the only one so far in a proper setting, and thought that of all the Splendor Seekers breezy Charley Schwab must be the nicest one to know.

13

The Winner

TWENTY-FIVE long years had passed since—you will recall—Henry Clay Frick and his young friend Andrew Mellon paused during a Manhattan sightseeing tour to sit looking with admiration and appraisal at William Henry Vanderbilt's Twin Mansion at 640 Fifth Avenue. Now, amazingly, this same Henry Clay Frick and family were ensconced as occupants of this Vanderbilt mansion.

The first factor behind this sensational social leap was the availability of the mansion, which after the death of Mrs. William Henry became the property of youngest son George Washington Vanderbilt. But he had removed himself to Asheville, North Carolina, where Richard Morris Hunt designed for him the noblest countryside mansion in America. Called Biltmore, it is set in the midst of a 130,000 acre barony.

Also involved was the great rise in the fortunes of Henry Clay Frick, who had $1 million on first viewing the Vanderbilt mansion and now had $77 million. Frick had been born in 1849 on a farm in Westmoreland County, Pennsylvania. His redheaded father was Swiss-Irish, his mother a daughter of the Germanic Overholt distilling family, who earned parental displeasure by marrying a lowly farmer. As a youth Henry Clay Frick displayed literary and artistic leanings, avidly reading the few magazines that came his way and nailing illustrations to his bedroom wall. But the Fricks were dirt poor (as the Overholts had predicted) and artistic inclinations were shelved in favor of earning a living.

After only thirty months of what might be called formal schooling, Frick went to work in a local grocery store, getting as pay his board and the right to sleep on the counter. Finally, he managed to take a business-school course in accounting, which won him a $1,000 a year job in the Overholt distillery. At twenty-one he became convinced of the importance of coke in the industrial processes of the future and persuaded Judge Mellon of Pittsburgh, Andrew's father, to finance his entry into the field.

Frick made his first million by age thirty and was hailed as Pennsylvania's Coke King. Yet in 1889 he elected to go to work for Andrew Carnegie as iron-fisted general manager, efficiency expert, and trouble shooter, a position necessary because the rapid expansion of Carnegie Steel had rendered its operations unwieldy. Despite the new post, Frick retained the old coke holdings and even sold his product to Carnegie. A seasoned plutocrat, he joined Andy Carnegie in shamelessly standing before the world to swear that Carnegie Steel lost money, when actually millions rolled in.

Frick believed the American workingman should perform his job thankfully, without protest over pay, hours, or working conditions. He held unions in contempt and coated his feelings in pompous words like "We propose to manage our own business as we think proper and right." Asked the secret of his own success, he replied, "Work and sleep"; then he added, "But hard work is the thing!" After ruthlessly breaking the Homestead strike, he became one of the least popular men in America. But popular opinion changed overnight to make him a sympathetic character when a young anarchist burst into his Carnegie Steel office, shot him twice, and plunged a knife into him seven times. Frick fought back courageously and survived.

Frick was medium sized, with strong, handsome features, a fast mind and extraordinarily quick movements—something his would-be assassin failed to consider. Both Carnegie and Frick were colossal egotists and personal conflict appeared inevitable. "F is a marvel," wrote Carnegie in his diary early in the game, but his feelings changed as Frick's prodigies in the management area began to overshadow his own super-skills as salesman and big-deal maker. A jealous Carnegie persuaded himself that in personable Charley Schwab he had found a better man than Frick. One of Carnegie's running resentments was the belief that Frick overcharged him for coke.

One afternoon in 1900, Carnegie visited Frick's office and requested his general manager to sell back his stock in Carnegie Steel at book value, pursuant to an agreement devised to enable the boss to rid himself of partners at will. While the book value of the stock was $4.5 million, actual value came to some $15 million. The two argued heatedly until Frick rose from his chair, eyes blazing. Carnegie took one look and raced out the door as fast as his size-five feet would carry him. Frick chased him down the hall. A fascinated observer reported that little Andy ran so fast the wind whistled through his silvery whiskers. In time, Carnegie was able to look with amusement at this encounter, but in Frick it ignited a searing hatred that never died.

Nor did the fracas settle anything. Frick sat in the catbird seat as Carnegie sold out to J. P. Morgan for $481 million. Of this, Carnegie kept his $300 million and divided the rest (except for the $4 million welfare fund) among the limited partners. Frick got $60 million as his share and, with $17 million of his own, became a Croesus of $77 million.

The Carnegie partners who shared in this bonanza were called the Pittsburgh Millionaires. Most of them elected to remain in Pittsburgh, where their sudden-wealth excesses have become legend. One had his wife's portrait painted by every conceivable type of artist; another bestowed automobiles on all and sundry. A few moved to New York and at least one set out for Paris. Asked if he planned to take his wife along, this fellow gave the classic answer, "Would you take a ham sandwich to a banquet?"

Frick was among those who moved to New York. He duly leased the Vanderbilt mansion and with wife, son, and daughter lived in seeming contentment among its marble halls. However, those who knew him were not so sure about the contentment, for the highly competitive Frick had adopted the guiding credo "Always the best." The Vanderbilt mansion, once the best, was now just the oldest.

Before Frick moved in, the Vanderbilt collection of paintings had been presented to the Metropolitan Museum of Art. This allowed the Pittsburgh Splendor Seeker space to hang his own works of art. For during his evolution from rich man to richer one, the artistic impulses of his youth burgeoned. At times he even did some sketching himself, a fact that made certain associates distrust him. He had acquired his first important painting in 1881—*In the Louvre*, by Luis Jiminez. Over the next twenty years, he bought the Barbizon works of Alma-Tadema, Bonheur, Ziem, and others. In 1899, he left Barbizons behind to buy Rembrandt's *Portrait of a Young Artist*. It marked his maturity as a collector; from there on his purchases were usually exceptional.

On his arrival on Fifth Avenue, Frick owned seventy-one paintings and was in a mood to dispose of some of them and build a new collection with the expenditure of $4–5 million a year. One dealer characterized him as a practitioner of Great Art—that is, interested only in Great Names and willing to pay Great Prices to get Great Paintings. Legend says he was vastly assisted in this by Sir Joseph Duveen, the English art dealer who spent much time in the United States. Duveen loved Old Masters with a raging passion and made an excellent living by acquiring works that pleased him and selling them to Yankee multimillionaires on whom his buoyant personality seemed hypnotic. Duveen's taste so dominated clients like Benjamin Altman, Joseph Widener, Samuel Kress, and Jules Bache that a lady paid tribute to one of these collections by murmuring, "How utterly duveen!"

Yet it is a mistake to see Frick as dominated by Duveen. This Maecenas knew exactly what he wanted in art—those Great Names and Great Pictures. Frick bought more from the Knoedler Gallery than he did from Duveen, with others like Wildenstein and Durand-Ruel also in the running. As his collection grew, he obviously needed surroundings of his own for display, and his mind dallied with the idea of erecting a mansion.

But the true catalyst in this matter did not come until the day Frick took a carriage ride through Central Park, accompanied by a male secretary. The trip was without incident until the carriage emerged from the Park in the vicinity of East Ninetieth Street. Here Frick spied an unfamiliar mansion surrounded by a blooming garden and leafy foliage. "Whose place is that?" he demanded. "That's Mr. Carnegie's new home," the secretary answered. Simmering hatred boiled anew. "Carnegie, eh?" he growled. "New home, eh? Why—I'll build a place that'll make his look like a miner's shack!"

Up to that point Frick's life in New York may have lacked real purpose. Now, however, he was gripped by a determination to outdo Andy Carnegie in the matter of a residence. In this, he was encouraged by Joseph Duveen, who saw in a Frick mansion the potentially ideal background for the finest procurable works of art.

To begin, Frick paid $2.4 million for the frontage on Fifth Avenue between Seventieth and Seventy-first Streets, extending east half the block. Here he met the first in a series of infuriating obstacles. On this property stood the Lenox Library, scheduled to move downtown to become part of the New York Public Library under construction at Fifth Avenue and Forty-second Street. But the Public Library was taking longer than expected to build, and an impatient Frick had to wait.

According to a biographer, the years between 1907–12, while Frick awaited the Lenox Library move, were hellish for his male secretaries and other underlings. As years passed, the Coke King became convinced that laborers on the downtown library were delaying only to annoy him, the enemy of labor. "Goddam them," he is quoted as ranting, "They're doing it just to get even with me. That library should have been finished long ago. Why, I'd like to give those contractors a few lessons in driving men!" He was also haunted by fears of death and wailed, "Carnegie's had his mansion for years. I want mine before I die! I've got to have it quickly!"

Especially galling to Henry Clay Frick was the fact that other mansions were blooming along Fifth Avenue. On the north corner of Seventy-eighth Street, tobacco magnate James Buchanan Duke had built a residence stemming in style from the Hotel Labbotière, an eighteenth-century adornment of the countryside near Bordeaux. High windowed, flat roofed, with balcony and impressive pediment over noble entrance, the Duke mansion contained fifty-four rooms. Through the windows on the first floor it was possible to see the surpassing dignity of its state rooms. Into this magnificence, Duke moved with his beautiful second wife, after a messy divorce from her predecessor; this second Mrs. Duke, it was said, had grown up with "a distaste for poverty." Shortly, a daughter named Doris was born to the couple.

Five-and-ten-cent-store pioneer Frank W. Woolworth was also drawing attention to himself at Fifth Avenue and Eightieth Street. Woolworth had lived there in suitable splendor since the turn of the century. One of the first to view the glories of the premises had been his eighty-year-old father, who reacted by saying, "This must have cost a lot of money, Frank." Woolworth replied, "Yes, father, but it was worth it." The old man shook his head. "Well, Frank," he said, "you always did like to lay it on thick."

In the downtown regions of Manhattan the Woolworth Building, tallest in the world, was rising to publicize the family name in unparalleled fashion. At the same time, in a prodigal gesture of paternalism, this Croesus was erecting the townhouses behind him at 4, 6, 8 and 10 East Eightieth. These were to be occupied by his married children. In the nearest lived his daughter and son-in-law, Mr. and Mrs. Franklyn Laws Hutton, parents of Barbara.

Woolworth was a self-made Splendor Seeker who thoroughly relished Fifth Avenue surroundings. A special reason was his mechanical organ, its infinite number of gadgets conceived and perfected by the owner himself. Woolworth could play no instrument, nor read music. Yet he was a fanatical music lover. His carved-oak and gilt-ceilinged drawing room on the second floor contained the inevitable millionaire's pipe organ, but his was different. The ingenious fellow had mechanized it to play organ and piano rolls at the push of a button. Ducts from the organ spread the music uncannily throughout the palatial house, with outlets in newel posts, chandeliers, and the like.

This was not enough for the musical millionaire. Further exercising ingenuity, he set vari-colored lights in the coves of the drawing room. By pressing different buttons, he could manipulate the lights to reflect the mood of the music. Usually he began by plunging the room into total darkness; then, as the music commenced, he played the lights subtly. Woolworth also devised special sound effects, so that thunder, lightning, and pelting rain could be simulated on cue.

Nor was that all. The inspired dime-store magnate ordered full-length oil paintings of musical immortals like Wagner, Beethoven, and Mozart. These were hung high in the music room. As their music began, a spotlight illuminated the painting, faintly at first, then increasing in a way to make the composer appear to enter the room.

With Frank Woolworth's organ and sound effects operating at full strength, the entire mansion seemed to shake. Musicians who attended his one-man concerts paid tribute to him as a master-interpreter of music and deplored the fact that Fate had not permitted him to be a symphony conductor.

Henry Clay Frick still fretted and fumed. He was not altogether idle, though, for with a lavish hand he was buying more works of art, including bronzes and porcelains. At the prodding of Joseph Duveen, he had hired the firm of Carrère and Hastings to design his mansion; they were also architects of the troublesome Public Library. Partner Thomas Hastings projected a low white-stone edifice that he called "a free treatment of eighteenth-century English architecture, with something of the spirit of the Italians." Duveen was already busy collecting masterpieces for this yet-to-be-commenced residence. On the death of J. P. Morgan, he bought from the estate eleven lightsome Fragonard panels commissioned by Louis XV in 1770 as presents for Madame Du Barry, who angrily rejected them as reflecting on her virtue. Duveen also bought Morgan's famed collection of Garland porcelains.

At last, in 1912, the Lenox Library moved and work began on the Frick mansion. Since everyone involved had been so well primed, the job was finished in the miracle-time of two years. For the interior decoration, Duveen imported Sir Charles Allom, who had earned his title by designing decors pleasing to King George V.

The canny Frick also employed the skills of Elsie de Wolfe, giving her responsibility for the second floor of the $5 million dwelling. Elsie had other duties as well. "It is your job to protect me from dealers," Frick told her. "I don't want to be bothered until after you have made up your mind about things. When you see anything I should buy, I shall go with you and look at it." Her fee would be ten percent of what he bought.

The first test of Frick's instructions came in Paris, where both happened to be. Ever a dynamo, Elsie heard that furnishings of the great Wallace Collection were to be placed on sale. Using Frick's name and her feminine wiles, she arranged a preview. But Frick had become a golf addict and seemed more interested in testing the links near Paris than in viewing art. She persisted and he grudgingly agreed to allow her half an hour. At the entrance to the building he asked if she approved the treasures on view inside. "Absolutely," she said. With that he proceeded to buy nearly everything in sight.

Elsie has recalled, "He went through the gallery like a streak, while I followed at his heels, aghast, as his purchases mounted up into millions of francs and I realized that in one short half-hour I had become tantamount to a rich woman."

The four-story Frick mansion at 1 East Seventieth Street —standing taller than it looks—was completed in 1914. Built of Indiana limestone that gives the impression of white marble, it appeared to one observer "a subtly sensuous Florentine palace." To others the English influence was apparent. Architect Hastings gave another interview in which he prosaically referred to his gem of a creation as a "house." Said he, "Mr. Frick's orders to

me were for a small house, with plenty of light and air and land."
He revealed that from the first Frick had visualized an eventual
museum. "He wished a house that was simple," Hastings went
on, "which would include galleries for his extraordinary
pictures—a house that would do to present to the city as a
museum."

At long last—this was Frick's triumph—a Fifth Avenue mansion looked as if it really belonged there. The white building,
lovely, serene, and striking, stood surrounded by an attractive
low wall, with well-kept greensward. Fittingly enough, the
monument to Richard Morris Hunt, most influential of Millionaires' Row architects, was across the way on the edge of Central Park.

It is safe to say that every Splendor Seeker along Fifth Avenue
had wanted his awesome residence to earn the admiration of the
public for himself and his activities. Only Frick achieved this
goal, with newspapers declaring that anyone capable of decree-
ing so superior a mansion must himself be a fine person. Said
one tribute, "This mansion, the latest private palace in the metropolis, differs as greatly in architecture, appointments, and atmosphere from those of other millionaires who have 'come out
of the west' as does its owner in personality, character, and
temperament from the owners. It is as modest and quiet in appearance and (one might say) in manner as its owner, and be-
speaks the character of this man."

Frick's emotions on finally entering his completed mansion do
not appear on the record. But then or shortly after he is quoted
as saying, "Now I can go up and laugh at that shack of
Carnegie's." Andy Carnegie, all anger spent, was so impressed
by the quiet beauty of the Frick mansion that he sent a message
to his old partner suggesting a reconciliation. Frick snorted.
"Tell Carnegie," he told the intermediary, "that I will see him in
Hell, where we are both going."

The Frick Collection did not become a public museum until
1935, following the death of Mrs. Frick. Then, enlarged and
improved but atmospherically unchanged, it opened to the public. In Frick's day few outsiders set foot inside. "This valuable
collection of paintings is a strictly private one," reported a 1916

guidebook, "and its contents are not generally known, Mr. Frick being averse to having a complete catalogue published."

As the cost of his collection rose toward an ultimate $30 million, the *Literary Digest* hailed Frick as successor to J. P. Morgan as America's foremost collector. Word spread through art circles that his English paintings were the finest part of his hoard. Among them were works by Reynolds, Hogarth, Romney, Gainsborough, Sir Thomas Lawrence, Hoppner, Raeburn, Turner, and others. His chief American painter was Whistler, represented by full-length portraits of Miss Rosa Corder and the Count de Montesquiou, both deriving from the collection of Richard Canfield, gentleman gambler. He also owned a Gilbert Stuart portrait of George Washington.

Frick's Old Masters included Titian's *Pietro Aretino*, purchased by the demon collector in 1905. Among his Rembrandts were the famed *Self-Portrait* and *The Polish Rider;* he also owned a Hals self-portrait, along with three other Hals paintings. He had two Veronese allegories, six Van Dycks, two Vermeers, and a Rubens. Frick was especially fond of Bellini's *St. Francis in Ecstacy*, in part because it had been plucked out of an ashcan in 1857.

Among his Goyas were *The Forge* and portraits of Spanish nobles; his El Grecos included the striking *St. Jerome, Portrait of Vincenzo Anastagi*, and *The Purification of the Temple;* he also possessed works by Velásquez and Murillo. Two Daubignys, four Corots, a Millet, Monet, and Troyon were visible on his walls, as were the Dutch moderns Jacobus Maris and Josef Israels.

Those who penetrated the Frick mansion found that most of the masterpieces were hung in the so-called West Gallery, a long room with French walnut woodwork and marble floor bordered with venial marble, covered in part by a rich Isfahan Persian rug; that the English influence was more apparent inside than out; that the high-ceilinged rooms blended into one another with unusual grace; that the Fragonard panels bought from J. P. Morgan had been given a room of their own; and that this Fragonard Room had been fleshed out by the hand of the ubiquitous Duveen with a marble fireplace from Marie Antoinette's mini-château in the Bois de Boulogne, a writing table from the same idyllic source, a Clodion tapestry, chairs covered with

Beauvais tapestry, a Riesener commode, and Houdon's bust of
the Countess de Galaya.

Amidst this grandeur, Frick lived with wife and family, which
now included his son's young children. Even the family quarters
radiated eighteenth-century flavor, one bedroom having delicate
Boucher panels. Frick had moved his Wall Street office to a
room of the mansion, but his interests had swung from finance
to art. Joyously he supervised the unpacking and hanging of
works bought from Knoedler or Duveen. Like Alexander T.
Stewart and Thomas Fortune Ryan before him he liked to sit
alone in his gallery communing with epochal possessions. At
night, his family safely abed, he slipped from divan to divan
absorbing the beauty of the ages around him. One biographer
wrote, "Mr. Frick did not merely admire and enjoy his beautiful
pictures; he loved them with a passion as tender as he felt for
little children." He especially appreciated portraits of pretty
women; if the female subjects were older he liked them to
look warm-hearted and wholesome, like those of Rembrandt
and Hals.

Inevitably, the Frick mansion possessed a pipe organ, placed
in an alcove at the foot of the grand staircase, with its golden
pipes part of the decoration above. On Saturday afternoons a
professional organist arrived to play such favored Frick selec-
tions as "The Rosary," "Sweet Alice Ben Bolt," "Largo," and
"Pilgrim's Chorus." A malicious writer has left us a description of
Frick on a Saturday afternoon as the organ throbbed—"in his
palace, on a Renaissance throne under a canopy, holding in his
little hand a copy of the *Saturday Evening Post.*"

Frick had small use for journalists or newspapers and usually
contented himself with scanning headlines. For bookreading, he
liked biographies of emperors and conquerors of history, or
modern books of an inspirational nature. Most of his opinions
were redolent of the pioneering past, but this man of only thirty
months' schooling uttered at least one remark that should please
Women's Lib. To a group of educators, he said, "Don't tell the
little girls fairy tales, teach them real things."

Life in cloistered surroundings did not altogether soothe Frick's rampant spirit. Andrew Carnegie, who had given millions for peace, was shattered by World War I. Frick saw world affairs through the eyes of a man of business and expressed annoyance when America loaned hundreds of millions of dollars to war-ravaged Allies. When Woodrow Wilson proposed the League of Nations at the end of the war, Frick's outrage doubled. The thought of his country joining a world peace organization with debtor nations seemed criminal.

"Well, I am opposed to this thing," he is reported as explaining. "Of course I am. I don't see how any experienced business-man could fail to be. Why, it seems to me a crazy thing to do." The passage of years may have showed us that President Wilson was his own worst enemy in the fight for the League, but at that time Frick seemed a villain for financing the fight against the world organization. Until he joined the fray, bringing Andrew Mellon with him, the forces opposing the League were broke.

Andrew Carnegie breathed his last in August 1919 and thus Frick had the satisfaction of surviving his hated opponent. But not for long. Frick himself died in December of the same year. His will showed that he must have pondered the case of Charles Yerkes, who had dreamed of bestowing his art collection on the people of New York. Alas, poor Yerkes!—he lacked the money to leave. Frick had it, and left an ironclad trust fund of $15 million to perpetuate his name and collection forever.

World War I brought grim days to citizens of the United States. Meatless Tuesdays, coal shortages, and casualty lists produced a state of mind that turned million-dollar mansions into prime examples of conspicuous waste. Both George F. Baker, the so-called Sphinx of Wall Street, and Otto H. Kahn, patron of the arts, erected lavish dwellings during the war years and came in for criticism as a result. Kahn's mansion, a pleasure dome on the Upper Avenue, roused particular anger because of the owner's Germanic background.

Other factors worked at negating mansions. The Sixteenth Amendment, establishing a national income tax, took effect in

1913 and slowly dampened extravagant spending. With the quiet city turning into a noisy metropolis, property taxes also intruded into the sphere of the ultra-rich. Lastly, the sons and daughters of these same rich, having passed uncomfortable childhoods in marble halls, had no desire to live there after inheriting the mansions.

But the main change stemmed from the twentieth century, which finally reached its stride after World War I. Among everything else, new times brought a demand for a more compact kind of city living—all at once apartment houses became smart and sophisticated. Park Avenue, lined with such dwellings, represented a fresh type of living for the wealthy. A few newly rich like Paul D. Cravath might opt for townhouses in the East Seventies, but for the most part multiple apartment houses became the thing. Social critic Bayrd Still believes they offered the ultimate in contemporary housing—"a symbol of the pullulating prosperity of the Twenties."

Park Avenue apartment houses might have lacked strong individuality on the outside, but within they could be duplexes and triplexes with baronial rooms. Overnight, quantity achieved victory over quality as Park Avenue won recognition as the richest street in the world, with 2,000 of its 5,000 families in the millionaire class. In 1924, when the handsome young Prince of Wales made a polo-playing visit to Long Island, he spent his evenings of frolic in the Prohibition-era night clubs of Broadway or at private parties on Park Avenue. Almost none of his precious time was passed on Fifth.

Still, Fifth Avenue possessed that superlative view of Central Park and apartments there would be of top value. So real-estate developers began dangling huge sums of money before the inheritors of mansions and in most cases the sons of the Splendor Seekers paid heed.

First to sell was Vincent Astor, who had been an undergraduate at Harvard when his father disappeared on the *Titanic*. During his first marriage Vincent lived in the parental white-marble Richard Morris Hunt mansion improved by Carrère and Hastings; he and his wife were aided by a retinue of twenty servants. Dutifully, the young man gave an annual Astor Ball and in other ways maintained his exalted family position. But by 1925 the mansion had grown oppressive and, after disposing of it for $3.5 million, Vincent Astor moved to a townhouse on East Eightieth Street. In this case, though, the buyer was not a builder of apartment houses, but a self-made millionaire who wished to present the property to Temple Emanu-El.

So the Astor mansion, once rivaling the White House in importance, vanished to make way for a synagogue. As with other mansions to follow, the demolition men had a hard time tearing this down, for the mansions of Millionaires' Row had been built to stay. Vincent Astor did not appear to be sentimental about his grandmother, and got rid of most of her possessions by impersonal auction. But he did order his father's bedroom and bathroom, including a huge marble tub, transported to his new residence.

Next to vanish were three Vanderbilt mansions. With no visible regret, the children of Cornelius Vanderbilt accepted $7.5 million for the majestic château facing Grand Army Plaza. With this, the public at last gained admission to Vanderbilt premises, for in the name of sweet charity people were allowed inside at fifty cents a head. This was the heyday of motion-picture glamour, and movie mogul Marcus Loew bought the Vanderbilt Moorish, Colonial, and other Rooms to be used as movie sets, executive offices, or picture-palace lobbies. Then the noble building fell to make way for the Bergdorf-Goodman department store.

Alva's singing-marriage château at the corner of Fifty-second Street vanished next, quickly followed by the Twin Mansion once occupied by the Mesdames Sloan and Shepard. Sad to say, the demolition of Alva's superb mansion attracted scant attention, for no Landmarks Commission existed at the time to protect relics of the past. Nor did the public appear to care. A boomtime world, eminently satisfied with things as they were, had no interest in preserving the monuments of days gone by.

That left only William Henry Vanderbilt's Twin Mansion and into it moved Cornelius Vanderbilt III and his wife, the former Grace Wilson. The marriage of these two, for which the bridegroom had renounced a $40 million inheritance, should have been a matter of living-happily-ever-after. It was not. Within a few years the couple that had sacrificed so much grew incompatible, causing their son to write, "The marriage, achieved in the face of such difficulties, deteriorated seriously over the years. I saw it happening and asked them why they didn't get a divorce. *People in our position don't get divorces*, my father said."

Each of the unhappy Cornelius Vanderbilts channeled energies in individual directions. The husband sublimated in yachting and military matters, becoming a Brigadier General in World War I. Grace Wilson Vanderbilt reached out to seize the tiara of top social leadership left by Mrs. Astor. Placing it atop her curly head, she began a lifetime of strenuous entertaining in this first and last Vanderbilt mansion. But first she ordered a $500,000 refurbishing by architect Horace Trumbauer.

Grandeur of a quieter sort was visible on Millionaires' Row as Mrs. Andrew Carnegie continued to occupy the Highlands dwelling at Ninetieth Street, paying a real-estate tax of $70,000 a year. The garden on which the lady lavished time and money in honor of her husband was cited as one of the costliest in the world. A guest at a tea party in the mansion found the interior "uncompromisingly gloomy and Victorian." Yet Mrs. Carnegie herself was young looking, charming to meet, and eager to press her conservative beliefs on others. This conservatism carried over into attire, for this possessor of at least $30 million owned a mink coat but preferred to wear cloth and never donned her collection of jewels. Her only extravagance was occasional dinner parties with excellent wines.

Twenty blocks to the south Mrs. Henry Clay Frick and daughter Helen Clay Frick lived with equal conservatism, choosing cotton over silk and cloth over fur. Their mansion would not become a museum until Mrs. Frick's death, and even then members of the family would continue to live on upper floors.

The Splendor Seekers themselves were a vanishing breed, most of them forced by old age to abandon their fierce drive for money and power. In quiescent terminal years, a few may have regretted a lifetime devoted to the Almighty Dollar. Once a newspaper reporter interviewed a Croesus who sat mummified in a wheelchair watching Fifth Avenue traffic. "Sir, what do you think about as you sit there?" the reporter was bold enough to ask. "Women," the wraith of a man answered.

For the most part, the mansions were slipping into the hands of the young. No longer were costume balls given in the fabulous ballrooms; now it was debutante parties for granddaughters and grandnieces. In the Charleston-dancing, gin-swigging Twenties, couples necked and drank from hip flasks in marble halls decorated by centuries-old tapestries. Said one writer, "The lilting melody of the cotillion orchestra has been drowned out by the blare and moan of the jazz band. The elaborate ball gown of an earlier day has been supplanted by the skimpy attire worn by girls of what Society pages call the Smart Set."

The mansions fell, some with a whimper, others with a bang.

The William Andrews Clark home departed noisily, with controversy in the air, its final hours paced by the auctioneer's hammer. Following the Senator's death in 1925, newspapers carried stories of his magnificent in-house funeral, with a full-size choir and so loud a barrage of diapason organ music that one mourner felt the Day of Judgment had come. Next, the contents of his will were printed. As expected, he left the best pictures of the Clark Collection to the Metropolitan Museum of Art, on condition that they be hung for all time in an exclusive, well-lighted gallery bearing his name.

This offer, with no funds attached to build a gallery or wing, was brusquely rejected by the Metropolitan, with the implication the Clark paintings would have been turned down under any circumstances. Learning from this, the family next offered the paintings to the Corcoran Gallery in Washington, along with funds to pay for a special wing. The Corcoran Gallery accepted and eventually a President of the United States presided over the opening of the Clark Gallery.

Next, the heirs sold the $7 million Clark's Folly for a paltry $3 million. It is touching to report that a single letter appeared in *The New York Times* suggesting that the Baroque mansion should be preserved for posterity. An editorial based on the letter ended with the rueful comment, "Built for eternity, it lasted less than twenty-five years."

Many Clark paintings still remained, even after the Corcoran gift, so it was decided to auction them off in the grand ballroom of the Hotel Plaza. With paintings removed, the bare-walled mansion was thrown open to a curious public at the usual fifty cents a head. Among those who paid to get in were Charlie Chaplin and a group of Hollywood friends.

Finally, the Clark furniture was auctioned off on the premises, with film companies again reaping publicity by purchasing entire rooms. Architects, decorators, and hotel managers also joined the bidding. Maison Cluny in Paris acquired the ceiling of the state dining room made from the Sherwood Forest oak. Prices on the whole were disappointing, though some rugs went for $16,000 and a set of Biblical sofa pillows fetched $7,200. Thus another mansion made way for an apartment house.

Senator Clark's children had been united in a desire to get rid of Clark's Folly as fast as possible. Not so the offspring of Isaac Brokaw, who came into possession of the family's duplication of Chenonceaux with the death of Mrs. Brokaw in 1925.

Old Isaac is enshrined in history as something of a ruffian. So vast was the power of millions, however, that his well-educated sons grew into men of high social sheen. When elder-son George Brokaw, then in his forties, fell in love with young, beautiful, and talented Clare Boothe, his manners were impeccable enough to render him the stiffest of suitors.

Nevertheless, George and Clare married, after deciding the mansion inherited by George as oldest son was too overpowering to live in. Instead, they took a Park Avenue apartment and made plans to sell the mansion to make way for an exclusive apartment-hotel. With this, the other Brokaw brothers rose up in wrath and took the matter to court. There George testified that the mansion cost more than $70,000 a year for upkeep and as a home depressed the human spirit. Nor had he been able to find anyone to rent the urban château, even at $25,000 a year. The case went to the Supreme Court, where George lost. Disconsonately he and Clare (who eventually became Clare Boothe Luce) moved into the gloomy mansion and remained four years before the marriage disintegrated.

Oddly, the mansions of Millionaires' Row attracted more attention during the Tragic Thirties than in the Teeming Twenties. In the midst of a Depression that brought hardship to nearly every American family, they seemed to represent a discredited past. An excellent case could be made for the fact that the greedy depredations of the Splendor Seekers had brought the nation to its current low estate.

Even the builders of apartment houses lacked money to buy and build during the Depression. So the remaining mansions of Fifth stood in a curious limbo. Newspapers occasionally focused on them to report that sixty-eight mansions and townhouses still lined the one-time Millionaires' Row, thirty-eight of them boarded up with litter on the steps. The rest were occupied by some eighty folk, usually old and eccentric. However, life must go on, and a baby had been born to the Bostwick family, whose millions stemmed from fortuitous association with the Rockefeller interests.

In the mid-thirties, *Fortune* devoted an issue to New York, with an article on Fifth Avenue's glorious past and less happy present. In words that might have been written in 1905, the editors extolled the onetime Millionaires' Row—

> Never in the history of the world had so much private wealth been concentrated on a single street. Here was no mere king surrounded by a rich nobility; here were dozens of kings and petty emperors vying with each other in power, in splendid appointments, in social positions, in indigestible food. It is true they were brash. It is true that their notions of splendor were more superficial than those of Europe. Nevertheless, their houses symbolized the most important social group of the late Nineteenth and early Twentieth centuries—the unregenerate dollar makers.

Having evoked a glorious image, the magazine turned statistical to report that the real-estate assessment on the remaining Fifth Avenue mansions amounted to $33 million; and that taxwise it cost Brigadier-General and Mrs. Cornelius Vanderbilt $200 a night to sleep in their Twin Mansion. In the past at least twenty servants had been considered necessary for a mansion;

now the number was ten. The wages of these ten amounted to an annual $14,000, with $600 additional for the elegant uniforms of butlers, footmen, and chauffeurs. Including gas, electricity, and general repairs, the minimal yearly upkeep of a Fifth Avenue home came to $30,000.

Of those living in such style Mrs. Cornelius Vanderbilt reigned supreme. An aristocrat with a keen sense of publicity, she had begun wearing a bejeweled velvet head-band on all social occasions, and few in the United States would fail to recognize her instantly in the photographs taken at openings of the Metropolitan Opera and other social events.

During the thirties, Mrs. Vanderbilt reached her hostessing pinnacle. It is safe to say that nearly every prominent figure in the English-speaking world at some time dined at her table. Not until a decade later did her relentless socializing grow mechanical. Then a guest whose name began with R looked around the dinner table to note that every other name began with R, except for a few S's below the salt.

If Mrs. Vanderbilt kept the fine traditions of the Four Hundred aglow, her son Cornelius IV opted for a later day. Likable and energetic, Cornelius aspired to be a journalist—an odd ambition for one of his background—and during the Depression became one of the busiest authors of books and magazine articles extant. Cornelius wrote not only about Society, but on political affairs and current events as well, infuriating his father and other crusty reactionaries by espousing the New Deal programs of Franklin D. Roosevelt.

Cornelius Vanderbilt, Jr., as he democratically signed himself, was eminently qualified to interpret phenomena like Barbara Hutton, who had stepped forth as the nation's Poor Little Rich Girl. Four years old when her beloved mother died, Barbara went to live with Grandpa Woolworth in the mansion with the mechanical organ. Grandpa died when she was nine. By that time her father had married again, an act the wilful child refused to condone. At age thirteen Barbara inherited $30 million and stood to gain far more with maturity.

With the country realizing Depression had come to stay,

eighteen-year-old Barbara provided distraction by giving herself a $60,000 coming-out party. Next she married, succumbing to the practiced wiles of a European fortune hunter. The anguished country watched these remote events with the same fascination a previous world had given the Four Hundred. But in a day of newsreels and tabloids, everyone could see that, for all her millions, Barbara Hutton wore a look of petulant melancholy. Plainly money had not brought her happiness. Not quite so wan was Doris Duke, who inherited $70 million from her tobacco tycoon father.

Glamour reappeared on Fifth Avenue in 1935, as the Frick Collection at last opened to the public. The lovely mansion had been slightly altered, especially by the addition of a noble inner courtyard with pool and playing fountains. At the gala, white-tie opening, Mrs. Carnegie and her married daughter were amazingly visible.

Occasionally, the auctioning of the art treasures of the Splendor Seekers brought Millionaires' Row back to the public eye. It happened with disposal of the Renaissance treasures of Thomas Fortune Ryan. The devout wife of this Croesus had died on 1917 and two weeks later the widower wed a Mrs. Cornelius Cuyler. The bride came of excellent family, but Ryan children behaved as if she were a Follies girl. The oldest Ryan son never spoke to his father again, and the financier's will cut him off with a solitary set of shirt studs.

Ryan died in 1928 and soon the fabulous home and Fifth Avenue garden vanished to make way for another apartment house. His magnificent Italianate collection was finally auctioned in 1933. Sir Joseph Duveen paid $10,500 for the Francesco Laurana bust of Catherine of Aragon, but other bids proved disappointing and the sale brought only $409,500.

Harry Payne Whitney died in 1930 and his sculptress wife Gertrude Vanderbilt Whitney used the old Whitney mansion as an urban residence. Finally, the Whitney collection, too, went under the hammer at an auction with uniformed ushers and soaring social tone. Again the bids turned out to be disappointingly low. . . . Today's outstanding members of the Whitney clan

are John Hay Whitney, onetime publisher of the New York
Herald-Tribune and Ambassador to the Court of St. James's, and
his sister Joan Whitney Payson, owner of the baseball Mets.

Over on Riverside Drive, Charles Schwab had lost his rare zest
for living with the death of his wife in 1932. Even the steel
industry failed to stimulate him and Bethlehem stockholders
actually made efforts to force his retirement. The master of the
ornate "On the Hudson" admitted to being anxious to sell his
mansion, but no buyers could be found for so superb a dwelling.
The suggestion was made that the City of New York take it over
as an official residence for Mayors. Peppery little Fiorello H.
LaGuardia reacted by shouting, "What, *me* in THAT!"

Schwab died in 1939, still the lord and master of "On the
Hudson." But with his death came the shocking discovery that
the steelmaster was nearly $2 million in debt. For eight years
after, the noble château on Riverside Drive stood empty and
forlorn. Finally, it was sold for $1.25 million and torn down for
an apartment complex. The owners had the grace to call this
Schwab House.

The agony of a second World War further diverted attention
from matters like mansions. Mrs. Grace Vanderbilt, now a
widow, had sold William Henry's Twin Mansion to make way for
a skyscraper and made plans to move herself into the 28-room
townhouse at Eighty-sixth Street once owned by William Starr
Miller. In the best tradition of the aristocracy she took her bathroom along. Before her departure, however, Mrs. Vanderbilt
opened the Twin Mansion at $20 a head for a formal dance to
benefit the USO.

With the post-war establishment of the United Nations in New
York, foreign countries began acquiring townhouses, and a few
mansions, as permanent missions or consulates. In the 1950's
American foundations, universities, and charitable organizations
started gaining possession of others. The Catholic Archdiocese
of New York moved into the midtown Villard mansion behind
St. Patrick's; for years, one of the residences was owned by the
publisher Random House. The James Buchanan Duke house
was presented by Doris Duke and other heirs of the tobacco
tycoon to the Institute of Fine Arts, a division of New York

University. The one-time Payne Whitney mansion next door became the Cultural Service of the French Embassy. For a time Columbia University used the Carnegie mansion as its School of Social Work; recently this was taken over by the Cooper-Hewitt Museum of Decorative Arts and Design. For nearly twenty years the Brokaw mansion functioned as headquarters for the Institute of Radio Engineers; then it was sold for a high-toned apartment house. The Otto H. Kahn mansion is the Convent of the Sacred Heart. The former Augustus Van Horne Stuyvesant mansion is the Ukrainian Folk Art Museum. And so it goes . . .

As the great city turned into a metropolis of glass and chrome skyscrapers and apartment houses, more people began thinking of preserving its architectural treasures. Gradually civic groups and concerned citizens formed to combat wanton destruction by real-estate interests. At length, the city created a Landmarks Commission that functions—too slowly, some think—to preserve the architectural relics of the past.

The clear winner in the mansion-sweepstakes of Millionaires' Row has been Henry Clay Frick.

Born in poverty on a Pennsylvania farm, Frick emerges as the only Splendor Seeker whose name has remained alive in the manner every Manhattan Croesus desired. Today the name Frick is synonymous with dignity of living and superior taste in art.

Furthermore, the edifice built by Henry Clay Frick seems destined to stand forever, not only perpetuating his works of art, but also offering a sample of how those Splendor Seekers lived. The founder might be shocked by the attire of some young art lovers who walk bra-less and surreptitiously over his Persian rugs and along his marble halls. But even by them his name is respected.

Yet all is not sweetness and light. The rapacity that clogged the minds of the Robber Barons was briefly visible in 1973, as the Frick Collection, speaking through Dr. Henry Clay Frick II, announced plans to demolish the handsome George Widener townhouse next door, to make room for a garden.

Once again, citizens rose to protest destruction of another beautiful remnant. But the Frick forces had moved with a speed, determination, and arrogance worthy of the founder himself. The Widener house was doomed.

So the ruthless spirit of the Splendor Seekers still lives on Fifth Avenue. But, for those who care to look, across the street from the Frick Collection stands the monument to a gentler Richard Morris Hunt.

BOOKS CONSULTED

(The author's thanks are due Mrs. Helen Worden Cranmer and Mrs. Beryl S. Austrian, for material on Society and Decoration respectively; and to Mrs. Ad Schulberg, literary agent.)

AMORY, CLEVELAND. Who Killed Society? New York: Harper & Bros., 1960

ANDREWS, WAYNE. Architecture, Ambition, and America. New York: Harper & Bros., 1955

———— Architecture in New York; a Pictorial History. New York: Harcourt Brace & Co., 1969

———— The Battle for Chicago. New York: Harcourt Brace & Co., 1946

———— The Vanderbilt Legend. New York: Harcourt Brace & Co., 1941

BALDWIN, CHARLES D. Stanford White. New York: Dodd Mead & Co., 1931

BEEBE, LUCIUS. The Big Spenders. New York: Doubleday & Co., 1966

BROWN, HENRY COLLINS. In the Golden Nineties. Hastings-on-Hudson: Valentine's Manual, 1928

BURNLEY, JAMES. Millionaires and Kings of Enterprise. Philadelphia: J. B. Lippincott, 1901

268 Books Consulted

CARNEGIE, ANDREW. Autobiography. Boston: Houghton Mifflin, 1920

CHANLER, MARGARET (Mrs. Winthrop Chanler). Roman Spring. Boston: Little Brown, 1934

CLEWS, HENRY. Fifty Years on Wall Street. New York: Irving Publishing, 1905

CROCKETT, ALBERT STEVENS. Peacocks on Parade. New York: Sears Publishing, 1931

CROFFITT, W. A. The Vanderbilts. Chicago: Bedford Clarke & Co., 1886

DE WOLFE, ELSIE. After All. New York: Harper & Bros., 1935

GLASSOCK, C. B. War of the Copper Kings. Indianapolis: Bobbs Merrill, 1935

HACKER, LOUIS M. The World of Andrew Carnegie. Philadelphia: J. B. Lippincott, 1968

HARRISON, CONSTANCE CARY (MRS. BURTON HARRISON). Recollections Grave and Gay. New York: Charles Scribner's Sons, 1911

HARVEY, GEORGE B. C. Henry Clay Frick. New York: Charles Scribner's Sons, 1928

HIRSCH, MARK D. William C. Whitney, Modern Warwick. New York: Dodd Mead & Co, 1948

HOLBROOK, STEWART. The Age of the Moguls. New York: Doubleday & Co., 1953

HOYT, EDWIN P. The Vanderbilts and Their Fortunes. New York: Doubleday & Co., 1962

JOSEPHSON, MATTHEW. The Robber Barons. New York: Harcourt Brace, 1962

KAVALER, LUCY. The Astors. New York: Dodd Mead & Co., 1966

LANDY, JACOB. The Domestic Architecture of the Robber Barons in New York City. New York University: Institute of Fine Arts, 1950

LEHR, ELIZABETH DREXEL (LADY DECIES). King Lehr and the Gilded Age. Philadelphia: J. B. Lippincott Co., 1935

LUNDBERG, FERDINAND. America's Sixty Families. New York: Vanguard, 1937

LYNES, RUSSELL. The Tastemakers. New York: Harper & Bros., 1937

McALLISTER, WARD. Society as I Have Found It. New York: Cassell & Co., 1890

MANGAM, WILLIAM. The Clarks, An American Phenomenon. New York: Silver Bow Press, 1941

MARCUSE, MAXWELL F. This Was New York! New York: Carlton Press, 1965

MARTIN, FREDERICK TOWNSEND. The Passing of the Idle Rich. New York, Doubleday Page, 1911

—— Things I Remember. New York: John Lane, 1913

MAYER, GRACE. Once Upon a City. New York: Macmillan Company, 1958

MORRIS, LLOYD. Incredible New York. New York: Random House, 1951

MYERS, GUSTAVUS. The Ending of Hereditary American Fortunes. New York: Julian Messner, 1939

—— The History of the Great American Fortunes. New York: Modern Library, 1939

PULITZER, RALPH. New York Society on Parade. New York: Harper & Bros., 1920

RALPH, JULIAN. Chicago and the World's Fair. New York: Harper & Bros., 1893

REED, HENRY HOPE. The Golden City. New York: Doubleday & Co., 1959

ROSS, ISHBEL. Taste in America; an Illustrated History. New York: T. Y. Crowell, 1967

RUSSELL, CHARLES EDWARD. Lawless Wealth; the Origin of Some Great American Fortunes. New York: H. W. Dodge, 1908

SAARINEN, ALINE. The Proud Possessors. New York: Random House, 1958

SHACKLETON, ROBERT. The Book of Chicago. Philadelphia: Penn Publishing, 1920

SILVER, NATHAN. Lost New York. Boston: Houghton Mifflin, 1967

STILL, BAYRD. Mirror for Gotham. Washington Square: New York University Press, 1956

TOWNER, WESLEY (completed by Stephen Varble). The Elegant Auctioneers. New York: Hill & Wang, 1970

TULLY, ANDREW. Era of Elegance. New York: Funk & Wagnalls, 1947

VANDERBILT, CORNELIUS, JR. Farewell to Fifth Avenue. New York: Simon & Schuster, 1935

—— Queen of the Golden Age; the Fabulous Story of Grace Wilson Vanderbilt. New York: McGraw Hill, 1952

VAN RENSSELAER, MRS. JOHN KING (with F. F. Van de Water). The Social Ladder. New York: Henry Holt, 1924

VILLARD, HENRY. Memoirs. Boston: Houghton Mifflin, 1904

VILLARD, OSWALD GARRISON. Fighting Years. New York: Harcourt Brace, 1935

WHARTON, EDITH. A Backward Glance. New York: Appleton-Century, 1934

WENDT, LLOYD AND HERMAN KOGAN. Bet a Million! The Story of John W. Gates. Indianapolis: Bobbs Merrill, 1948

WINKLER, JOHN K. Incredible Carnegie. New York: Vanguard, 1931

——— Morgan the Magnificent. New York: Vanguard, 1930

——— Tobacco Tycoon. New York: Random House, 1942

SPECIALIZED SOURCES: American Institute of Architects Guide to New York City—Catalogues of Astor, Clark, James Henry Smith, and Yerkes auctions—History of Architecture and the Building Trades in Greater New York—History of New York Real Estate, Architecture, and Building—Mr. Vanderbilt's House and Collection—Real Estate Record—Rider's New York—Valentine's Manual

PERIODICALS: American Architect & Builder—Architectural Record—Collier's Weekly—Frank Leslie's Weekly—Harper's Weekly —Literary Digest—McClure's Magazine—Metropolitan Magazine —Munsey's Magazine—Popular Biography—Town Topics

NEWSPAPERS: New York Herald—New York Sun—New York Times—New York World

INDEX